Magical Arrows

THE MAORI, THE GREEKS,
AND THE FOLKLORE
OF THE UNIVERSE

Gregory Schrempp

Foreword by Marshall Sahlins

THE UNIVERSITY OF WISCONSIN PRESS

The University of Wisconsin Press

3 Henrietta Street
London WC2E 8LU, England

5   4   3   2   1

Printed in the United States of America

    Grateful acknowledgment is made for permission to publish the following:
    Figure from *The Raw and the Cooked* by Claude Lévi-Strauss. Copyright © 1969 by Harper & Row, Publishers, Inc. Reprinted by permission of HarperCollins Publishers.
    Extract from *Myths and Tales of the Jicarilla Apache Indians* by Morris Edward Opler. Reproduced by permission of the American Folklore Society from the MEMOIRS OF THE AMERICAN FOLKLORE SOCIETY, Volume XXXI, 1938.
    "Antinomy and Cosmology: Kant Among the Maori" by Gregory Schrempp. Reprinted from *Myth and Philosophy*, ed. Frank Reynolds and David Tracy by permission of the State University of New York Press. © 1990 State University of New York.
    Extracts from *The Lore of the Whare-Wānanga* by S. Percy Smith. Reprinted by permission of the Polynesian Society, Auckland, New Zealand, from Memoirs of the Polynesian Society, Vol. III.

Library of Congress Cataloging-in-Publication Data

Schrempp, Gregory Allen, 1950–
    Magical Arrows: the Maori, the Greeks, and the folklore of the universe /
Gregory Schrempp; foreword by Marshall Sahlins.
        238 pp.   cm.—(New directions in anthropological writing)
    Includes bibliographical references and index.
    ISBN 0-299-13230-7   ISBN 0-299-13234-X
    1. Cosmology. 2. Cosmology, Ancient. 3. Mythology, Maori.
    4. Maori (New Zealand people)—Social life and customs.
    5. Zeno, of Elea. I. Title. II. Series.
    BD511.S37   1992
    113′.09—dc20   91-33076

For my father,
and in memory of my mother

Contents

Foreword

IF A PARADIGM shift may be likened to an intellectual earthquake, an event that changes the topography of received knowledge, then reader of Gregory Schrempp's *Magical Arrows*, prepare for some big shocks. Lest I be accused of hyperbole, how else can one introduce a text that opens up a new field of comparative cosmology wherein Zeno of Elea, the Maori sage Te Rangikaheke, Arthur O. Lovejoy, intellectuals of the Ojibwa, Tikopia, Bororo, and Jicarilla Apache, and Claude Lévi-Strauss all converse with one another on universal themes of being whose most general metaphysical expression is provided by Immanuel Kant and whose most popular narrative version is the race of the tortoise and the hare?

Yet as Gregory Schrempp argues, grand cosmological issues can be found even in little folk tales. Nor is it accidental that for Zeno and Lévi-Strauss both, the determination of big issues appears as a transformation from mythos to logos: the first confronting space, time, motion, and infinity in the race of Achilles and the tortoise; the second addressing the same kinds of problems, if from the particular perspective of logical intelligibility, through the cosmogony of the Ojibwa or Bororo Indians. Meanwhile, Schrempp is elegantly demonstrating that Kantian antinomies of reason appear in the contrasts between narrative and genealogical versions of Maori cosmogony. Respectively representing creation through acts of will and a natural causality, unconditioned cause and infinite regress, these alternative narrative and genealogical genres reproduce the unresolvable contradictions of the transcendental dialectic—in explication of which Kant himself did not hesitate to use the figure of genealogy. Happy combination, this startling synthesis of Kant and the Maori philosophers, since it allows Schrempp to make the point, as against a certain postmodernist indulgence in ethnographic disarray, that contradiction is not the negation of a structural logic but its sequitur. Yet more important, in these inspired juxtapositions of the principles of order that support integrated forms of being—which is what he takes cosmology to be—Schrempp gives us a veritable comparative ontology. The reason this is so important is that cosmology thus expresses in the most abstract terms, which is also to say the most logically productive terms, the principles that organize other dimensions of social existence, such as kinship and political relations, or even economic practice. Here Schrempp specifically makes a logical claim, not necessarily a causal one. All the same, by treating Maori kinship, for example, as a modality of cosmological principles, he recasts traditional anthropological understandings in original ways, indeed in this case revives a field that had become an endangered intellectual species.

Like the blind men and the elephant (to enlist mythos once more in support of logos), everyone is likely to grasp this wondrous text in some particular aspect and elaborate images of it that are consistent with his or her scholarly experience. My own elephant is the relation between cosmology and society in Polynesia: in particular the "dual formulation" of the principles of order encoded in myth, ritual, and social practice that Schrempp describes for the Maori; and in general his return to the classic problems of Durkheim's "sociological epistemology" and its unsuccessful attempt, as against Kant, to derive the categories of understanding from the structures of society.

By "dual formulation" Schrempp means the two different schemes the Maori use to construct their universe, the recurrent exchange between certain unitary and binary forms that inhabit their cultural order from cosmogony to sociology, from the system of myth to the structures of actual existence. Attending the origins of the universe and the beginnings of humanity, these coexisting forms of "the one and the two" are not merely thus imagined but also historically practiced in various patterns of salience, alternation, and combination. Logically distinct yet not existentially incompatible, they are found in the organization of concrete social groups, in kinship, in chieftainship—even, one might add, in the famous Maussian enigmas of "the gift."

In part, this is how the elephant seems to me because the same dual formulation is widely distributed in the Polynesian islands. It appears in Fiji as the interchangeable contrast between a unitary lineage organization of the social totality, an encompassment of the whole in the ancestry of a divine king (*yavusa* system), and the scheme of society as a synthesis of indigenous and immigrant peoples, joined by the marriage of a daughter of the land with a stranger-king from the sea, and then ordered as a diarchic kingdom under a ritual paramount from the foreigners and a warrior-king from the originals (land-sea or *vasu* system). Again, Samoa has been described in the same general way by Bradd Shore: organized at various levels and in different domains by a synthesis of "symmetrical" and "complementary" relationships. Such structures conjugate classic oppositions of Polynesian culture, as between powers of conquest and powers of reproduction, war and agriculture, legitimate authority by descent and usurpation, the sociality epitomized by the ranked relationship of older brother–younger brother as against the alliance effected through the "sacred" bond of brother and sister. All these and other contrasts that regional specialists will easily identify represent a continuous interplay of monism and dualism.

So Schrempp finds a Maori scheme of "the one and the two" in different gestalts of hierarchy that are much like the Fijan system. One the one hand, authority is vested in a senior chief whose succession to the ancestor of the group entails the inclusion of its members as differentiated forms of his own person. Here the model is the self-affirmation of the divine ancestor of mankind, Tū, who incorporated his brother gods, the ancestors of foods, in acts of cosmic cannibalism. On the other hand, the group is construed as the descendants of an original people and a wandering chief whose heroic virtues of encompassment imitate rather the fertilizing god Tāne, the one who gave rise to humanity and species of multiple things through cosmic acts of copulation. The first encoding an autonomous masculinity and the second its mediation by a transformative femininity, the two find a sociological parallel in descent groups formed by principles of agnation that allow or include membership by cognation. But then, is not the coexistence of "the one and the two" manifest also in Mauss's celebrated text on the gift of tribal valuables? Belonging always to the donor even as it passes to another, the gift thus expresses the force of a higher unity—which for the Maori is an ultimate common ancestry— of those who exchange. Hence the pragmatic aspects of "inalienability" and "debt" by which anthropologists (since Mauss) have sought to explain the necessity to reciprocate. If the Maori rather emphasize the spirit of the gift, the *hau*, is this not the way they represent the pervasive powers of transformation between "the one and the two"?

Not that the paradigm shift initiated by Gregory Schrempp in this work consists in substituting symbolic causes for economic or sociological ones. As I see it, what Schrempp accomplishes is the revelatory inclusion of the social and the practical in the symbolic, as dimensional forms of a cultural order of cosmological proportions, which understanding of what there is, is a necessary condition of any causal explanation. Thus his engagement with Durkheim's sociological epistemology. For all Durkheim's deference to the ideal nature of society and the relative autonomy of collective representations, his argument about the Aristotelian categories of class, cause, time, and the like grounded them in the social morphology. The categories were mental reflections on, and of, the way people were de facto organized. Something needs to be explained here about why this argument has ever since remained appealing even though its logical inadequacies have been known for a long time. Anthropologists have known them at least from the time of Rodney Needham's criticism of *Primitive Classification* (Durkheim and Mauss), to the effect that society is alredy constructed by the mental operations of which it is supposed to be the source. The social groups presumed to be the model for classes of other things and beings could not be perceived as such without the a priori notion of class. For the Maori, Schrempp adds the observation that the metaphysical form—here the Kantian category of quantity, integrating the dichotomy of unity and plurality by totality—is at once more definite and extensive than its specific manifestations in kinship. Organizing a greater variety of phenomena, the metaphysical form retains an existence in representation and practice independently of the social relations that more or less conform to it. Indeed, so far as the indeterminate Maori concept of descent is realized in determinate ancestral groups, it is by conformity to the formal model of totality as the oneness of manyness: for example, the way the Maori chief encompasses the group by referring to it in the first person singular, the famous "kinship I."

One may easily anticipate the accusations of "idealism" that Schrempp's discussion will elicit. Yet the hard-headed social scientists who raise such Cries of Alarum in the name of the realia of praxis are then likely to miss the larger area of unconscious agreement between Schrempp's position and their own regarding the way cultural orders are fashioned. Consider, for instance, the current vogue for explicating diverse cultural phenomena in terms of "power." It appears in this respect that functionalism is no longer practiced in name, only in reality. Power and its correlates such as "hegemony" have become an intellectual black box into which all kinds of cultural content are sucked. But leaving aside this reduction of cultural forms to functional effects (of domination), there remains a large residual resemblance to Schrempp's perspective in the notion of power as a cosmological principle of order—a principle prior to people's experience and constitutive of their institutions. For on one side, to adopt Durkheim's characterization of the coercive social fact, power is understood to impose ways of seeing, believing and thinking that could not have been arrived at spontaneously. This means that people's perceptions of the world, and *a fortiori* their practices, are no simple reflex of experience but are organized by transcendent cultural values. On the other side, notions such as Gramscian hegemony or the ubiquitous power-without-a-sovereign of Foucault amount to political doctrines of the Invisible Hand: superordinate values of order that inhabit the specific structures of ordinary existence, such that in living everyday family life or gender relations people unconsciously produce and reproduce the totalized system of their own submission. If all this seems convincing—as also Durkheim's sociological epistemology—it is probably because it rests on a foundation similar to Schrempp's analyses of the Maori: the sense that general cultural schemes are at work in the organization of people's empirical experiences, customary actions, and social institutions.

All the same, there is something in Schrempp's text, even apart from its monumental or elephantine proportions, that has not been well served by this introduction. For it is simply, charmingly and humorously written—a great read.

MARSHALL SAHLINS

Acknowledgments

IN COMPLETING this study, I am struck by the different strata of intellectual debts that are displayed in it. The first of these belongs to a period of graduate study in the Folklore Institute of Indiana University in the mid-1970s, and reflects in particular an abiding interest that I have in the nature and power of "little" narratives. It turns out that these are relevant to the study of cosmology, for many of the world's great visions of the whole—the ultimate totality—are built up from seemingly minor and familiar stories, such as the tale (known all over the world in slightly different versions) of the race between the tortoise and the hare. Many stories about the origin of the universe are built out of the most familiar and unexceptional of life experiences. The Maori story of the universe that will be considered in the course of this study, for example, is neither more nor less than the story of a particular family— the dissention it experiences and the forms of cooperation it manages to maintain.

Another, and more obvious, element of this first, folkloristic stratum in my study will be seen in the labeling of "motifs" according to the quasi-mathematical formalism of Stith Thompson's *Motif Index of Folk Literature*. Scorned even in the 1970s as precisely that which modern folkloristics is *not* about, the *Motif Index* is a masterpiece of cosmology in an atomistic mode, belonging to the same intellectual epoch that brought us A. O. Lovejoy and Benjamin Lee Whorf. These great figures were cosmologists, all no doubt taken up at some level in the spirit of modern quantum theory. Thompson's *Motif Index* is one answer to what Lovejoy posits as the constitutive question of cosmology: How many things are there in the universe? Thompson gives us a complete litany, from a "Creator" (A0) to "Unique exceptions from curse" (Z357), with many other interesting things (such as F911.3.3 "Animal with men in its belly playing cards, etc.") in between. Thompson's work also manifests, in its own way, the dual intellectual imperatives that Kant, in portraying the character of cosmological thought, saw as giving rise to "transcendental dialectic" or the "antinomy of pure reason," that is, the permanent, irresolvable dilemmas that are induced by the attempt to enumerate completely. For if the goal is a complete enumeration or set of discriminations, the activity of attempting to reach this goal negates its possibility, since any act of discriminating poses itself as a model for some further discrimination. The *Motif Index* (as does many a cosmology) contains strategies for satisfying both imperatives. On one level it declares its own completeness, specifically by beginning and ending with, respectively, the first and last elements from a system that is widely acknowledged as complete, the Roman alphabet; this is a gesture which, moreover, has numerous resonances in popular ("everything from A to Z!") and traditional religious ("I am the Alpha and the Omega." Revelation 1:8) culture. Yet, not unlike the power of containing infinite utterances that is possessed by the finite set of letters in the alphabet, the *Motif Index* locks in forever the possibility of further motifs through a (theoretically limitless) decimal involution, which gives us, for example, T541.2.1.1 "Child born of splinter in hand (foot)"—where even the "foot," now in parentheses, threatens to become a distinct thing-in-the-universe.

A second main stratum of my study belongs to archival and field research in New Zealand. The approach to the Maori material to be considered in the following is fundamentally textual. The main data are original manuscripts written in the nineteenth century by Maori cosmographers, and are now housed in various New Zealand archives. I began working on them during a year that I had available through a Department of Education Fulbright grant for doctoral dissertation research abroad (1981); during this time I was associated with the Anthropology Department of the University of Auckland. In 1982, I held a position at the Centre for Maori Studies and Research, University of Waikato. There I worked within a number of projects, many related to specifically contemporary concerns such as education and economic development. But I was also centrally involved in the construction of a reader on the study of *whaikōrero*, or traditional Maori oratory (Mahuta, Schrempp, and Nottingham 1984). That work has influenced the present study in certain ways; for instance, the recurrent emphasis in *whaikōrero* on tribal identification by features of landscape is one of the sources of the emphasis on "place" and topography that is recurrent in this analysis of cosmogony.

I was fortunate enough to receive an invitation to live, for the duration of the university position, in a Maori community, that of Wāhi Marae, which, along with Ngaruawahia Marae, is the center of the "king" movement and the home of the reigning *arikinui*, or Queen, Te Atairangikāhu. Although the nature of my involvement carried me more in the direction of contemporary political issues than traditional cosmology, the stay at Wāhi nonetheless contributed in two main ways to the present work. One influence lies in the realm of ritual, for I was invited to participate in virtually all the annual cycle of *hui* (gatherings) that are organized around the king movement. The ritual of *hui* appears to be one element of contemporary Maori culture that has particularly strong continuities with pre-European Maori society. The *hui* that I experienced are the source of the speculations about the relation of *hui* ritual to cosmogony that I have presented, some in an earlier paper (Schrempp 1985) and some here.

The second way in which the experience at Wāhi contributed directly was in the opportunity it afforded for further work in the Maori language, which I made the single highest priority of my stay in New Zealand. The language of the documents written in the last century is distinctive enough vis-à-vis contemporary usage that it is sometimes designated as classical Maori; it differs in some ways from what is being taught in the universities and within language revitalization programs. The time at the *marae*, in which I had numerous opportunities to listen to and speak with fluent older speakers, was very helpful in the process of developing enough knowledge to work with the earlier texts, since language appears to begin where analytical grammar leaves off. I am grateful to the people of Wāhi for one of the most interesting and educational experiences of my life.

Of the many scholars and friends who generously assisted me in New Zealand, I would particularly like to mention Robert Te Kotahi Mahuta, Bruce Biggs, Pat Hohepa, Judith Huntsman, Antony Hooper, Robin Hooper, Isla Nottingham, Jane McRae, Sharon Dell, Valerie Sallen, Roger Green, Toon van Meijl, Steven Webster, Michael Goldsmith, and Ray Harlow. I am especially grateful to Jenifer Curnow for a number of thoughtful comments on my analyses and transcriptions of Maori texts. I gratefully acknowledge the members of the staffs of the Anthropology Department, University of Auckland, Centre for Maori Studies and Research at the University of Waikato, Maori Studies at Victoria University, the Auckland Public Library, the National Library in Wellington, and the Hocken Library in Dunedin.

My research in New Zealand culminated in a doctoral dissertation, "Maori Cosmogonic Thought," in the Anthropology Department at the University of Chicago, for which Marshall Sahlins served as chair. I am grateful beyond words for his support during my days as a student and since then, during the long work of revising and augmenting my dissertation research toward this book. I am also grateful for the advice and guidance of the other members of my doctoral committee, David Schneider, George Stocking, and Valerio Valeri, all of whose influence, I believe, will be seen in particular parts of my argument. Frank Reynolds and David Tracy of the Divinity School at the University of Chicago have also been especially supportive of my work; they provided in their interdisciplinary colloquium "Religion(s) in Culture and History" a forum in which to explore many of the concerns of this book. A number of other individuals have read various drafts or parts of drafts along the way: Henry Glassie, Richard Bauman, John McDowell, Hasan El-Shamy, Roy Wagner, Elizabeth Traube, David Konstan, John Bowen, David Aronson, Raymond Fogelson, Webb Keane, Daniel Segal, Miriam Rabban, Phillip McArthur, Judith Neulander, Michael Mason, Theresa Vaughn and Elizabeth Locke. I have profited a great deal from all their comments. The series editors for this book, James Clifford and George Marcus, have both provided me with useful and detailed commentaries at a number of points. I am grateful for the help of the staff of the University of Wisconsin Press, and especially for Robin Whitaker's detailed copy editing. It goes without saying that the scholarly responsibility for the project as a whole and all its details are my own.

At the time of completing this study, the issue that is least resolved in my mind is the question of how to approach the relation of individual and collectivity in the analysis of any style of intellectual life. For the subtitle of my book, I have settled on two collective terms ("the Maori," "the Greeks") not just for purposes of formal symmetry, but also because I was continually impressed by the collective dimension—the many reworkings by different individuals of shared or borrowed ideas and themes—in both ethnographic cases. However, I caution that the collective terms imply *not* that the concerns treated here are thought to characterize exhaustively the intellectual content or spirit of either the Maori or the Greeks, but only that in each case these concerns seem to have formed a significant common focus, or point of interchange, between many thinkers within each of the cultural traditions. I regret that at this moment I am not able to pursue in more detail the study of the individual/collective dynamic within each tradition, and a comparison of them; my sense is that this would be a fascinating study, one that would be very revealing in relation to present-day attempts to come to terms with inherited intellectual concepts such as "myth" and "philosophy."

I am grateful to the Auckland Public Library for permission to publish the extracts from Te Rangikaheke's writings (GNZMMSS 43, 44, 81) that appear in my study. I also thank the National Library of Australia for permission to cite the manuscript of Matiaha Tiramōrehu (National Library of Australia MS 4017) in my discussion of the cosmogonic accounts that were published by John White in *The Ancient History of the Maori*.

Magical Arrows

Sages and Sophists

Human reason has this peculiar fate that in one species of its knowledge it is burdened by questions which, as prescribed by the very nature of reason itself, it is not able to ignore, but which, as transcending all its powers, it is also not able to answer.

—Immanuel Kant, opening line, Preface to first edition of *Critique of Pure Reason*

Y E T   W E   K N O W that humans not only pose answers to the unanswerable, but also often locate the most fundamental principles of their lives in times and places that will never be encountered as matters of direct sensory experience. The capacity for cosmologically vesting existence—and especially of creating mythically and/or ritually mediated experiences of times and places that are otherwise beyond the realm of the senses—is a remarkable, if not defining, characteristic of the human species. The question of course arises whether the capacity for cosmological vestiture might be an exclusively human characteristic, whether, for example, "cosmology" has any meaning in speaking of the minds of, say, nonhuman animals or gods (humans picture gods within or without a cosmos, but do gods do the same for humans?). The present study is confined to the human species, though, mindful of a potential hubris in this sort of delimitation, I leave the question open whether cosmology can be extended in any meaningful way beyond human consciousness.

The concept of cosmology also has an interesting status within contemporary ethnological theory. The term shows a remarkable capacity for deflecting inquiry away from the most basic questions, toward specific ones. Recent ethnology has produced a vast number of valuable studies of particular cosmological accounts and systems, but the large, general questions—such as, What human expressions can be called cosmological? or, Why do humans

engage in cosmological speculation at all?—tend to be submerged in the fascination of the particular. The imprecise definition of "cosmology" seems also
to be accompanied by a feeling that elaboration is unnecessary, as if in the case
of this concept it is admissible to rely upon our "gut feeling." One would indeed have to search at length to find another term more reliant on the assumption of intuitive obviousness, such that any specific attempt at definition is
unnecessary.

What do we mean by "cosmology"? In part we seem to point toward formulations that involve a quest for *ultimate* principles and/or grounds of the
phenomenal world and the human place in it. But cosmology often—and this
aspect stems perhaps from the Greek notion of *kosmos*—seems also to carry
for us a concern with wholeness and integratedness, as if cosmological principles are not only ultimate principles, but also principles of *order* in the
broadest sense, that is, principles engendering and supporting a way of being
that is cognitively and emotionally integrated and whole. In these two kinds
of concerns—the impetus to seek the "ground" of the present order, and the
impetus toward integratedness and wholeness—there is already a potential tension, since the quest for a ground is implicitly a resting of one thing on another,
and thus involves a regression from any given state, whereas the impetus toward
wholeness may engender the task of finding closure, as a condition for
wholeness. The possible tension within cosmology is a matter that we will
return to in a number of ways within this study.

While "cosmology" connotes, in part, descriptions of physical universes,
ethnological concerns often gravitate more toward moral concerns that are
sometimes embedded in such portrayals. In some cases, there is little or no
concern for a physical portrayal of the universe; that is, we sometimes encounter "cosmology" used as an almost exclusively moral term. This suggests
another source for the tendency to leave the concept of cosmology in a nebulous
state. That is, the notion of cosmology is nearly axiomatic to certain styles
of humanistic research; many forms of "symbolic" and "interpretive" analysis,
for example, depend, to one degree or another, on the assumption of an impetus toward ultimate principles of integratedness and order, especially moral
order, within given forms of social life. One source of the nebulous quality
of cosmology thus no doubt lies in the axiomatic or quasi-axiomatic character
that this concept takes on—its existence, that is, not just as an object of study,
but also as a set of framing assumptions with which one carries on a certain
kind of study.

It is not unusual for particularly central concepts to remain poorly defined.
One can find, throughout the history of ethnology, numerous magical concepts
whose evocative power seems to be proportional to their nebulousness—or

perhaps nebulousness is a necessary condition of evocative power. But whatever the source, there is a kind of ultimate unsatisfactoriness in the persistent use of a term which one is unwilling to confront, at least periodically, in regard to the most basic question: What does it mean?

The emphasis that I accord to attempting to distill a basic character (and indeed, is a "theory" any more than an extended version of the same pursuit?) for this phenomenon is motivated by my interest in and admiration for the Durkheimian tradition of comparative sociology, which was organized on the principle of different students each choosing a particular type of "social fact" and considering it cross-culturally (quite in contrast with the Boasian/American pattern of each student focusing on one particular culture). A nearly indispensable part of the Durkheimian monograph was a formal delimitation of the phenomenon under investigation; most readers will recall Durkheim's (1965:62) definition of "religion," or Mauss's (1967:10–11) delineation of the three principles of "exchange." One finds a similarly framed general definition in most of the now classic monographs of the Durkheimian tradition. On the other hand, my sense of a relative lack of interest in trying to articulate a Durkheimian "essence" for cosmology is no doubt related to the fact that the majority of the works I am familiar with on this topic are in the American tradition, which, from the time of Boas onward, has, in varying degrees, tended toward uncertainty if not skepticism regarding the possibility of cross-culturally valid categories.

Yet, while my analysis is in some important sense more on the Durkheimian than the Boasian side of the issue, the stance of approaching cosmology as if there is the possibility of articulating some basic character is here taken up in a spirit different from that which motivated Durkheim himself—and the tempering here also no doubt stems from the influence of the Boasian tradition. The value of seeking the essential character of a phenomenon cross-culturally lies, in my view, not in the expectation of adding another element to a "periodic table" of social facts, but rather in the belief that juxtaposing phenomena bearing a cross-cultural "family resemblance" can be a particularly thought-provoking, creative venture, one whose outcome cannot be predicted in advance. In many ways it is the moment of juxtaposition—the reading of one formulation in the light of another—that is the value. I do suspect that we can, if we try, clarify what we have in mind by "cosmology," and that we can discover at least fragments of an essential character of this phenomenon. But, this aside, there is a distinctive value in the comparative moment itself. It amounts to a kind of intellectual "effervescence" that can emerge in the process of comparison, and which indeed at some level must be the ultimate motivating factor in all cross-cultural research. The experience at issue stems not exactly from the perception of commonalities or the perception of differences, but perhaps from a tension between the two. I suspect that the comparative moment's potential to enliven and fascinate stems from a source deeper than merely academic pursuits, and belongs, as it were, to the basic condition of being human, to the inescapable necessity in human life of dealing with "self" and "other," and of doing so on many different levels simultaneously.

To the critic skeptical of even this modified Durkheimianism, one of curtailed ambition and open outcome, I would reply that the alternative present in much contemporary ethnology is not a true skepticism but a sort of halfhearted skepticism, characterized as much by an unwillingness to give up a concept as by the lack of a sense of obligation to come to terms with it. At the least I would claim that the form of hubris implicit in my approach, the invocation of a unifying essence that might end up an evanescent and "sort of" unity, is not particularly a worse form of hubris than that involved in the unwillingness to give up a term which one regards as undefinable; the one form of hubris is merely more concentrated, and the other more dispersed. The concept of cosmology, or in certain cases the cosmological axiom, is thus one that I do not seek to overthrow—I accept that it is an appropriate axiom for the study of at least some societies—but rather one which I hope to engage and bring to the surface, clarify, and in certain respects, resituate.

ZENO, KANT, LÉVI-STRAUSS, AND THE PURSUIT OF COSMOLOGY

By a roundabout and retrospective process, the hero of my tale, insofar as a general theory of cosmological thought is concerned, turns out to be the pre-Socratic philosopher Zeno of Elea. While working on Maori and several other cosmological traditions, I found myself returning continually to three sources of a theoretical perspective. One was Lévi-Strauss—not the usual Lévi-Strauss, but rather a small and for the most part ignored corner of Lévi-Strauss's theory of myth, which will be explicated in the course of my arguments. A second was the classic work in "history of ideas" by A. O. Lovejoy, *The Great Chain of Being*, a work specifically about Western cosmology, but which seems to me to have implications beyond any single tradition. The third source was the fascinating—some would say, bizarre—arguments about cosmology that occur in Kant's "Transcendental Dialectic," the second of the two main parts of the *Critique of Pure Reason*. Because of the influence it exerted on the founding figures of Boas and Durkheim, nearly all students of ethnology are aware of the general tenor of Kantian epistemology, particularly the notion of "*a priori* categories of the understanding," as laid out in the first part of the *Critique of*

Pure Reason. Indeed the development of contemporary cross-cultural perspectives is scarcely imaginable apart from the inspiration that founding figures drew from the basic arguments contained in the first part of the *Critique of Pure Reason*. The same cannot, however, be said for the arguments of the second half of the *Critique*, the "Transcendental Dialectic," which attempt to portray, among other things, the consequences that flow from applying the a priori categories beyond the bounds of experience. Just as in my treatment of Lévi-Strauss, so in my treatment of Kant: it is the lesser-known side of the perspective that I will explore. In both cases, the lesser-known side is also potentially subversive with respect to the notion of "rationality"; and it is thus perhaps not accidental that it is the lesser known.

What these three figures—Lévi-Strauss, Lovejoy, and Kant—have in common is Zeno. And thus by a kind of triangulation from my main "modern" sources, Zeno emerges as the primordial inspiration of the approach that I take. Though I do not claim to be able to give a minute historical contextualization of Zeno, in the manner of a specialist in pre-Socratic philosophy, this would, in a sense at least, be irrelevant to my purposes anyway. While it may be that Zeno entertained views on space, time, and matter specific to his historical moment, which only the most highly specialized scholar could hope to retrieve, there is the other Zeno as well: the Zeno who has escaped the bounds of his historical moment, to visit subsequent times and regions, and to exercise his strange art. Whatever the difference in surrounding intellectual and cultural context between Zeno and those who came after him, these seem never to have precluded the latecomers from appreciating the logical difficulty that Zeno has called to attention.

My basic claim is that Zeno provides a perspective propitious for beginning, and at least getting a ways into, cosmology considered cross-culturally. To put it another way, I argue that Zeno is able to capture certain characteristics of the nature, intellectual source, and even tangible "matter" (e.g., images, idioms, symbols) of Western cosmology at a general enough level that one might seek to move into other cosmological traditions through him. And at the same time Zeno's perspective provides a reflexive vantage point from which to examine the status of cosmology in contemporary ethnological theory, one that offers a way of bringing certain subliminal Western orientations to light, and providing a basis to make those orientations themselves a part of the analysis.

My invocation of Zeno is thus not in the spirit of a deus ex machina, brought in to tidy up a situation that is conceptually very messy. The "bringing in" is really a "drawing out" of ways in which Zeno's predicament has shaped and reflected central issues in the Durkheimian perspective (including the perspective of Lévi-Strauss). There are thus two main interrelated dimensions to my study. One is an examination of ethnological theory, with an emphasis on the Durkheimian tradition in light of the perspective of Zeno; the other is that of turning the issues that are developed in this study to the issue of cosmology considered cross-culturally. As for Zeno's idea of cosmology, the values that I see might be tentatively grouped under several broad concerns, each of which I will return to a number of times within my experiment.

First, there is, implicitly, in Zeno's paradoxes a portrayal of the cos-mological activity and how one might be led into it—a portrayal, if you will, of the essential character of cosmological thought. This activity seems to be a part of, possibly a precondition for, analytical reason. At issue is the poten-tial of analytical reason to create or fall into infinite recursiveness or regress in its basic activities. Zeno's paradoxes all revolve around portrayals of a kind of basic mental activity of "dividing up"; but they add a further concern. Although dividing might be a modality of consciousness, consciousness, in Zeno's portrayal, cannot be reduced to merely the sum of particular acts of mentally dividing. As portrayed by Zeno, dividing is something that takes place within, or produces, a consciousness of dividing or an *idea* of dividing. The consciousness of dividing (as opposed to dividing as an activity of conscious-ness) becomes a source of speculation in its own right, and particularly so with respect to the question of the "totality"—the ultimate bounds—of this activity. Zeno's paradoxes thus suggest that cosmology—in the sense of the raising of speculations lying beyond any empirical situation—may be immanent in the way in which consciousness is conscious of its own activity. This of course is not the only approach that is worthy of consideration regarding the origin and nature of cosmological speculation; Zeno's is an "intellectualist" theory, and certainly it must be admitted that there are emotional imperatives to cosmological speculation as well. Perhaps the ultimate questions will concern how and why "rational" and "emotional" impulses combine in cosmology. But even if incomplete, Zeno's portrayal of cosmology demands considera-tion both on its own merits and because it raises some issues closely related to foci long-taken as worthy mainstays of cognitive and cross-cultural cognitive research, but as yet inadequately explored.

Zeno's paradoxes are also suggestive with respect to what we might call the "matter" of cosmology. Most immediately I call attention to the con-crete idioms, symbols, and images that are found in many cosmologies. Zeno invoked the image of a race, and that of an arrow in flight, among others. Kant (1965:452), in an argument that derived directly from Zeno, invoked genealogy—or the retrospective searching for one's ancestors, and ancestors of ancestors—as a metaphor of the problem of the cause of the cause, or in other words of the regresses into which reason is led by one of its own necessary forms. But such images—the race, the arrow in flight, genealogy—are not limited merely to Western cosmology; they are found as cosmological idioms throughout the world, and Zeno's perspective may help to illuminate why this is so. As there may be a cosmological propensity in the categorizing capacity itself, so there may be a sort of cosmological potential in certain kinds of images; that is, there may be images that are concrete and cosmologically speculative at the same time. If this is so, then perhaps we also have here the beginning of the answer to the question posed above regarding the interpenetration of "rationality" and "emotion" in cosmology. That is, while reason can apparently entertain abstractly the idea of seriation or regress, the more usual and interesting kind of cosmology may reside in a more embodied speculation—about the extension of the universe not as space but as *our* home, the "home of mankind" (see Boas 1887), or of regress not in time but of *our* ancestors in time.

There is, in Zeno, a consistent theme regarding the ultimate outcome or ending point of reason applied to cosmology: this venture, in Zeno's portrayal, ends in paradox, or pairs of seemingly equally necessary but mutually exclusive propositions about the character of the universe. Inspired in part by Zeno, Kant developed his own treatment of cosmology in terms of his doctrine of "the antinomy of pure reason," or the claim that reason applied to cosmology ends up "divided against itself" (1983:81)—drawn, that is, toward sets of contradictory propositions about such issues as the cause, extent, and decomposability of the universe. It is important to note that in both Zeno and Kant the claim is stronger than merely a claim that, as matters lying beyond empirical investigation, there is no basis for adjudicating between different possibilities that may be suggested regarding such issues. Rather the claim is that, in its own fundamental nature—in the very principles through which it is constituted—reason ends up at odds with itself, ultimately producing irresolvable conflicts when applied to cosmological issues.

The idea that cosmological speculation has paradox or antinomy as a part of its fundamental character is a notion that, whether or not universal, is clearly not limited to the Western cosmological tradition; the very inclusion of the Kantian perspective in this analysis is motivated by the fact that one of the cosmological traditions that I have researched, that of the Maori, typically takes two forms, suggesting contrastive answers on a number of basic issues regarding the nature and shape of the cosmos. The enterprise of Zeno and Kant is appropriately characterized not so much as a cosmology, but as an analysis of cosmological thought, specifically an attempt to lay bare the processes through which cosmological thought ends in antinomy. The Zenoian/Kantian notion of the conflict of reason applied to cosmology, or, more precisely, the Zenoian/Kantian attempt to portray how such conflict develops, provides at least a point of contact between several traditions which seem to share a sense of the ultimately paradoxical character of the cosmological endeavor.

Perhaps the most important, and, certainly to me, the most fascinating, aspect of cosmology to which Zeno can provide entree, is the set of problems inhering in the issue of "representation." Though these problems are legion, it is possible to delineate two foci for which a certain definition of perspective has been achieved. The first of these involves what have been called folk genres, namely, the variety of communally based popular representational frames belonging especially to vernacular tradition. In relation to such genres, there is a long-standing tendency to link cosmology with "myth." But while this is not totally unwarranted, it is also too restrictive. Zeno's "Achilles" paradox contains an allusion to one of the most widespread folktales on earth—a race between two physically unequally matched animals, won by the more clever. That Zeno has seized upon a cosmological potential in a popular folktale can be taken as an allegory for the study of cosmology in relation to folk genres: that is, the whole issue should be dislodged from traditional assumptions and declared "open" for further investigation. I suspect we will find cosmological issues or concerns broached in a wide variety of different popular frames, including epic, riddle, litany, and even proverb, as well as many genres unique to particular societies. There has been a tendency in recent decades among academic folklorists to broaden the term "folklore" beyond such recognized traditional forms, to encompass and in a sense valorize virtually all forms of vernacular discourse. For present purposes, however, the more popular notion of folklore—which would be more likely to call to mind silly little tales of not much account—will suffice; for I mean to show that such familiar little images are, in philosophy and mythology, and within and without Western knowledge, precisely the stuff out of which some of the most grand mental creations have been brought to life.

But beyond the level of folk genres, there is a second realm of issues of representation brought home to us in Zeno's paradoxes, specifically, those involved in the now long-standing—though admittedly loosely formulated—contrastive pair "mythos" and "logos." This contrast has been approached in many ways, including as a polarity within Western intellectual history (Detienne 1986; Vernant 1982). The polar terms are not always formulated in precisely the same way (and, as Detienne's analysis reveals, the terms "mythos" and "logos" have undergone important historical shifts in meaning). Despite the variation, however, there is a recurrence of basic themes, one of which—the contrast, roughly speaking, between the presentation of a lesson in a traditional story, on the one hand, and presentation in a logical or mathematical argument, on the other—will figure centrally in this analysis.

The issues surrounding the mythos/logos pair have been manifested in ethnological theory; indeed it would be a worthy project to analyze the history of ethnological theory from the perspective of this polarity. One of the more interesting contemporary manifestations of something like this polarity has arisen within the context of African studies. Specifically, there is a tradition of some complexity and depth in which European ethnologists have utilized the concept and terminology of philosophy in the analysis and representation of African traditional wisdom and worldview, often with an attendant notion that traditional African expressive forms embody an implicit philosophy, perhaps a specific ontology. The recent response registered by indigenous African writers has been mixed. For example, Kwame Gyekye (1987) agrees with the idea of a continuity between traditional worldview and philosophy, while Paulin Hountondji (1983) argues for a discontinuity—such that African "philosophy" must be seen as yet to come. Hountondji calls attention to the fact that the disposition of European ethnologists to treat African traditional wisdom as philosophy was, in certain cases, part of a pernicious political agenda, specifically that of religious conversion; and one gets the feeling that this forms an important component of the generally negative regard in which Hountondji holds the ethnological project of articulating implicit philosophies.

Hountondji is no doubt correct in the observation that a pernicious agenda might in some cases have been attached to the tactic of representing traditional wisdom as philosophy. But insisting on a radical *discontinuity* between traditional wisdom and philosophy could also form part of a pernicious agenda (a point which arises in this debate in regard to Lévy-Bruhl, who argued that non-Western thought often rested on principles radically at variance with what many Western thinkers have regarded as the sine qua non of rationality, i.e., the "law of contradiction"). The attempt to show either continuity or discontinuity is potentially pernicious, but what makes it finally so is not an emphasis on either continuity or discontinuity per se, but the larger agenda within which either emphasis is taken up.

There is a perfectly legitimate term that combines the idea of similarity and difference, namely, "analogy," which points to similarity within difference. I find it impossible to do away fully with (at least ideal typical) concepts of myth and philosophy, yet I am equally struck by analogies between the mythic and the philosophic, as though there are alternate, but parallel, paths through the same terrain. It is these analogies that I particularly intend to explore, and I find Zeno to be a sort of primordial inspiration in thinking about them. Zeno's formulations intrinsically bring together and juxtapose elements from two poles: the tangible, popular story, and a skeptical, logico-mathematical, analytical spirit. In the more detailed discussion that will follow, I impute to Zeno a motive that is impossible to prove, namely, that the juxtaposition is part of an overall strategy of comparison of forms of representation. If this interpretation be judged overzealous, as an attempt, on my part, to effect a retrospective imposition on the historical Zeno, then I must point out that the juxtaposition itself—between popular tale and mathematical argument—yet remains as an undeniable fact of Zeno's portrayal, something for which there must exist some conscious or unconscious motive.

I admit to having slipped, in the process of writing this work, into a "Zeno as first and best" syndrome. This, however, is not a view of Zeno as first and best in the world, or of Zeno as the beginning of human mental evolution, but rather of Zeno as first and best in what my own cultural/intellectual tradition offers to me in terms of a way of thinking about the nature of cosmology. The kind of cross-cultural approach that I envisage—indeed the only one that seems possible to me—involves not a denial or "trashing" of one's particular intellectual heritage, but the discovery and self-critical use of those parts of it which, perhaps by virtue of seeking the vulnerable underpinnings and challenging the boundaries of that tradition, seem to offer ways both of objectivizing it vis-à-vis other traditions and of passing beyond its borders. In approaching Maori cosmology through analytical perspectives associated with such Western thinkers as Zeno, Kant, and Lévi-Strauss, I do not make the claim that the Maori "have" philosophy (though I am also not claiming that they "do not have" philosophy). My claim is that there is an analogy between some of the concerns and forms characteristic of some classical Western philosophers and Maori cosmology. I see Western philosophy as one form of discourse addressing concerns that are broader than Western philosphy, that is, concerns that are confined neither to the West nor to philosophy. The only sense in which philosophical discourse may be "special" is that some forms of philosophy may create, by virtue of their particular kind of cold abstraction, the possibility for certain kinds of comparisons between different cosmological traditions that we know in terms of the particular tangible stories that they tell. This possibility shows itself even within the corpus of Zeno's various paradoxes, most of which are, at some level, the same "logical" dilemma, but portrayed in different images. Much that is most compelling in many of the accounts I compare— particularly their artistic quality—cannot be captured in this philosophical abstraction. If the particular form of abstraction that is characteristic of philosophy has as its strong point the possibility it creates for acting as a comparative vehicle, the aesthetic/artistic aspect of cosmology or cosmological narrative is what it intrinsically surrenders to achieve this goal.

As noted earlier, Zeno is a problematic figure in his own tradition. Who and indeed what was Zeno? He has been assimilated to mathematics and philosophy, but he could as well be assimilated to a tradition of entertainer, a purveyor of popular puzzles and brain-teasers. The puzzles that Zeno peddled have been developed into the most complex forms of mathematics (e.g., they are sometimes said to be at the root of calculus), but Zeno's own professed form of representation also encompassed the popular story or image. Even among contemporary Western people, it is for a minority that Zeno exists as a mathematician or philosopher; for the majority, he exists as a popular puzzler tied to definite embodied folkloric images. The idea that the modern world retains from Zeno only the disembodied mathematical problem receives a splendid refutation, for example, in Tom Stoppard's "modern" drama *Jumpers*. *Jumpers* revolves around the juxtaposition of different moral philosophies; but the moral concern is given a cosmological ambience through a focus that shifts between arenas of different spatial magnitudes—bedroom, home, university, nation, and a British exploratory mission to the moon—the last of which gives rise to, among other things, a sense of the progressive disenchantment of the cosmos. The cosmological ambience—serious, complex, and farcical all at once, in keeping with the general tenor of the play—is also created in part through numerous allusions to Zeno's and derivative metaphysical paradoxes, often expressed in overlaid images, such as a philosopher's attempt to hit a target with an arrow (which goes awry and strikes, instead, his pet hare, Thumper). Finally, like the Achilles paradox itself, which in turn seems to be emulating the popular tale of the race between the tortoise and the hare, Stoppard's plot unfolds amidst a juxtaposition of two kinds of agility, physical and mental; specifically, the main characters are analytical philosophers and metaphysicians who are also amateur gymnasts ("jumpers"). The more usual "modern" treatment of Zeno's paradoxes involves a passing over of the tangible images so that the mathematical arguments can be developed; it is as if Stoppard passes over the mathematical arguments in order to tap the cosmological resonances of the popularly known Zenoian images.

These and other occasions of juxtaposition of mythos and logos suggest one further point regarding the danger that Hountondji has called to attention of imposing philosophy where it doesn't exist. Specifically, in arguing that African wisdom is not philosophy, Hountondji perhaps makes philosophy into a more monolithic entity than it ever actually is. Philosophical discourse frequently contains, or is even motivated and built around, elements that are traditionally associated with the other thing to which it is contrasted, that is, myth. Kant—the philosopher's philosopher—while plodding through the most abstruse, tortured mathematical abstractions about the nature of cosmology,

suddenly starts talking about genealogy, and imagining an infinite regress of
his ancestors, which is precisely one of the ways that the Maori portray cosmogony. What many a reader remembers from Hegel is the scenario of the
Master and the Slave, that is, the dialectic of consciousness, embodied. The
motive force of the scenario lies ultimately in a hierarchical impetus, and in
the specific dynamics that constitute and flow from it; this is of course a kind
of scenario not unknown in myths of the origin of the cosmos (several variations will be considered in the course of this study).

At one point (pp. 147ff.) I call attention to a way in which Maori cosmology
itself presents an abstract analysis of its own form. The first phases of the
cosmic genealogy do not fully take the standard Maori form of a human
genealogy. They take the form rather of a series of repeating mathematical patterns (that of a regularly compounding numerical sequence); and this pattern
gradually turns into a more typical Maori human genealogy. Thus, if "philosophical" cosmology often has recourse to narrative scenario, there are clearly
instances in which Maori cosmology, which is dominantly narrative, also
makes recourse to a mathematical abstraction or characterization of its own
project. There is a difference between Zeno's approach and that of the Maori,
but it is a difference within which numerous parallels also manage to appear.

It would be incomplete and unfair to Zeno to end other than with a reference
to his subversive character. At least a part of Zeno's reputation rests on an image
of him as intrigued by the limitations and the seemingly ultimately self-
subverting character of rationality as he envisioned it. Though I will spare the
reader from an attempt to portray Zeno as the first to "deconstruct" Western
rationality, it does seem to me that the character of Zeno's doubts and probings
might be not inappropriately raised as emblematic of the present age's sense
of deep despair regarding the possibility of solid first principles. Yet, if there
is something disturbing and nihilistic about Zeno, there is something
regenerative in the form in which the paradoxes are cast; for the paradoxes combine abstract nihilism with tangible marvel. Though abstractly the same problem, pondering the plight of Achilles attempting to catch the tortoise is, for
some at least, a more intriguing exercise than pondering how it is that two vec-
tors are able to intersect. Moreover, Zeno's way of putting it raises a question
that formal geometry can all but totally avoid, namely, the relation of its principles to the experienced world.

The main chapters can be summarized as follows:

In chapter 1, I deal with a lesser-known and little-acknowledged part of
Lévi-Strauss's theory of myth—to show that, in a small but significant corner
of his vast edifice, Lévi-Strauss is a bearer of specifically the problems of Zeno.
The analytic of Zeno is, in Lévi-Strauss, ethnologized, that is, made into a

perspective of cross-cultural analysis. The ethnologization, and not the perspective itself, is the Lévi-Straussian innovation.

In chapter 2, I attempt to broaden the exposition of chapter 1, to give a sense of the deeper historical significance of Zeno's problem, so that Lévi-Strauss emerges as a recent recurrence of a perspective that has been manifested in numerous contexts, from the classic formulation of the Chain of Being, to Durkheim's defense of rationalism in the face of the philosophy of pragmatism, as espoused by William James and Henri Bergson.

Chapters 3 and 4 are discussions of Maori cosmology in terms of the perspective set up in the foregoing chapters. The Maori possess a particularly elaborate cosmological tradition, one with which I have developed some familiarity. My overall emphasis is on the commonality of pursuit between the "philosophical" cosmology of Zeno (and his derivatives) and the "mythological" cosmology of the Maori. I hope to show that the two can be thought-provokingly juxtaposed, that is, that the juxtaposition is a venture that produces new questions and insights, in both directions. Chapters 3 and 4 serve mainly to set up my main attempt at a theoretical characterization of Maori cosmology, which is set forth in chapter 5.

Chapter 6 centers around the images that fascinated Zeno (the race, the arrow in flight, etc.), and points out some instances of cross-cultural recurrence of these or similar images in cosmological contexts. The imagery of cosmologies/cosmogonies from various parts of the world often exhibits resemblances which, I argue, Zeno's perspective and the perspectives that stem from it help to illuminate. The aim of the final chapter is thus to suggest some of these further possibilities of analysis.

If I have one more hope for this work it is that it might make a contribution to the connection that has existed and yet potentially exists between philosophy, on one hand, and, on the other, the variety of disciplines that empirically study cultural traditions cross-culturally (including anthropology, folklore, cognitive science, and others). This latter set of disciplines has given us a sense of the variety and richness of cosmological speculation, but classical philosophy has given us a better sense of ways to situate and envision cosmology as a kind of intellectual enterprise. It is important to note that the kind of interest that I bring to philosophy is not the same as the philosopher's. Philosophy for me is a source of perspective, theory, and inspiration for conducting cross-cultural study. The model here again is Durkheim and his students, who, though philosophically trained, were less obsessed with the detailed analysis of the internal force and coherence of various philosophical positions and arguments than with the ways in which basic ideas and principles from philosophy might be opened up within the broader context of cross-cultural study. They seem to have regarded cross-cultural study as potentially benefitting from the tapping of philosophy as a source of perspective. But at the same time, they seem to have seen philosophy as potentially benefiting from the new kind of evaluation and critique that the trying out of philosophical arguments in cross-cultural perspective made possible. The studies by Durkheim and his students formed a particularly fertile moment in the history of ethnology—and this, I believe, owes in part to the ways in which these scholars were able to conjoin philosophical and ethnographic concerns.

For Kant, the fact that cosmological speculation ends ultimately and unavoidably in antinomy was reason for dismissing speculative cosmology—as least as far as any substantive scientific claim was concerned. Yet even in the event of this rather nihilistic conclusion, Kant argued that what was wanted was not so much a dismissal as an opening up to a broader perspective, that of "anthropology." That what Kant had in mind was not anthropology in the contemporary ethnographic sense is of no significance here. What is important is the necessity that Kant saw of situating epistemology, or at least the epistemology of cosmology, within a broader framework. Kant called for a continuance of the study of speculative metaphysical cosmology—now, however, no longer organized around the question of the metaphysical truth of such accounts, but around the question of why humans engage in producing them, for "the question does not concern the objective validity of metaphysical judgments but our natural predisposition to them, and therefore does not belong to the system of metaphysics but to anthropology" (1983:102).

Chapter One

The Great Race

S O N U M E R O U S are the parallels between, on the one hand, Lévi-Strauss's representations of certain myths which, *ex hypothesi*, recount the origin of discrete categories, and, on the other, the representation of *motion in the famous "Achilles" paradox posed over two millennia ago by the Greek philosopher Zeno of Elea, that one might compose an origin story that founds the one representation on the other.[1] Before attempting to explore this suggested affinity between the perspectives of Lévi-Strauss and Zeno, it should be noted that, quite apart from this specific imputation, Zeno's paradoxes of motion are, by any measure, highly contemporary. On the level of contemporary popular culture, for instance, many mathematical "brain teasers" are, at base, versions of Zeno's paradoxes. More generally, one would be hard put to find other instances of formulations of this brevity (the paradoxes of motion are known mainly through brief characterizations by later philosophers) that have elicited, over the centuries, such a continuous chain of commentary and discussion, right down to the present. In recent commentaries it has become fashionable—to such an extent that it might be regarded as a near mandatory rule, at least within the Anglo-American Zeno genre—to open by citing the words of the late Bertrand Russell: "Zeno's arguments, in some form, have afforded grounds for almost all theories of space and time and infinity which have been constructed from his time to our own" (cited in Salmon 1970:5).

There are of course numerous other themes and theories in Western thought—for example, Anselm's Ontological Proof—which have had a pretty good run, that is to say, which have possessed whatever quality it is that, for periods of centuries, compels other writers to develop their own position in some sort of relationship to it, at least mentioning and thereby showing their awareness of it. But the paradoxes of Zeno are more than this. It is as if they possess some sort of absolute perenniality and resilience that guarantees their reemergence, perhaps in some slightly different form, after each new intellectual watershed. They are, if anything is, metaparadigmatic, that is, always there as a kind of logical exercise or sounding-board against which any emergent perspective can try itself out. In the common regard they are considered to embody some original, founding articulation of the nature of the world. As such they are a little like sacred texts; and, once again like sacred texts, they have spawned over the centuries commentaries and commentaries on commentaries, imparting to many of these, as if through the contagion of the sacred, a part of the numinous quality inhering in the original message.

THE PARADOXES

The Achilles paradox can perhaps be assumed to be part of the common knowledge of Westerners, and this folkloric level constitutes a very real and genuine dimension of its existence. However, for the present analysis something more definite is required; and partly for this reason I will begin with the basic classical texts, from Aristotle and Simplicius, through which the paradox is known to us. They are preceded, however, by a text of Aristotle on one of the other of the four paradoxes of motion, the "Dichotomy," to which Aristotle's discussion of the Achilles refers, constructing itself as an extension (the texts in the following discussion have been drawn from the collection assembled by H. D. P. Lee [1967]).

> T1. Aristotle:
> There are four arguments of Zeno about motion which give trouble to those who try to solve the problems they involve. The first says that motion is impossible, because an object in motion must reach the half-way point before it gets to the end. This we have discussed above . . . . Hence Zeno's argument makes a false assumption when it asserts that it is impossible to traverse an infinite number of positions or to make an infinite number of contacts one by one in a finite time. For there are two senses in which length and time and, generally, any continuum are called infinite, namely either in respect of divisibility or of extension. So while it is impossible to make an infinite number of contacts in a finite time where the infinite is a quantitative infinite, yet it is possible where the infinite is an infinite in respect of division; for the time itself is also infinite in this respect. And so we find that it is possible to traverse an infinite number of positions in a time in this sense infinite, not finite; and to make an infinite number of contacts because its moments are in this sense infinite, not finite. (Lee 1967:43)

> T2. Aristotle:
> The second is the so-called Achilles. This is that the slower runner will never be overtaken by the swiftest, since the pursuer must first reach

the point from which the pursued started, and so the slower must always be ahead. This argument is essentially the same as that depending on dichotomy, but differs in that the successively given lengths are not divided into halves. The conclusion of the argument is that the slowest runner is not overtaken, but it proceeds on the same lines as the dichotomy argument (for in both, by dividing the distance in a given way, we conclude that the goal is not reached: only in the Achilles a dramatic effect is produced by saying that not even the swiftest will be successful in its pursuit of the slowest) and so the solution of it must be the same. (Lee 1967:51)

T3. Simplicius:
    This argument also bases its attempted proof on infinite divisibility but is arranged differently. It runs as follows: If there is movement the slowest will never be overtaken by the swiftest: but this is impossible: therefore there is no motion. . . . The argument is called the Achilles because of the introduction into it of Achilles, who, the argument says, cannot possibly overtake the tortoise he is pursuing. For the overtaker must, before he overtakes the pursued, first come to the point from which the pursued started. But during the time taken by the pursuer to reach this point, the pursued advances a certain distance; even if this distance is less than that covered by the pursuer, because the pursued is the slower of the two, yet none the less it does advance, for it is not at rest. And again during the time which the pursuer takes to cover this distance which the pursued has advanced, the pursued again covers a certain distance which is proportionately smaller than the last, according as its speed is slower than that of the pursuer. And so, during every period of time in which the pursuer is covering the distance which the pursued moving at its lower relative speed has already advanced, the pursued advances a yet further distance; for even though this distance decreases at each step, yet, since the pursued is also definitely in motion, it does advance some positive distance. And so by taking distances decreasing in a given proportion *ad infinitum* because of the infinite divisibility of magnitudes, we arrive at the conclusion that not only will Hector never be overtaken by Achilles, but not even the tortoise. (Lee 1967:51)

I turn now to a consideration of Lévi-Strauss's manner of representing and analyzing certain myths that, *ex hypothesi*, deal with the origin of discrete categories. Because these particular analyses form one of the least explored themes in Lévi-Strauss's writings, the relevant passages will be quoted at more length than is perhaps necessary for purposes of summarizing the argument. Indeed, they can be quoted in near entirety, a point which reveals how minutely they bulk within the corpus. Systems built upon the structured interrelationship of discrete elements, or course, form the main focus of Lévi-Strauss's analysis; the problem of the *origin* of discrete categories—this includes particularly the concern that certain myths appear to show with this problem of origin—emerges as a kind of "sideshow," but one in which, its residual character aside, Lévi-Strauss raises some of the most momentous issues that are to be found in his work.

The themes that will be considered here have a beginning of sorts in Lévi-Strauss's analysis, in *Totemism*, of an Ojibwa myth recounting the origin of the five Ojibwa totemic clans. The story recounts that six anthropomorphic supernatural beings emerged from the ocean to mingle with humans. One of the six, whose glance was fatal to humans, was caused by the other five to return to the waters, while the other five remained with the Indians and "became a blessing to them"; from the five derive the five totemic clans. The Ojibwa story is held in abeyance while Lévi-Strauss moves on to consider some of Firth's data on Tikopia. Lévi-Strauss calls attention to the story of Tikarau, presenting a summary, from which the following is excerpted:

> A long time ago the gods were no different from mortals, and the gods were the direct representatives of the clans in the land. It came about that a god from foreign parts, Tikarau, paid a visit to Tikopia, and the gods of the land prepared a splendid feast for him, but first they organized trials of strength or speed, to see whether their guest or they would win. During a race, the stranger slipped and declared that he was injured. Suddenly, however, while he was pretending to limp, he made a dash for the provisions for the feast, grabbed up the heap, and fled for the hills. The family of gods set off in pursuit; Tikarau slipped and fell again, so that the clan gods were able to retrieve some of the provisions, one a coconut, another a taro, another a breadfruit, and others a yam. Tikarau succeeded in reaching the sky with most of the foodstuffs for the feast, but these four vegetable foods had been saved for men. (Lévi-Strauss 1963:25–26)

After noting various similarities between this Tikopian myth and the Ojibwan one, Lévi-Strauss points out: "In both cases, totemism as a system is introduced as *what remains* of a diminished totality, a fact which may be a way of expressing that the terms of the system are significant only if they are *separated* from each other, since they alone remain to equip a semantic field which was previously better supplied and into which a discontinuity has been introduced" (1963:26). While some further comments regarding these arguments occur in *The Savage Mind* and elsewhere, the most highly developed form of this argument regarding the origin of discreteness occurs in *The Raw and the Cooked*. Several different myths and fragments of myths form the data around which the argument is organized, the following (from Colbacchini's collection) being one of the most critical:

M3. Bororo. "After the flood"

After a flood the earth became reinhabited; but previously men had been increasing to such an extent that Meri, the sun, was afraid and looked round for a way to reduce their numbers.

He therefore ordered the entire population of a village to cross a wide river by means of a bridge made from a tree trunk, which he had specially chosen because it was not very strong. It did, in fact, snap under the load; and all the people perished, with the exception of one man called Akaruio Bokodori, who could only walk slowly because his legs were deformed.

The hair of those who were sucked into the whirlpools turned wavy or curly; the hair of those who drowned in calm waters was fine and smooth. This became clear after Akaruio Bokodori had brought them all back to life by incantations with a drum accompaniment. He brought back first the Buremoddodogue, then the Rarudogue, the Bitodudogue, the Pugaguegeugue, the Rokuddudogue, the Codogue, and finally the Boiugue, who were his favorites. But of all these newly returned people, he welcomed only those whose gifts he approved of. He shot down all the others with his arrows and so was dubbed Mamuiauguexeba "killer" or Evidoxeba "cause-death." (Lévi-Strauss 1970:51)

With the additional information that the "-gue" endings may be plural forms that indicate human groups, Lévi-Strauss suggests that M3 and the rest of the interrelated set of myths in question here, on both physical and social levels, have to do with various ". . . domains, each of which was originally continuous, but into which discontinuity had to be introduced in order that each might be conceptualized. In each case, discontinuity is achieved by the radical elimination of certain fractions of the continuum. Once the latter has been reduced, a smaller number of elements are free to spread out in the same space, while the distance between them is now sufficient to prevent them overlapping or merging into one another" (1970:52).

Lévi-Strauss notes that despite the overall similarity of process—the construction of discreteness through deletion of some members of a continuum—each of the three myths nevertheless constitutes ". . . an original solution to the problem of the change-over from continuous quantity to discrete quantity" (1970:53). To summarize Lévi-Strauss's discussion: the Ojibwa solution is most economical, for deletion by only one allows space between the remaining five. In contrast with this transition from finite to (lesser) finite, the Tikopian solution is pictured as a leap from the potentially infinite to the finite:

The Tikopian solution is more costly: originally foodstuffs were indeterminate in number, and it was necessary to jump from this state of indetermination—that is, from a high and even theoretically limitless figure,

since there was no list of the original foodstuffs—to four, in order to en-
sure the discrete character of the system. We can guess the reason for
this difference: the Tikopia clans are in fact four in number, and the
myth has, at great cost, to jump the gap between the imaginary and the
actual. (1970:53–54)

Lévi-Strauss's formulation of the Bororo solution contains yet another
novelty, in contrast with the formulation of the two previous solutions. For the
"problem of infinity" (that is, of the indefinite, which Lévi-Strauss suggests
in the Tikopian case carries the implication of the possibility of the "theoretically limitless") is now coupled with a hierarchical concern, implied in the
use of different length segments to represent graded units of cultural value.
The problem is not merely that of the possibility of infinite extension of
equal length segments (as in the case of Tikopia: see the diagram of Tikopia
in Figure 2), or that of the possibility of infinite but "egalitarian" divisibility
within a limited segment, as suggested in Figure 1. The issue is, rather, a differential segmentation within the same continuous series, in which differential length of segments represents also differential placement within a hierarchy.
It can be seen in Figure 2 (Lévi-Strauss's Figure 4) that this particular
characteristic differentiates the Bororo solution from the "egalitarian" Ojibwan and Tikopian instances.

1.
2.
3.
4.
5.
n.

Figure 1. Degrees of divisibility

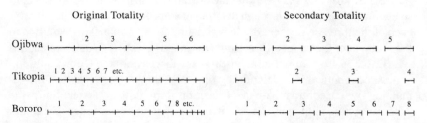

Figure 2. Lévi-Strauss's (1970:54) representation of the transition to discontinuity.

Men had to become less numerous for the most closely related physical types to be clearly distinguishable. For if we admit the existence of clans or tribes bearing *insignificant* gifts—that is whose distinctive originality is as weak as one cares to imagine—we should run the risk of finding that between any two given clans or communities there was an unlimited number of other clans or other tribes, each one of which would differ so slightly from its immediate neighbors that they all would ultimately merge into each other; whereas in any field a system of significances can be constructed only on the basis of discrete quantities. (1970:52–53)

In relation to the Ojibwan and Tikopian formulation,

the Bororo solution is an original one. . . . It looks upon continuity as a sum of quantities, at once very numerous and all unequal, beginning with the smallest and extending to the largest. The main point, however, is that the discontinuity, instead of resulting from the subtraction of one or another of the totalized quantities (the Ojibwa solution) or from the subtraction of a considerable number of equal and interchangeable total-ized quantities (the Tikopia solution), is achieved, in the case of the Bororo, by making the smallest quantities bear the brunt of the operation. Bororo discontinuity consists therefore of quantities unequal among themselves, but chosen from among the largest, and separated by inter-vals that have been created in the original continuum by using the space previously occupied by the smallest quantities (Figure 4). (1970:54)

Of the three cases—Ojibwa, Tikopia, and Bororo—it is perhaps with the analysis of the Tikopian case that the Achilles has the most overt similarities. Some of Lévi-Strauss's comments on the Bororo origin myth are suggestive of issues which in certain respects go beyond those implicated in the Achilles, and which will necessarily lead to a broader quest for the origins of Lévi-Strauss's analytic. On the other hand, the relation of the Tikopian case to the Ojibwan case is the reverse: much of what is characteristic of the Tikopian case is characteristic also of the Ojibwan case, but in a diminished way. This situa-tion is implicit in Lévi-Strauss's presentation itself, which takes the form of a progression through three ethnographic cases which, with respect to the par-ticular issues under consideration, form an ascending scale of complexity.[2]

ZENO AND LÉVI-STRAUSS

The parallelism between Zeno's Achilles paradox and Lévi-Strauss's analysis of the Tikopian Tikarau story (and extending to some extent to his analyses of the Ojibwan and Bororo stories) is of a special character. It might be described as inhering in a certain cluster of traits which themselves are of several levels, some being "structural" and others relating to "content." While the precise significance and particularly the interrelation of the traits may vary between the two formulations, the same set of traits nevertheless shows up in both instances, as if there is some sort of affinity between them. Some of the main ones can be outlined as follows:

1. The main and broadest point of similarity between Achilles as analyzed by Zeno and Tikarau as analyzed by Lévi-Strauss lies in both analyses' focus on *two forms of discourse and their interrelationship.* We have on the one side, in each case, a kind of narrative that involves the great heroes of the past, with their power to effect marvelous and memorable events, and, on the other side, a kind of mathematical diagram that claims to represent some aspect of those events. Without pretending a thorough familiarity with all the historical dimensions and nuances of the distinction, we will consider each of the two analyses here as embodying, and indeed deriving its fundamental impetus from, a contrast of mythos and logos, in the general sense in which I employ the contrast. The projects of Zeno and Lévi-Strauss each grow up around a contrast between starkly different forms of representation, one which, in narrative color and detail, conjures up (to use Radin's term) the "life-blood" of the great heroes, and, in contrast to this, one which represents this in the form of a pure, one-dimensional mathematical extension devoid of mass (i.e., line segments).

The evaluation of the significance of the distinction—including the most critical fact: that it exists at all—of course itself constitutes one of the oldest and richest issues in Western intellectual history. One position is that the logico-mathematical re-presentation constitutes a higher form of understanding; under one possible interpretation this is the position of Zeno, since, according to his argument, the mathematical re-presentation leads necessarily to the dismissal as illusion of the possibility of what is recounted in the narrative. Under this interpretation, Zeno's arguments thus perhaps form an early instance of one of the themes underlying much of Western social thought, namely, "the schema of the conquest of mythos by logos" (Gadamer 1975:242).

Other interpretations are possible. Without arguing that the logico-mathematical form of understanding is necessarily superior, the possibility of re-presenting the working of one mode of discourse in the form of the other constitutes a significant affirmation of the unity of the human mind; so the point of making the translation is not so much to displace one with the other permanently, but rather to demonstrate that it can be done. Something like this would appear to be the position of Lévi-Strauss. There are of course also voices that proclaim this sort of re-presentation itself as illusory or as instrinsically inappropriate (e.g., as sterile and unavoidably reductionistic).

The presence of "myth" in the formulation of Zeno is a bit more oblique than in that of Lévi-Strauss. For in the former the mythic content—the calling up of the figure and, by implication, the world of Achilles—is not strictly necessary, since the paradox of motion can be perfectly well stated without it. One of Aristotle's comments (T2) regarding the Achilles makes this point: ". . . it proceeds on the same lines as the dichotomy . . . only in the Achilles a dramatic effect is produced by saying that not even the swiftest will be successful. . . ." The element of dramatic effect is noticed also by Simplicius (T3), whose account of the paradox pits Achilles specifically against a tortoise, shifting the dramatic effect from the speed of Achilles to the slowness of the tortoise, or to the contrast between them, so that "not only will Hector never be overtaken by Achilles, but not even the tortoise." Alfred North Whitehead (1979:69) begins his classic analysis of the paradoxes of motion: "Eliminating the irrelevant details of the race and of motion—details which have endeared the paradox to the literature of all ages. . . ."

But, despite these commentaries, the invocation of myth (or at least of an "epic" that is highly mythically tinged) ought perhaps not be regarded dismissively as a mere appeal to dramatic effect. While the invocation of Achilles, and by implication the world of heroes, may not be strictly necessary for an exposition of Zeno's technical arguments against the possibility of motion, it may be necessary for some larger intellectual purpose. Specifically, Zeno may be attempting to confront an entire habit of thought. In many societies the relation of the present human world to a past world of gods and/or great ancestors is pictured as a relation of overall diminishment of potentials and powers, including in particular kinetic powers of motion and metamorphosis. Deeds, such as traversals of great distances or physical transmutations, that are accomplished by the gods and the great ancestors with ease and extravagance are retained by humans either not at all or else in some limited way. (The theme is not inconsistent with Lévi-Strauss's view of origin myths, such as those considered above, as depicting a transition that involves a material impoverishment.) The invocation of myth by Zeno is thus perhaps motivated by a more profound intention: to oppose the disclosure and methods of logico-mathematical thought precisely to the form of discourse or mode of thought that *most liberally* asserts all that logical thought would, in Zeno's view, demonstrate to be illusion. Certainly this is true at least in the case of motion, where the exemplary case was to be found not in the world of mere humans, but in the demigod "Achilles the swift" or "fleetfooted Achilles," as he is invariably introduced by Homer. (The power that the figure of Achilles had on the Greek imagination can be seen in the familiar example of Aristotle's *Poetics*, where Achilles is easily the most frequently invoked literary character.)

The paradox as it is presented in the Simplicius account may be a composite form, in which Achilles steps in, so to speak, for the hare in the well-known animal tale of the race between the hare and the tortoise (Thompson K11.3

"Hare and tortoise race: sleeping hare"). Given the fact that this tale is among those attributed to Aesop, and the demonstrated stability from Homeric to modern times of basic folklore forms (see Thompson 1946:272ff.), no great leap is necessitated in supposing that the "plot" of Zeno's Achilles paradox is built, in the Simplicius version, upon a combination of mythical epic and the still widely known folktale of the race between the hare and the tortoise. There are similarities between the myth and the tale that would facilitate the syncretization. The two runners, Achilles and the hare, are the same tragic figure: acknowledged as the swiftest within their class (of humans in one case, animals in the other), both ultimately are defeated in part by their own false sense of invulnerability.

The element of trickery figures prominently in these myths and tales: it is central to Tikarau's success, and of course it was, according to at least one popular account, ultimately through a clever deception, where a military campaign had failed, that Troy was conquered. In relation to the tale of the tortoise and the hare, it is interesting to note that there is another closely related tale, of equal or greater geographical distribution, again still widely known, that involves success through trickery (Thompson K11.1 "Race won by deception: relative helpers"; also Aarne Type 1074). Thompson's summary is as follows: "One of the contestants places his relatives (or others that resemble him) in the line of the race. The opponent always thinks the trickster is just ahead of him. (Told of animals or of men; often of the hare and the turtle.)" The same basic plot, in other words, can oscillate between the situation of the champion's defeat through the trickery of the disadvantaged on one hand and his defeat through overconfidence on the other; such tales can caution those whose outward appearance seems to warrant self-confidence, and to console those whose visible attributes seem not to warrant it—and thus the message of the two variants is the same: there is a proper amount of self-confidence.

The element of success through trickery is in fact one of the most widespread themes of mythology and folktale. The fact that clever deceptions are recounted in a positive light, evoking admiration and glee, is a factor which Victorian anthropologists often called to attention in order to illustrate the savage's inherent delight in treachery and the general want of morality belonging to his grade of existence. But if there is a conclusion to be drawn regarding morality, it is only that, as is similarly the case in the genre of spy novels, morality is usually applied within a restricted range. And yet if the morality lesson was wrongly drawn by Victorian anthropology, life-values are in fact implicated in such tales, and in a way that involves more than a word of caution or consolation. What has not been adequately recognized in such tales is a dimension that stands directly opposed to the Victorian interpretation:

namely that, as a life-value, force almost always emerges precisely as less efficacious than the use of the mind (cf. Detienne and Vernant 1991:13).

Probably no cultures have given more emphasis to athletic prowess than Polynesian ones, where, among other things, tales of great athletes abound. In the Maori case, the whole system of establishing initial claims to tracts of land involves a sort of athletic code: the fearlessness and endurance, swiftness and agility, of the early navigators culminate in certain ancestors and their canoes reaching and traversing certain tracts of land first, and thus having a claim to them. But this athletic code is punctuated by instances of victory through clever deceit. One well-known story for instance (e.g., see Kelly 1980:49–50) recounts how the members of a later-arriving canoe set up a *tūāhu*, or ceremonial marking post, which has been carefully dried over a fire, so that, when the various contenders for the tract of land compare their claims, this *tūāhu*, even though the newest, looks to be the oldest; and the land in this case goes to the losers of the athletic contest but the more clever. But more generally what may be at issue in this brief but unequivocal overturning of the code is a value system's self-reflection, in which, in the triumph of brains over brawn, a purely athletic code, if not wholly transvalued, is at least called into question with regard to its adequacy as a life-strategy.

While this consideration of the theme of trickery in myth and folktale has been a bit of a digression, a point is to be made in regard to Zeno. That is, quite without the aid of "critical philosophy," myths and folktales themselves often pose essential confrontations between qualitatively graded levels of mental activity, with the aim of showing the superiority of one to the other. This confrontation between unimaginative force and cleverness, as present in the world of myth and folktale, may not be totally extraneous to Zeno's purposes in implicating these worlds in his paradoxes. For Zeno is attempting to open up yet another confrontation, analogous but, perhaps as Zeno would see it, one step further along the scale of mind: between the ordinary cleverness that is rooted in pragmatic pursuits, on one hand, and, on the other, a realm of abstract, logical, contemplative thought, in which many of the presuppositions of even clever pragmatic reasoning would necessarily have to be dismissed as illusion.

The issue of myth in the two contrasts, Zeno's and Lévi-Strauss's, could be explored further. There is, for instance, the point of the recurrent connection of the key personages to the sea. Achilles is born from a sea mother and earth father, and Tikarau from a sea father and earth mother. The six Ojibwa creatures are from the sea. Finally there is the twofold implication of water in the Bororo story (M3), in the first instance in the fact that the account begins by citing a flood after which the earth becomes reinhabited, and in the second instance in the use of the river to reduce again the numbers and make possible the discreteness and differences between things. All these can perhaps be seen in the larger context of Lévi-Strauss's concern, in that part of *The Raw and the Cooked* (1970:188, passim), with "creative" and "destructive" water. In the Bororo account the water not only destroys in the sense of reducing the population, but at the same time it also creates the characteristics that differentiate the physical types of the survivors (those who go into the whirlpool coming out with wavy or curly hair, those who go into calm water having fine and smooth hair). No doubt there are culture-specific values in each case belonging to this motif. Common, however, to these stories about the beginning of classification, is the element of water, which, as a substance that is both eminently continuous and divisible, can be seen perhaps as the "natural symbol" of the great continuum over against which the order of the discrete emerges, and at the same time of the possibility of that emergence.

2. In addition to the general point that the analytics of both Zeno and Lévi-Strauss take their impetus from a concern to relate two forms of discourse, there is a more specific convergence between the two analyses. For the ultimate problem that both articulate is the same: *the logical gap between the infinite and the finite.* In one case the issue is that of effecting a transition from a potentially infinite series of classifiers to a finite set, since an infinite series of classifiers poses certain threats to a classification, or even precludes it as a possibility. In the other case the logical gap is presented as unavoidably present in the idea of motion, since in order for any object to move a finite distance (the Dichotomy) or to overtake another object that is moving (the Achilles) it would first have to reach an infinite series of intermediate points. In each formulation, Lévi-Strauss's and Zeno's, the goal, as it were, is the finite, and the notion of the infinite interposes itself problematically—for Zeno, insolubly. As noted earlier, Lévi-Strauss's description of the problem of "any two given clans" corresponds to Zeno's Dichotomy; here it can be added that the presence of the additional principle of gradation in the Bororo case eventuates in a diagrammatic representation that is, as alluded to earlier, the same as that associated with the Achilles, namely, an infinite linear series made up of continuously proportionately smaller segments, which represent either the sequential segments run by Achilles in catching up to the last starting point of the tortoise or of the tortoise in moving ahead in the time it takes Achilles to reach its last starting point.

It could of course be objected that Zeno's Achilles and Lévi-Strauss's analysis of the Bororo myth are perhaps not the same in all respects, since in the Achilles the line might be thought to represent motion specifically. But that is a debatable point; it could be argued that in the paradoxes of motion what is most essentially diagramed is not motion (which is admitted subjunctively, only to be denied as a possibility anyway) but rather space. The paradox consists of the problem that the idea of space, thought of as infinitely divisible, presents to the idea of motion. The Dichotomy projects the infinite in the form of an infinite division of a given space, while the Achilles projects it in the form of an infinite extension. The argument of the latter is that the double action of two objects, one behind and trying to overtake the other, could result only (despite the fact that each new extension is less than the last) in the outcome of an infinite extension. Viewed this way—as fundamentally about the division or extension of space—the paradoxes of motion have a profound relationship to other paradoxes posed by Zeno, particularly the paradox of plurality, which, like Lévi-Strauss's analytic, without implicating the particular issue of motion, addresses the problem of the divisibility of being in general. The following is one of a large number of variants of this paradox, many being attributed to Zeno, others, such as the one below, being attributed to his master, Parmenides:

> T4. Simplicius:
> Parmenides had another argument which was thought to prove by means of dichotomy that what is, is one only, and accordingly without parts and indivisible. For, he argues, if it were divisible, then suppose the process of dichotomy to have taken place: then either there will be left certain ultimate magnitudes, which are minima and indivisible, but infinite in number, and so the whole will be made up of minima but of an infinite number of them; or else it will vanish and be divided away into nothing, and so be made up of parts that are nothing. Both of which conclusions are absurd. It cannot therefore be divided, but remains one. Further, since it is everywhere homogeneous, if it is divisible, it will be divisible everywhere alike, and not divisible at one point and indivisible at another. Suppose it therefore everywhere divided. Then it is clear again that nothing remains and it vanishes, and so that, if it is made up of parts, it is made up of parts that are nothing. For so long as any part having magnitude is left, the process of division is not complete. And so, he argues, it is obvious from these considerations that what is is indivisible, without parts, and one. (Lee 1967:13)

But despite the similarity of the fundamental issue and its diagrammatic representation, Zeno and Lévi-Strauss arrive at opposite conclusions regarding the significance that is to be attributed to these. For Lévi-Strauss the notion of infinitesimal gradation suggests the possibility—that is, the threat—that at some point distinctions finally disappear, so that one can logically pass from one end of a qualitative continuum or "space" to the other through infinitesimal gradations. For Zeno, on the other hand, the point is precisely that, irrespective of level of magnitude, the logico-mathematical possibility of a midpoint within any segment remains, so that any passage through a spatial continuum is therefore precisely not possible.

The fact that analytics based on similar terms and considering the same logical problem arrive at opposite results is a matter of moment, whose full implications cannot be treated cursorily. Ultimately, however, the inversion of results would seem to stem in large part from the fact that while Zeno is finally concerned with "pure" logic (which for him may ultimately contradict sensory evidence), Lévi-Strauss is in this case operating within his concept of a "concrete" or "tangible" logic. Insofar as concrete logic is "logic" it can be assumed to be bound by the forms and limitations—those of "the human mind"—as a "pure" logic. But there is this critical difference: insofar as a concrete logic is "concrete"—in the sense that its essential operators consist of tangible qualities such as tones, colors, and scents—then it is constrained by whatever inherent limitations there are in the whole neuropsychological apparatus of sense-perception. The issues here are several, but one of the most fundamental is that of the "perceptual thresholds," within which distinctions, and therefore structural oppositions, are possible in the various sensory continua that furnish the terms. In the end Lévi-Strauss's concern is not the logical problem of infinity as a logico-mathematical idea, but rather the problem that this logico-mathematical idea poses for a logic that is, ex hypothesi, at the same time intrinsically concrete. Put another way, the logical "loop" that, when applied within the realm of pure mathematical space results in a mere infinite regression, applied in the realm of tangible logic results in something more dire: the nonopposability of the terms and thus collapse of the system.

But this difference, while critical, does not throw off the basic analogy between the analytics of Lévi-Strauss and Zeno, and indeed in one sense rather confirms it. For Zeno too recognized the applicability of the analytic of infinite divisibility within the epistemology of perception. Perhaps the least known of Zeno's paradoxes, the "Millet Seed," while founded on the notions of divisibility and infinity, differs from the paradoxes of motion precisely in that the notion of divisibility is applied directly to sensory data, posing the question of the extent to which sense data as such can be regarded as divisible.

T5. Simplicius:
"Tell me, Protagoras," he said, "does a single grain of millet or the ten thousandth part of a grain make any sound when it falls?" . . . This was the way Zeno used to put his questions. (Lee 1967:109)

3. These considerations regarding the notion of threshold bring us to yet another parallel between the analyses of Zeno and Lévi-Strauss, this one in-

volving a similarity on the level of concrete content, namely, the appearance in each of *the figure of the great runner.* I might at the outset hazard the generalization that in mythologies great athletes tend to be mediators, and perhaps in several senses. Their physical abilities, often deriving from a divine or partly divine parentage, place them above the ordinary order of humans and in the vicinity of the gods.

But, secondly, in line with the previous considerations, we might ask whether their mediating ability has something to do precisely with the fact that they operate outside of normal thresholds, many of which are temporal in character. Certain myths propose a link between speed and sight in that the runner is said to be faster than sight or faster than thought. But of perhaps greater importance would be some concept—already rather diffusely present in ethnological theory—of cultural thresholds within which potentially meaningful acts must fall in order to register as such. Perhaps the exemplary case is that of "the gift," which, following Mauss, imposes and operates within a definite set of quantitative and qualitative prerequisites and limits, and which, following an incipient theme in Mauss that has been further developed by Bourdieu (1985:162ff., passim), transpires only within a set of necessary temporal constraints. A return that is the wrong kind, or too big or too little, *or too fast or too slow*, does not register as a return but as something else—a taunt or an affront.

There is perhaps in myth, in the case of difficult and logically problematic transitions, a tendency toward prestidigitation or its opposite, that is, to invoke figures that are not only qualitatively and quantitatively exceptional but also temporally out of phase with expected natural or cultural rhythms. In all three of the cases analyzed by Lévi-Strauss there is something of this type. In the Tikopian case, the transition is effected because Tikarau is too fast (or more precisely, because he is able, through feigning a limp, to build up the illusion that he is slower than the rest, only to throw off that illusion—but then actually to stumble so that his theft is not complete). The transition in the Bororo case is effected because Akaruio Bokodori, with his real deformity, is slower than the others. In the one case in which the figures are not described as exceptional in locomotion, that of the Ojibwa totemic beings, nonetheless there is a differentiation that even more directly implicates a perceptual threshold, for one of them possesses powers of sight so strong that it kills humans; the transition is effected because this condition dictates that this being return to the waters, thus, according to Lévi-Strauss, allowing the others to spread out and in so doing become more distinct.

In addition to the appearance in the analyses of both Zeno and Lévi-Strauss of the great runner, Achilles and Tikarau, there is the further parallel of the defect, which, as noted above, is also shared by the Bororo character. Akaruio Bokodori limps; Tikarau pretends to limp and then later actually does stumble; Achilles' single vulnerability lies in his heel (this theme is not actually in Homer, but is known from other sources; it is not unlikely that Homer was aware of it). The theme of lameness, as any fervent reader will be aware, is indeed one of the favorites of Lévi-Strauss, and is one that tends to come up specifically in the context of analysis of cosmogonic myths, where it invariably is seen as providing a form of mediation between initial and final states of the world. In "The Structural Study of Myth" (1967:212) an early instance of this theme occurs in reference to some of the characters of the Oedipus myth, where it is linked to the theme of autochthony. And the point is made that "in mythology it is a universal characteristic of men born from the Earth that at the moment they emerge from the depth they either cannot walk or they walk clumsily."

Particularly in the second and third volumes of the *Mythologiques*, Lévi-Strauss links the transition from continuous to discrete (and generally from nature to culture) to the theme of the establishment of periodicity through the segmenting of temporal continua. Within the context of this broader concern, it is noted, "Limping is everywhere associated with seasonal change" (1974:463). With data from various widely dispersed areas of the world, Lévi-Strauss suggests that as a dimension of the general concern with periodicity in the form of the transition of seasons, the irregular gait of a limp provides a "diagrammatic expression" of the desire of some societies "to *shorten* one period of the year to the advantage of another" (1974:464), for example, to lengthen the salmon season in relation to the other seasons.

But commensurate with the opposite conclusions that are drawn (see above), Zeno's and Lévi-Strauss's runners come to opposite fates. Tikarau has a feigned vulnerability as a guise over real soundness and therefore (partly) succeeds, whereas Achilles has a real vulnerability under the supposition of invulnerability and is ultimately overcome. Success or failure resonates through the entire analytics of each. In Lévi-Strauss's framework, in the *Mythologiques*, the runner's success parallels, and casts some of its aura upon, the larger project, which on several levels—between different mythologies of neighboring groups, and between, as suggested above, something like mythos and logos— affirms the possibility of passage in the form of translation (". . . my ambition being to discover the conditions in which systems of truths become mutually convertible and therefore simultaneously acceptable to several different subjects . . ." [1970:11]). But in the case of Zeno the failure of the champion parallels the pervading sense of the inherent vulnerability of the ways in which the world is ordinarily thought of. Mythos and logos lead to irreconcilable views of the world; seemingly one must be abandoned as illusion. The seeming obliviousness of Zeno to certain "commonsense" notions, for instance that one runner can overtake another, can be seen perhaps in the context of a style of thought that was experiencing its optimistic "first blush," and affirms in a way a point that Lévi-Strauss alludes to: that Western science had its origins not, as some radical empiricist view might have it, in a stricter adherence to and more direct and immediate inference from the tangible qualities that appeal to the senses, but, rather, in a readiness to abandon the senses (see esp. Lévi-Strauss 1978:5ff.).

The contrasting attitude, that of relative rapprochement of mythos and logos, can be seen in the historical context, much broader than the discipline of anthropology, in which the view of logos as the single epitomizing achievement of humanity—and the single "norm" for civilization or individual life—is, for many, experiencing a "last blush."

4. But despite the fact that Lévi-Strauss and Zeno occupy different corners with respect to the fundamental issue of the interrelationship of mythos and logos, there is an equally fundamental sense in which they belong to the same broad intellectual tradition. This is a particularly complex issue which cannot here be worked out in all its intricacy; but, in approximate terms, I refer to *a certain tendency to link ultimately the notion of logical intelligibility with the notion of stasis.* There is a notable absense in Lévi-Strauss's representation of the transition from continuous to discrete series, namely that—perhaps analogously to motion in Zeno's diagrams—the transition itself is not represented, but only the static initial and final states.

On the other hand, however, there is a sense in which Lévi-Strauss's fuller scheme does contain a representation of the possibility of transition (which could also serve as a representation of motion): as noted before, while the notion of an infinitely divisible continuum suggests to Zeno the impossibility of motion, it suggests to Lévi-Strauss precisely the possibility (or threat of the possibility) of transition between all the members of a segmented continuum. But Lévi-Strauss's acceptance of this possibility and of its formal representation ultimately is turned into a kind of roundabout rejection. For while Lévi-Strauss accepts motion (he has no problems with the possibility of a runner; and, more abstractly, recognizes the possibility—the threat—of transition through the original continuum, and, again, the possibility of the transition from a continuum to a series of discrete segments), it is an acceptance in which the possibility of transition is given existence just long enough to banish it forever as a possibility. The transition away from the continuous and to the discrete—and, more important, away from the possibility of at least certain kinds of transitions—is, *ipso facto*, viewed as a transition to a system that is "logically richer" (1970:53). This is only one of many points that suggest the general tendency in Lévi-Strauss to link logical possibility, or better, the possibility of logic, to orders of invariants.

There are many other examples, and they show up in interesting ways. For instance, in his debate with Sartre, Lévi-Strauss did not really deny the dialectic, but rather insisted that dialectical thought is really analytical thought set in motion (see esp. Lévi-Strauss 1966:251ff.); this implies that what constitutes the central logic in this form—which is considered by many to be an intrinsically dynamic logic—is something static that can be abstracted from it. Lévi-Strauss's picking out, in this case, the static aspect of an apparently dynamic form, illustrates a recurrent theme in his theory of human mentality. For in many cases (including the one being analyzed here, the transition from continuous to discrete in traditional cosmogonies; and, again, in a different form, in the notion of "*bricolage*"), motion (change/transition/event), far from being denied, is posited as the first principle, the initial situation. Over against this the mind works by seeking ways to reduce change to changelessness, trying to form a structured representation of the detritus of a primordial flux, which tends to be taken as a given and not subject to further analysis *as such* (the only possible analysis of it consists precisely in the attempt to reduce it to structure). According to Lévi-Strauss, this is what the cosmogonies that he considers attempt to do; but the process of stoppage that Lévi-Strauss sees in cosmogonies is in many respects merely a narrative depiction situated, at the beginning of time, of an operation that Lévi-Strauss views the mind as carrying on all the time.

If the connection of all this to Zeno seems to have been misplaced, without attempting to work out the details, I suggest that a main point of connection will be found in the intermediary, Henri Bergson. Bergson's (1911:308ff.) treatment of Zeno occurs directly adjacent to his classical argument that the mind should be regarded as working like a "cinematograph" or like a "kaleidoscope," that is, as forming stopped pictures of a kind of primal motion that is characteristic of all being. Bergson, *on the level of matter*, rejects Zeno's argument against the possibility of motion, and, instead, accords to motion a primal character. But Bergson maintains an even more profound continuity with Zeno, for the proof of the impossibility of motion, discounted (indeed inverted) as a theory about matter, is retained in principle as an argument about the working of the mind. For Bergson, who appears to be followed by Lévi-Strauss on this point, although motion is not denied in the world of things, it is yet regarded as in some fundamental way anathema to reason.

There are, to be sure, insightful counterthemes in Lévi-Strauss, for instance, the comment on Maori society alluding to the possibility of an "evolutionary" socio-logic, and moreover the implication, in discussions of "hot" societies, that "event" can be a principle of explanation. But these are not subtly developed and remain set against the general drift; we get neither the explication of what a "hot" socio-logic would be nor even any firm assurance that there could be such. Lévi-Strauss seems to accept the general idea that in some sense formal disciplines of logic, mathematics, and science have been developed in the most complexity within the Western intellectual tradition, so that there is this twist: logic as a formal abstract tool is most highly developed precisely in those societies whose forms of sociality, committed as they are to history in the sense of "event," have most fully surrendered it, where society itself, that is, can no longer serve as its locus and subject matter.

The positions of Zeno and Lévi-Strauss can be put in even broader contexts, though only vaguely at this point. For, many cosmogonies, theologies, and philosophies, Western and non-Western, ancient and modern, in one way or another posit a cosmogonic antinomy or question as to whether the fundamental nature of what is, is still and inert, or active and in motion. Zeno's formulations can be seen as proposals relating to this great debate, theories about which took a variety of forms in classical Greek philosophy. The next chapters, on the Chain of Being and on Maori cosmogony, will deal with other versions of this antinomy. For present purposes it is enough to note that in terms of an age-old and geographically widespread cosmological antinomy, Lévi-Strauss's sympathies, at least with respect to the issue of what is humanly intelligible, fall in some fundamental way on the same side as Zeno's. For both, the intelligible world is the static world. For Zeno, the other seems to be illusion; for Lévi-Strauss, the other is a sui generis order which he tends to regard as inscrutible *as such*. Intelligibility is a matter of placing upon that order an interpretation which itself may be a kind of illusion—since, following Lévi-Strauss's penchant for optical metaphors, one might conclude that in the end it is "all done with mirrors"—but an illusion which, in a mode consistent with a given society's view of the world, provides some fragile intelligibility and degree of workability. Creative as it is, the implicit allusion to Zeno and the race which occurs in Lévi-Strauss is not the first occurrence within the Durkheimian tradition. It is, in certain essentials at least, a replay of Durkheim's response to the dangerous new philosophy of pragmatism (an incident that will be considered at a later point [chapter 5]).

One other aspect of the difference between Lévi-Strauss's and Zeno's analyses consists of the fact that the same logical problem (the transition from infinite to finite) appears within different "genres," one whose purpose is to found, and one whose purpose is to confound. That there is in each analysis (Zeno's and Lévi-Strauss's) something like the opposition of mythos to logos has already been discussed. But in Zeno there is something else as well. For while the underlying analysis that gives rise to the issue is essentially logico-mathematical in nature, and while the content in which it is couched and presented is that of myth and folktale, the ultimate framing attitude of speech genre is one that has always been a common ground of Western science and folklore, namely the "puzzle" (I am not attempting to be too subtle here about the variety of distinctions folklorists make between such things as conundrums, riddles, enigmas, and so on).

So, between the formulations of Zeno, on one hand, and those of Lévi-Strauss, on the other, which proceed through the same abstract principles, there is a major genre gap, which in turn correlates with the opposite conclusions, as noted above, that they reach regarding the significance of the idea of infinite divisibility. The example can be useful in suggesting something about the relationship of the two genres. For, despite the fact that the two genres seem generally to embrace opposite attitudes of mind—the one apodictic, the other fundamentally stymied—they may in fact be very close and interposable. If myth is ready to lay down fundamental truths and paradigms with an attitude of sacred certainty, this attitude may be inspired by precisely the great riddles that loom behind those certainties. Myth and riddles both deal with very fundamental issues, and the transition from "It is this way!" to "Is it this way?" is both facile and fragile, particularly in grand cosmological speculations. There are cases in which cosmogony is a riddle rather than a myth (or perhaps something in between: a mythic riddle or a riddling myth). The Vedic cosmogonies—interesting as well for their numerous parallels in structure and content with Polynesian ones—are a primary example; the attitude of the hymns is often enigmatic and riddling, for example:

> Who really knows? Who will here proclaim it? Whence was it produced?
> Whence is this creation? The gods came afterwards, with the creation of
> this universe. Who then knows whence it has arisen?
> Whence this creation has arisen—perhaps it formed itself, or perhaps it
> did not—the one who looks down on it, in the highest heaven, only he
> knows—or perhaps he does not know. (O'Flaherty 1981:25–26)

The analysis of "genres" in relation to cosmogony could of course form an entire analysis in its own right. Here the general point will suffice: besides the content and structure of a cosmogonic narrative, the attitude of mind as reflected in a particular speech category forms another issue to be heeded inasmuch as it is a "variable."

As noted above, the position of Lévi-Strauss regarding the historically fateful distinction of mythos and logos would, particularly when seen in contrast with a perspective like Zeno's, seem to be one of supporting an attitude of rapprochement: they are not identical, but they are in some wise inter-translatable. What can be thought naturally in one can be at least crudely and with difficulty re-presented in the other. This attitude of relative rapprochement is evident in other ways also, one of which has to do with a recognition of certain commonalities between the insights on the human condition that are achieved, on one hand, in traditional mythologies, and, on the other, in Western science. It is a case of turning against the smugness of nineteenth-century scientific evolutionism—not, however, so much by the "usual method" of empirically discrediting findings and listing the sins of the practitioners, but rather by showing the mythic quality of the scientific vision by demonstrating the currency in many traditional mythologies of certain fundamental ideas which Western evolutionism tended to regard as its own privileged insights.

The general theme of a transition from nature to culture in Lévi-Strauss itself undergoes a transition (this was first called to my attention by Valerio Valeri). It is transformed from a concern, in the first edition of *Elementary Structures*, that was influenced by the notion of an actual transition from state of nature to state of culture somewhere in the course of human prehistory, to, in later editions and works, the recognition of something like this transition as a recurrent theme in various traditional mythologies or ideologies. A specific instance of this general transition can be observed with respect to the cosmogonic themes that are being considered here. In the case of these cosmogonic themes, the shift is observable not so much in the contrast between early and late Lévi-Strauss, but rather between the earlier formulations within the Durkheimian tradition and those of Lévi-Strauss. For particularly in *Primitive Classification*, Durkheim and Mauss picked up strongly on the common nineteenth-century theme, perhaps known most widely from Tylor, of human mental evolution as following a course from a state of confused and blurred mental associations and images to one of more objective and discrete categories and classifications, as epitomized in Western science:

> Not only has our present notion of classification a history, but this
> history itself implies a considerable prehistory. It would be impossible to
> exaggerate, in fact, the state of indistinction from which the human mind
> developed. Even today a considerable part of our popular literature, our
> myths, and our religions is based on a fundamental confusion of all
> images and ideas. They are not separated from each other, as it were,
> with any clarity. Metamorphoses, the transmission of qualities, the sub-
> stitution of persons, souls and bodies, beliefs about the materialization
> of spirits and the spiritualization of material objects, are the elements
> of religious thought or of folklore. Now the very idea of such trans-
> mutations could not arise if things were represented by delimited and
> classified concepts. The Christian dogma of transubstantiation is a

consequence of this state of mind and may serve to prove its generality.
However, this way of thinking exists today only as a survival. . . .
(Durkheim and Mauss 1972:5)

The small part of Lévi-Strauss's writings that deals with cosmogony or
origins might be said to be similarly occupied with this transition from confused to discrete, which is linked to the more general theme of transition from
nature to culture. Moreover the theme of this transition occupies roughly the
same part and proportion in Lévi-Strauss's work as it does in Durkheim's and
Mauss's; for, in both cases, Lévi-Strauss, and Durkheim and Mauss, the main
concern is with the organization of given systems, and the concern with the
origin of those systems surfaces as a small and residual, but distinct, inquiry.
But the *difference* between the formulations of Durkheim and Mauss, on one
hand, and Lévi-Strauss, on the other, constitutes a specific instance of the
general shift noted above. For, in Durkheim and Mauss, the evolution out of
an initial state of indistinction is a generic evolution posited for mankind by
nineteenth-century science; in Lévi-Strauss, the evolution out of an initial state
of indistinction is called to attention rather as reflecting a fundamental human
concern that recurs in various forms in many of the world's mythologies. It
could of course be argued that this transformation of the theme by Lévi-Strauss
is merely a form of forcing Western concerns onto non-Western materials. But
on the other hand—and this is the interpretation that at this point seems more
plausible—it could simply be taken as one of many indications that even the
grandest paradigms of Western social science are, at base, often folk notions
recast within the rhetoric and style of "science."

Chapter Two

Cosmogony Today, Cosmogony Yesterday: The Further History of the Chain of Being

You may remember that I have written that myths get thought in man unbe-
knownst to him. This has been much discussed. . . . But for me it describes
a lived experience, because it says exactly how I perceive my own relation-
ship to my work. That is, my work gets thought in me unbeknownst to me.
—Claude Lévi-Strauss, *Myth and Meaning*

ONE OF THE myths that thinks itself in Claude Lévi-Strauss is the one that is known particularly by virtue of Arthur O. Lovejoy's classic exercise in the history of ideas, *The Great Chain of Being*. Any attempt to summarize Love-joy's explorations, however, will inevitably take on a kind of fleshless character. After all, Lovejoy's work spans nearly two and a half millennia of Western philosophy, and, despite the many colorful threads that Lovejoy manages to weave together, we are assuredly getting only "highlights"; any summary therefore will be highlights from the highlights. One could merely state the three main principles—"plenitude," "continuity," and "gradation"—which would be a summary of sorts. But this too is highly unsatisfactory, since it conveys nothing of the moral values, traditional rhetoric, metaphysical and poetic sen-sibilities, in short, of the various dimensions of worldview that engender and accompany this complex of ideas. Much of what is fascinating about the Chain lies in the reworking of the major patterns in terms of the thousand variations in detail, tone, and arrangement; yet most of this will admittedly be lost here.

However, any invocation at all of the Chain might be perceived as a detour into matters properly medieval. I will argue that, on the contrary, the concerns of Lovejoy's work are of great relevance to some recent anthropological in-terests. Moreover, the past to which these principles belong is not necessarily all that distant. Eighteenth- and nineteenth-century anthropology, in its

39

adherence to a notion of a hierarchy of racial types, may have been conditioned in part by the principles of the Chain of Being (see Stocking 1968:113, 119). While it is hoped that the specifically racialist applications are no longer viewed as intellectually compelling, the complex itself is still very much alive. And the main foci that make up Lovejoy's analyses would indicate why: the main concerns lie with the logic of some of the most fundamental and fertile ideas in Western thought regarding the principle of hierarchy, and moreover, particularly in the long sections on medieval thought, such concerns invariably occur within the context of a religious worldview that was incessant in its commitment to a "totalizing" perspective and principles of explanation.

The highlights that follow are presented merely for the purpose of getting started; it is simply accepted, as noted earlier, that this is a case in which a summary cannot claim to be a substitution for the larger work, which, anyway, is assumed to be one of general familiarity. Most of the examples and illustrations derive in some way from the *ur*-text, that is, from Lovejoy's work. In addition there is a highly interesting recapitulation and development of the Chain in an article by Formigari (1973), and a few further illustrations derive from that. However, in many cases I have overlaid other or further interpretations, so that the presentation here, while owing most of its inspiration and illustrations to these two sources, cannot necessarily be considered as authorized by either of them. It should be recognized that, as is already evident in the foregoing, I am permitting myself a kind of reification that will inevitably be involved in speaking, for the sake of convenience, of certain recurrent themes, actually quite diverse in their detailed formulation, as though they form a monolithic construct (named the Chain).

PLENITUDE, CONTINUITY, GRADATION (IMPULSION)

The complex itself, although composed of several propositions, can nonetheless perhaps be caught most fully in spirit by thinking of it the way that Lovejoy tends to: as fundamentally an answer to a particular question, namely, How many beings ought the world contain? The intellectual tradition that Lovejoy examines is, despite great diversity of historical epoch and philosophical system, united in the general principle by which it answers: *It ought to contain all possible kinds.* The first and most important principle of the Chain is the principle of plenitude.

Associated with the principle of plenitude are two closely related ideas, each of which can be seen as deducible from plenitude (although plenitude is not deducible from either of them [cf. Formigari 1973]), and each stressing different of its logical implications. One of these is the principle of continuity, or the notion that "nature does not pass from extreme to extreme *nisi per medium*" (cited in Lovejoy 1960:79). Each species should begin where another leaves off. There should be no sudden leaps between kinds in nature—a corollary of the principle of plenitude in that a leap would indicate a qualitative gap within which something could exist but doesn't. The idea has as one of its epitomizing expressions the notion of nature's *horror vacui*.

The third principle is that of gradation, or the notion that on some scale of goodness, some things are better than others. Gradation, too, is deducible from the principle of plenitude, though by another route, namely by the principle that ". . . *non essent omnia, si essent aequalia*: "if all things were equal, all things would not be" . . ." (1960:67). Although one could, logically, choose any criterion (for instance, size or color) and derive, from the principle of plenitude, that all possibilities within that scale should exist, nonetheless, in medieval formulations, in such scales (particularly those involving sensory, intellectual, and motile powers, all of which were thought to be powers of "soul") the temptation of assigning a moral evaluation was simply too great to resist, so that most *scala naturae* were at the same time scales of moral perfection. Though he does not regard it as the most consummate expression of the Chain, Lovejoy begins his account with Plato's mytho-philosophical cosmogony, the *Timaeus*, where he finds arguments of sorts for plenitude in several formulations, such as the notion of the original Living Creature, and more particularly in the "one-universe" argument. According to Plato:

> God therefore, wishing that all things should be good, and so far as possible nothing be imperfect, and finding the visible universe in a state not of rest but of inharmonious and disorderly motion, reduced it to order from disorder, as he judged that order was in every way better. It is impossible for the best to produce anything but the highest. When he considered, therefore, that in all the realm of visible nature, taking each thing as a whole, nothing without intelligence is to be found that is superior to anything with it, and that intelligence is impossible without soul, in fashioning the universe he implanted reason in soul and soul in body, and so ensured that his work should be by nature highest and best. And so the most likely account must say that this world came to be in very truth, through god's providence, a living being with soul and intelligence.
>
> On this basis we must proceed to the next question: What was the living being in the likeness of which the creator constructed it? We cannot suppose that it was any creature that is part of a larger whole, for nothing can be good that is modelled on something incomplete. So let us assume that it resembles as nearly as possible that of which all other beings individually and generically are parts, and which comprises in itself

all intelligible beings, just as this world contains ourselves and all visible creatures. For god's purpose was to use as his model the highest and most completely perfect of intelligible things, and so he created a single visible living being, containing within itself all living beings of the same natural order. Are we then right to speak of one universe, or would it be more correct to speak of a plurality or infinity? ONE is right, if it was manufactured according to its pattern; for that which comprises all intelligible beings cannot have a double. There would have to be another being comprising them both, of which both were parts, and it would be correct to call our world a copy not of them but of the being which comprised them. In order therefore that our universe should resemble the perfect living creature in being unique, the maker did not make two universes or an infinite number, but our universe was and is and will continue to be his only creation. . . .

The construction of the world used up the whole of each of these four elements. For the creator constructed it of all the fire and water and air and earth available, leaving over no part or property of any of them, his purpose being, firstly, that it should be as complete a living being as possible, a whole of complete parts, and further, that it should be single and there should be nothing left over out of which another such whole could come into being. . . . (Plato 1981a:42–45)

The notion of all possible kinds was not, within a Platonic context, necessarily an imprecise answer, for a world of possible forms defined in advance, so to speak, what could have existence. Yet, as Lovejoy points out, there was also the twist that, despite a tendency to view this world of possible forms as the most fundamental verity, a mere form was regarded as less good than one that had existence as well. The notion that lack of existence is somehow a delict is highly recurrent, taking on historically a number of variations, one of which consists of the notion that there is a kind of impetus-to-be residing in mere possibility. As Leibniz, centuries later, wrote, "In possible things, or in their very possibility or essence there is an exigency to exist, or (so to speak) claim to exist; in a word, . . . essence of itself tends towards existence" (cited in Formigari 1973:328). In the Middle Ages, as will be considered in more detail, the notion of this impulsion raised from various angles the question of whether God was constrained to create. So recurrent is this theme of an impulsion, bridging "potential" and "actual," that one might reasonably think of it as a fourth main idea belonging to the complex that Lovejoy analyzes (though it is of a different order in that the other three are, loosely speaking, structural, while this one is, in a premodern sense, existential). As noted before, plenitude is the fundamental concept, continuity and gradation being, through different channels, deducible from it. The idea of impulsion is similarly also closely related to plenitude: in the notion that all possible things ought to be, plenitude stresses "all possible things" and impulsion stresses "ought to be," but shading into something like "strive to be."

As one might suspect, the Middle Ages were one of the Chain's best periods, this despite, and no doubt because of, the fact that the essential regard in which it was held was one of ambivalence. Perhaps the most recurrent theme in Lovejoy's treatment of the medieval adaptations is precisely that ambivalence. On the one hand, the Chain was compelling in relation to the assumption of a designed, orderly cosmos, from each part of which, and in their interrelation, it ought to be possible to read the mind of the Creator. But on the other hand, ". . . it was impossible for a medieval writer to make any use of the principle of plenitude without verging upon heresies" (Lovejoy 1960:69). Following Lovejoy, within the framework of an ambivalent acceptance, the Chain gave rise, in medieval thought, to three great interrelated antinomies—the first having to do with freedom versus determinism in the will of God, the second with the problem of evil, and the third with alternative intentions, and hence alternative interpretations of the inner nature of God—that can be read from the Creation.

The first issue, that of freedom versus determinism in the will of the Creator, can be seen as the development of the notion that the lack of existence of something that could exist constitutes some sort of delict or defect. Was the Creator free to create gratuitously and at whim, or was he constrained by his own perfection not to allow defect? The problem inheres in the variety of criteria of moral perfection that was available to medieval thinkers. On the one hand it would be an imperfect God that would allow defect, but on the other it would also be an imperfect God that would be constrained by other than his own will.

The second antinomy rests on much the same issues as the first, but in regard to the problem of evil. For a possible moral implication of the notion that all possible things ought to exist is that evil things too should exist. Was the perfect Creator constrained to create that which was less than perfect? that which was evil? One particularly intriguing development within this line was the theme of a *justification of evil by reference to totality*, so that, for instance, Thomas Aquinas felt constrained to write, in a fashion out of character with his larger formulation, that "a universe in which there was no evil would not be so good as the actual universe" (cited in Lovejoy 1960:77). The Chain was implicated in the ongoing rumination on the "problem of evil" within yet another train of thought which, Lovejoy argues, reached its zenith in terms of both positive expression and cynical reaction in the eighteenth century, namely, within a kind of "necessitarian optimism" holding that the world must be as it is, and that it is therefore the "best of all possible worlds."

The third great antinomy, related to the first two, is the problem of what is to be read from the Creation regarding the nature of the Creator. One argument would have it that a plenitudinous creation constitutes a necessary self-expression of the Creator's inner nature; but this is directly opposed to another view, regarded by many as compelling, that is, that the Deity's nature is essentially quiet and self-contained. And so two sorts of idea existed in precarious balance and sometimes conflict, one, as Lovejoy (1960:82–83) summarizes it, of "unity, self-sufficiency, and quietude, the other of diversity, self-transcendence, and fecundity," or, again, as between a view in which "the One is undivided and eternally at rest in its own self-sufficiency" and the notion of a "restless 'active principle,' which is manifested in becoming, motion, diversification" (1960:93–94). According to the one argument, fullness and diversity in themselves reveal a necessary attribute of the divine nature; and it is in terms of this argument that one can understand, for instance, Aquinas' argument that a universe containing angels and stones is better than a universe containing only angels (1960:77). It is again in terms of this antinomy that one can understand some of the paradoxical language about the divine nature, such as Fludd's phrase, "When One shall be Variety" (cited in Lovejoy 1960:95).

No doubt because of their "totalizing" orientation, the principles of the Chain appear recurrently in attempts to comprehend the arrangement of the heavenly bodies. In these contexts plenitude in some cases became synonymous with infinitude. Perhaps the most elaborate development of this theme is to be found in Giordano Bruno; to cite just one of a myriad of arguments: ". . . if infinite active power doth actuate corporeal and dimensional being, this being must necessarily be infinite; otherwise there would be derogation from the nature and dignity both of creator and of creation" (cited in Singer 1950:233).

Kant too was influenced by the argument:

> If, again these star-systems are viewed as members in the great chain
> of the totality of nature, then there is just as much reason as formerly to
> think of them as in mutual relation and in connections which, in virtue
> of the law of their primary formation that rules the whole of nature, con-
> stitute a new and greater system ruled by the attraction of a body of in-
> comparably mightier attraction, and acting from the centre of their
> regulated positions.
> . . . But what is at last the end of these systematic arrangements?
> Where shall creation itself cease? It is evident that in order to think of it
> as in proportion to the power of the Infinite Being, it must have no limits
> at all. (Kant 1970:137–39)

While Lovejoy writes extensively of a transformation that took place in the eighteenth and nineteenth centuries in which, particularly in the biological but also in the cosmographic applications, the Chain was "temporalized," nevertheless he has nothing to say regarding Darwin; and the analysis in fact terminates at approximately the time of the appearance of Darwin. Although not the first implication of the Chain within a temporalized scheme, the eighteenth century nevertheless marks one of the most radical shifts in terms of large-scale application and general acceptance of the idea that the plenitude of the universe is not necessarily all given at any one time, but rather through a temporal process. Everything that can be, will be, but not necessarily all at once. While this sort of evolutionism has a number of superficial similarities to the later Darwinian type, at a deeper level, and particularly in terms of the different worldviews that these two types of evolutionism tend to engender or accommodate, they could hardly be more radically opposed. For in place of the notion that, according to a design, all things that can potentially be are at some time actualized, Darwin substituted the notion of "transmutation of species," with the implication that species themselves are contingent and mutable, having a kind of shifting, statistical character.

The notion of transmutation was particularly at odds with the traditional applications of the ideas of plenitude and continuity, where such mutations would be inconceivable. Something changing into something else—and thus of necessity leaving its place in the scheme—would mean that a gap would be created. Perhaps more significantly, to fall back on Plato's one-universe argument, anything that changes into something else can change only into something that already exists. So, in terms of two of the most fundamental qualities of the traditional Chain—the inherent teleology, and the immobility (by which I mean here that the scheme or design itself remains constant even though the actualization may be construed as a temporal process)—Darwinism was firmly at odds with the traditional Chain.

Following what is unspoken but seems implicit in Lovejoy, there is thus good reason to say that Darwinian evolutionism marked the end of the Chain as a potent intellectual scheme in the West (and that, of its many applications, it met its death, not inappropriately, in the realm of biology). On the other hand, however, there would be a certain logic in calling Darwinian evolution a transformation rather than a termination (cf. Formigari's [1973] treatment of Darwin). For even though in terms of the implications for how the world order came to be and is maintained, Darwinian evolution challenges the traditional Chain in its most fundamental implications; nonetheless in abstract principle there is a continuity between the Chain and Darwinian transmutation, namely, in the principle of continuity itself. For the same principle of "infinitesimal gradation," which, in the traditional Chain, forms the basis for an ordered, immobile scheme based on the maximum number of forms (see

Lovejoy 1960:90), serves in Darwinian evolution as the very basis for the claim that *any one* form can, so to speak, gradually turn into another one by passing through an infinitesimally graduated set of intermediaries. Retrospectively it can of course be seen that the Chain, in the principle of continuity, contained the seeds of the destruction of the traditional worldview with which it is most closely and persistently implicated over two millennia. The nineteenth-century debates between the various forms of the temporalized Chain and Darwinian evolution form one of the most intriguing moments of Western intellectual history: no two ideas were more similar and more different (see Schrempp 1983).

Earlier it was noted that Lévi-Strauss's analytic of myths recounting the origin of totemic systems goes through a progression in complexity in considering, in turn, the myths of three different societies, Ojibwa, Tikopia, and Bororo. We are now in a position to articulate more precisely the nature of that analytical progression.

The analysis of the Ojibwa myth rests essentially on the principle of continuity (the six beings are interpreted and diagramed contiguously, one beginning where the last leaves off). The analysis of the Tikopian myth is based upon the principles of continuity (as previous) and plenitude (the "high and even theoretically limitless" series of original foodstuffs [Lévi-Strauss 1970:53]). The Bororo analysis implicates continuity (as previous), plenitude (the possibility of "an unlimited number of other clans" [1970:52–53]), and gradation (because the clans form a kind of *scalum culturae*, diagramed as a "sum of quantities, at once very numerous and all unequal, beginning with the smallest and extending to the largest" [1970:54]). The three basic principles comprised in Lévi-Strauss's analytic of cosmogony are precisely the principles that, following Lovejoy, have from time immemorial formed the basis of Western cosmography. The main transformation is that the Chain is now a technique of specifically sociological analysis. In place of a general ontological angst regarding the possibility of the "infinity of kinds of beings between any two kinds of beings" (Lovejoy 1960:331), we have a specified sociological angst: the fear of discovering that "between any two given clans or communities there was an unlimited number of other clans or other tribes" (Lévi-Strauss 1970:52–53).

Common to all three ethnographic cases analyzed by Lévi-Strauss is the notion of a reduction—the creation of a discrete order through the deletion of some members—which, as far as I know, is a distinctive analytical innovation by Lévi-Strauss, an innovation, moreover, that is closely related to the issues comprised in structuralism. We can imagine a further chapter for Lovejoy's history, one perhaps entitled "Structuralizing of the Chain of Being" to complement his chapter "Temporalizing of the Chain of Being." The main purpose of the present chapter is to continue this sort of prolegomenon to the study of cosmogony. But it may be possible as a secondary effect to lay the basis for a future chapter in Lovejoy, since, it is suggested, Lovejoy's work fairly well articulates the tradition that is thinking itself in Lévi-Strauss, or rather, in that residual part of Lévi-Strauss that is concerned with the analysis of cosmogony.

In the way that the principles of the Chain underwent various transformations within the philosophical systems and worldviews characteristic of various epochs (of which its historicization in the eighteenth century constitutes a ready example), so also has Lévi-Strauss's version of the Chain been shaped in particular ways in terms of dominant concerns of the structuralist worldview. The most diagnostic of these is already evident, namely the overriding concern with insuring the possibility of opposability, or "difference"—expressed in the recognition of a recurrent pattern of reduction of a chain, or, more tersely, in the maxim, suggested by Lévi-Strauss (1979:431), that as nature abhors a vacuum, culture abhors a plenum. Despite the fact of his having brought to social science the cutting edge of mid-twentieth century linguistic theory, there are those who have always felt the presence in Lévi-Strauss—it is meant as a compliment—of a solidly and profoundly medieval strain.

This hypothesis of the Lévi-Straussian transformation of the Chain is easily accommodated within the more general intellectual transformation that was suggested earlier, all the elements of which point to a sort of progressive imputation of a universal mythic quality to Western social science. That is, the theme of a nature-to-culture transition conceived as a privileged European scientific perspective is, in Lévi-Strauss, eventually displaced by the recognition of the nature-to-culture transition as a cross-culturally recurrent theme in myth. Moreover, the idea that human mental evolution is constituted specifically in a transition from indistinction to the recognition of discreteness undergoes, in its transmission from Durkheim and Mauss to Lévi-Strauss, a trade-in on similar terms. So, here as well, the Chain of Being, which, in the Western intellectual tradition, formed in the eighteenth and nineteenth centuries a Eurocentric ordering of the world's peoples, is transformed by Lévi-Strauss into the hypothesis that something like its basic principles appears recurrently in the envisioning of social order by various of the world's peoples.[1]

There is little prima facie reason for rejecting the hypothesis of Lévi-Strauss's link to the tradition of the Chain. While Lévi-Strauss's thought has evolved in a post-Darwinian world, and while he gives no indication of rejecting biological Darwinism, nonetheless a good part of his own method seems singularly uninfluenced by the basic character of that view, a fact which at least in part has to do with the purported "timeless" orientation of the societies that he specializes in studying, but which may reveal broader sympathies as well (see point 4 of the Zeno–Lévi-Strauss comparison—pp. 33–35).

For Lévi-Strauss as for Durkheim, there is an analogy to be made between biology and society or between biological and social "morphology." Durkheim took the structural analogy in an explicitly evolutionary direction, positing different types of social forms that represent a line of development of society considered generically (see especially *The Rules of Sociological Method*, chapter 4 [1982]). It is sometimes argued that a general form of social evolutionism, based on something like Durkheim's scheme of social morphology, is still present in Lévi-Strauss. Whether this is so or not, the truly intriguing point is that, in one of his last major discussions of the theme of continuity, that in *The Naked Man*, Lévi-Strauss subjects modern biological evolutionism to an interpretation that confounds what is for many its defining point—namely, continuity in development—and asserts, in effect, that what appears as continuity is ultimately discontinuous.

That is, as previously discussed, many of Lévi-Strauss's earlier formulations appear to follow Bergson in accepting a primordial motion or flux as a condition of all being, and the stopping of it as a condition of the mind. In Lévi-Strauss's later argument, however, it is as if the state of flux exists, rather, in a middle ground between mind, which knows only discontinuity, and nature, which also *at its ultimate level* knows only discontinuity. The theme appears most forcefully in Lévi-Strauss's discussion of the diagrams of D'Arcy Wentworth Thompson, which illustrate, in Lévi-Strauss's words, that "it is possible, by means of a series of continuous transitions, to move from one living form to another and, with the help of an algebraic function, to deduce the outlines or external differences . . . which make it possible to distinguish at a glance, from their shape, two or more kinds of leaves, flowers, shells or bones, or even whole animals, provided the creatures concerned belong to the same botanical or zoological class . . ." (1981:676).

However, Lévi-Strauss also calls attention to a passage in which Thompson himself notes that the principles of classification necessarily impose discontinuity. And then Lévi-Strauss adds the argument that this recognized condition of the mind—that it needs to introduce discontinuity in order to classify—has only just now been shown by a recent discovery of modern science to be not just a condition of the mind, but a general condition of biological nature:

> With the discovery of the genetic code, we can now see the objective
> reality behind this theoretical requirement for a principle of discontinuity
> operating in the processes of nature and in the constructions of the human

mind, to limit the infinite scale of possibilities. Only in a mythic universe . . . could the species be so numerous that the differential gaps between them became imperceptible. And if the myths themselves conform
to a similar principle of discontinuity, this is because, in reconstituting
the properties inherent in the world of the senses, but whose objective
foundations they could not be aware of, they were simply making a
general application of the processes according to which thought finds
itself to be operating, these processes being the same in both areas, since
thought, and the world which encompasses it and which it encompasses,
are two correlative manifestations of the same reality. (1981:678)

FURTHER ADHESIONS

One other point can be made regarding the Chain in Lévi-Strauss. That is,
certain other *indirect* features that often accompany the Chain of Being also
show up in Lévi-Strauss, usually in the general vicinity of the expositions of
his cosmogonic analytic. I will briefly mention a few of many such features,
which, invoking a venerable old anthropological term, we might refer to as
adhesions.

One profound parallel is to be discovered in the similar ways in which Plato,
within the text that Lovejoy cites as a sort of rough beginning point of the tradition of the Chain, and Lévi-Strauss, within one of his discussions of totemism,
argue the impossibility of anything new coming to be, within the systems
they are respectively discussing. In both Plato's *Timaeus* and Lévi-Strauss's
Totemism, the exhaustive character of the original cosmic inventory is advanced
as a condition which *ipso facto* precludes the coming into being of anything
new. At several points Lévi-Strauss suggests that Polynesian societies, and
Maori in particular, are "evolutionary" in that they posit the origin of man
not merely through a vague notion of descent from some original being, but
rather through a line of intermediate beings that form a gradual transition
(1963:30ff.; 1966:232ff.). (In the precise way in which Lévi-Strauss makes
this point, it is of questionable validity in the case of the Maori; nevertheless
it could be rephrased in such a way that the broader point would hold.) This
view, he asserts, is different from and incompatible with totemism, which,
". . . as in certain games of patience, lays all its cards on the table at the beginning of play: it has none in reserve to illustrate the stages of transition between the animal or vegetable ancestor and the human descendant" (1963:31).

The argument is reminiscent of Plato's claim, noted earlier, that there could
have been only one creation, "inasmuch as there was nothing left over out of
which another like Creature might come into existence" (1981b:32–33). In the
case of Plato the issue is the coming to be, *in toto*, of a second universe (in

the form of a second comprehensive Living Creature—the first of which contained all possibilities); in Lévi-Strauss the issue is the coming to be, within a given universe, of a single new entity. But both ground the static and "unproductive" nature of the system not, in this instance, in some abstract commitment to stability, but in a formal, axiomatic property of the system, namely, that it is defined as full-at-inception.

Another parallel is to be found in a certain moral insight implicated or allowed by this axiomatic fullness, namely, the need for and simultaneously the provision of a means for justifying the defective. It occurs within the analysis, discussed above, of the three totemic myths, in reference to the recurrent theme of physical defect within them. While free of any theological implication, and while involving concerns specific to his particular concept of structure, the argument nevertheless has resonances with traditional theodicy. We might consider it, for instance, in relation to an argument made by Giordano Bruno, that it is "not permissible to carp at the vast edifice of the mighty Architect because there are in nature some things that are not best, or because monsters are to be found in more than one species. For whatever is small, trivial or mean serves to complete the splendor of the whole" (cited in Lovejoy 1960:119).

And thus there can be no "grade of being which, in its own place in the series, is not good in relation to the whole body" (Bruno, cited in Lovejoy 1960:119). Lévi-Strauss argues:

> Mythological figures who are blind or lame, one-eyed or one-armed, are familiar the world over; and we find them disturbing because we believe their condition to be one of deficiency. But just as a system that has been made discrete through the removal of certain elements becomes logically richer, although numerically poorer, so myths often confer a positive significance on the disabled and the sick, who embody modes of mediation. We imagine infirmity and sickness to be deprivations of being and therefore evil. However, if death is as real as life, and if therefore everything is being, all states, even pathological ones, are positive in their own way. "Negativized being" is entitled to occupy a whole place within the system, since it is the only conceivable means of transition between two "full" states. (1970:53)

A third element consists in a propensity toward astronomy. While perhaps the majority of formulations that Lovejoy treats have to do with some innerworldly sphere, particularly the chain of living beings, the principles of the Chain also appear recurrently in the context of attempts to discover the order of the universe as manifested in the multitude of heavenly bodies. In regard to this astronomical propensity, it might simply be noted that *The Origin of*

Table Manners, a work in which the principles of the Chain have a particularly noticeable presence, also happens to be Lévi-Strauss's *De Caelo*, containing extended treatments of various constellations, night and day, sun and moon, "the days and the seasons," and "the stars in their courses" (the other volumes of the *Mythologiques* also deal, though to a lesser extent, with these themes).

A fourth set of elements consists in what might be referred to as the traditional hortatory adhesions of the Chain. One of these is humility. As Lovejoy (1960:122ff.) points out, while there were some interesting inversions of the theme, for instance in Pascal, the various expressions of the vastness of the cosmic edifice, and hence the smallness of man, were readily implicated in the service of the traditional religious emphasis on this virtue. In the case of Lévi-Strauss we merely have to turn to the closing section of *Table Manners*, entitled "The Moral of the Myths," to find the humility lesson, expressed precisely in a contrast between an attitude of deference to the world, on one hand, and, on the other, a compulsion to destroy its myriad forms:

> We . . . find that mythology . . . conceals an ethical system, but one which, unfortunately, is far more remote from our ethic than its logic is from our logic. If the origin of table manners, and more generally that of correct behavior, is to be found, as I think I have shown, in deference towards the world—good manners consisting precisely in respecting its obligations—it follows that the inherent ethic of the myths runs counter to the ethic we profess today. . . . For, since childhood, we have been accustomed to fear impurity as coming from without.
>
> When they assert, on the contrary that "hell is ourselves," savage peoples give us a lesson in humility which, it is to be hoped, we may still be capable of understanding. In the present century, when man is actively destroying countless living forms, after wiping out so many societies whose wealth and diversity had, from time immemorial, constituted the better part of his inheritance, it has probably never been more necessary to proclaim, as do the myths, that sound humanism does not begin with oneself, but puts the world before life, life before man, and respect for others before self-interest. . . . (1979:507–8)

Intriguing and humanistically compelling as the above lesson on humility taken in itself might be, there is the following intellectual problem: although the lesson on humility implicates a contrast between the "savage's" deference to the world and Western civilization's disposition to destroy its natural and cultural fullness, only slightly earlier in the same volume there occurs another comparison of traditional and Western—specifically in a contrast of classical Roman and American Indian society—implicating the same terms, but in which they are reversed. For in the latter comparison, plenitude is on the side of the Romans, and a stance against plenitude on the side of the American Indians. The attribution of the stance against plenitude is referred back to and presented as an elaboration on the theme of the reduction of an original series, recounted in the three totemic myths that we have considered. The antiplenitude stance, moreover, in this discussion, aligns with societies committed to an atemporal regime, whereas espousal of plenitude aligns with societies committed to history. The comparison has to do with, *ex hypothesi*, certain fundamental differences between Roman and Indian mathematical systems:

> This power of multiplication, feared by the Indians as a deadly threat, was regarded by the Romans as offering them their chance of survival. For them, there was something exhilarating in the procedure which consists in repeating the same operation several times on the product of the preceding operation. They were intoxicated by the vistas of the future opened up by the progressive gradation of the groups. . . . In short, from a yet static formula, they derived the hope of a process of historical evolution, whereas the Indians, unable to tolerate any events other than those they encapsulated within the already enacted time of myth, wanted those events to have a finished character which would guard them against any possibility of development, apart from the repetitive development of periodicity.
>
> This difference in attitude with regard to high numbers admirably reflects the contrast between a society which is already determined to be historical, and others which are also historical no doubt, but most unwillingly, since they believe that they will lengthen their duration and increase their security by excluding history from their being. It is an old saying that nature abhors a vacuum. But might it not be said that culture, in the primary form in which it opposes nature, abhors a plenum? This, at least, is the conclusion suggested by the preceding analyses. (Lévi-Strauss 1979:430–31)

Perhaps there is ultimately no contradiction in this reversal of terms because of the fact that the level of analysis tends to shift simultaneously with the reversal. That is, perhaps we are to take it that it is the cultural commitment to "put a vacuum where there has been a plenum" (1979:431) that leads to an attitude of deference to physical nature; conversely, it is a cultural commitment to "putting a plenum where there was a vacuum" (1979:431) that ultimately leads to the attitude of quiescence in the face of the destruction of physical nature as has occurred in the West—so that cultural vacuum goes together with natural plenum, and cultural plenum with natural vacuum. Lévi-Strauss writes:

> By rejecting and fragmenting nature, culture strives in the first place to
> put a vacuum where there has been a plenum. And when it opens itself
> to change, it allows itself the complementary possibility of putting a
> plenum where there was a vacuum; but at this point, it must bow to the
> inevitable and use for its purposes forces which it formerly condemned,
> since history, which provides it with the means of this reversal, inter-
> venes in culture as a kind of second nature: that nature which men se-
> crete during the historical process, as they cover up the past with ever
> new layers and press the old layers ever further down, as if to fill in the
> yawning gap between themselves and a world that nature itself, now
> plundered and enslaved, is on the point of abandoning. (1979:431)

But a separation of levels along these lines is not entirely convincing. If the
commitment to a vacuum in the sense of a deletion of the Chain is cultural,
then so—it would seem—would be the inclination of the "savage mind" to build
up elaborate, maximally discriminating classifications (emphasized in *The
Savage Mind* and elsewhere).[2] Moreover, in two of the three totemic myths
an ambivalent attitude could be read in the form that the deletion takes—namely,
that the deletion, though seen as necessary, is by the smallest possible amount
(in the Ojibwa case, by one; in the Bororo, by the smallest members of the
continuum).

Moreover, Lévi-Strauss makes the interesting argument elsewhere that the
"primeval continuity" appears in some cases to be invested with a "power"
that ". . . is still to be felt at those rare points where it has survived its own
self-destructiveness: either to the advantage of men, in the form of poisons
they have learned to handle; or to their disadvantage, in the form of the rain-
bow over which they have no control" (1970:280). Lévi-Strauss's arguments
regarding the plenum and the vacuum are abstruse and cannot be pursued in
further detail here. The point that I wish to make here is that if I am correct
that Lévi-Strauss's implication of the Chain reveals a kind of contradictory
attitude—reflecting and attributing both attraction to and rejection of the principle of plenitude—then in this respect his analysis falls right into the tradition, since this is the more-or-less standard attitude that this principle of thought
seems to elicit.

In brief, the fifth and also final traditional adhesion that I wish to point out
(though there are many others) is that of ambivalence. It is possible that the
ambivalence stems from an ambiguity and self-negating quality that inheres
in the principle of plenitude itself. If we want a similar though alternative expression of why the philosophers in various traditional societies have apparently
seen it necessary to introduce a principle—in the form of a deletion—that expresses the necessity of settling for a little less than the maximum possible

(might this also be a part of the logic of sacrifice?), we can do no better than cite one of Lovejoy's summary comments regarding the principle of plenitude: "When its consequences were thus fully drawn, it confronted the reason of man with a world by which it was not merely baffled but negated; for it was a world of impossible contradictions" (1960:331).[3]

A world of impossible contradictions. The idea that *the attempt to think the totality of being lands reason in a realm where it ends up negating itself in endless dialectic*, or, in other words, that ". . . rationality, when conceived as complete, as excluding all arbitrariness, becomes itself a kind of irrationality" (1960:331), is the idea that Kant elegantly and tortuously philosophized (see chapter 5), that Lovejoy historicized, and that Lévi-Strauss ethnologized—after Zeno gave his name to it.

Chapter Three

Maori Cosmogonic Thought:
A Text of Orientation

THE PRESENT CHAPTER considers a Maori narrative with particular reference to the cosmogonic orientation of the larger mythology, and more generally, of Maori society. This chapter and the one that follows are limited to cosmogony as it is recounted in prose narrative form; together these two chapters form a preamble to the attempt made in chapter 5 to bring together these prose narratives with the other form in which Maori cosmogony is recounted, namely the form of genealogy. The inspirations for the present analysis derive from a number of perspectives, particularly those considered in the previous chapters, in which Zeno, or more precisely Lévi-Strauss's ethnologization of Zeno's approach to the cosmos, forms a main point of orientation.

One particular tenet of Lévi-Strauss's perspective, however, poses immediate difficulties, namely, the emphasis that is accorded to the analysis of all the variants of a particular myth. The concept and definition of variants are in themselves difficult enough. The issue is compounded by complexities in Maori ethnography and ethnology that are coming into focus at the present time. One of the more imposing debates concerns the question, To what extent does the notion of a single Maori people reflect an indigenous social conception? One argument would have it that the unitary notion is largely a European fabrication, or else was fabricated in response to the European presence.

In terms of method, the way in which that question is answered could be of moment. For if one were to accept the notion of a single Maori people, then one might approach all the indigenous cosmogonies of New Zealand as partial images of the same object, each incomplete in itself, but together forming a total view—a view that exhausts all possible vantage points for viewing the common object. If, on the other hand, one were to take the position that emphasized the relative autonomy and social and cultural distinctiveness of various major tribal groupings, then the analysis of the various versions of cosmogony might more appropriately take the form that it takes in the *Mythologiques,* in which one begins with the accounts belonging to a particular tribal area, and then moves outward to explore transformations within mythology and society and culture more generally. One—arbitrarily—picks a given text with which to begin.

The analysis here will tend toward the latter method, for several reasons. Firstly, while the cultural and social diversity characteristic of Maori society is likely not as great as that which is to be found through the expanse of the Americas, it is certainly not insignificant; the cosmogonic accounts of the Maori themselves picture the process of biological speciation, and cultural speciation among different tribes, as developing through specifically oppositional processes. Secondly, in line with this, the latter method is prudent: less has to be undone if one, in setting up a perspective, overestimates heterogeneity, only to discover a greater than expected unity of view, than if one underestimates heterogeneity, only to find his formulation unraveling at every turn and ultimately unable to be sustained. Finally, there is an inescapable practical point: many of the Maori formulations are extremely intricate and complex; and to attempt to incorporate immediately into a unified picture all formulations that are in some way related would be not only imprudent but also, practically, impossible. More is to be gained by initially working closely, even at the risk of partiality, with a particular "text of orientation" than by opening up the analysis too early. At the same time, I hope to show that in doing this it is possible to reveal patterns significant and compelling enough that, when the analysis is opened up, it will gather in much.

The version that I will consider in this excursus is, perhaps largely by virtue of historical accident, probably the most widely known (at least in the Western world) of the many cosmogonies that have been written by Maori cosmographers. Some of these are to be found only in archives, whereas others, like the one considered here, exist both in archives and in published form. The version in question was written in the mid-nineteenth century by the Arawa chief Te Rangikaheke, who was employed to teach George Grey about Maori language and customs. It was subsequently published several times by Grey, in Maori and English, with various degrees of faithfulness to the original, and is most popularly known to English readers from the translation that appears in Grey's *Polynesian Mythology.* In the transcriptions that follow, I have basically followed those that Grey published in the appendix to his *Ko Nga Moteatea* (1953). I have, however, compared Grey's transcriptions with the original manuscripts and with some more recent transcriptions by Jenifer Curnow (1983, 1985), and have made some emendations to Grey's transcriptions on the basis of these comparisons. I have not on the whole tried to improve upon Grey's method of punctuation (see Curnow's discussion of the issue of punctuation [1985]). Translations are mine, though made in consultation of Grey's and Curnow's. Agathe Thornton (1987) has also written on these accounts, emphasizing especially the issue of oral versus literary style.

A main feature of the analysis below will be the separation into levels or "schemata," following the example of Lévi-Strauss in "Asdiwal"—but, *mutatis mutandis*, expressly with the notion of cosmogony foremost. Since a sort of minimal definition of a cosmogonic narrative is one that recounts how the world comes to assume its present state from some previous state, the schemata will be patterns of change between initial and final states. As indices of change I am using the simplest possible indicator, one stemming from the tradition of the Chain of Being, namely, the quantitative indicator: How many kinds of things ought the world contain? The schemata are defined by transitions that take place in the amount of stuff in the world, under the assumption that each of these changes is significant. Even though, however, the base criteria by which this analysis takes its cue for defining a schema is quantitative, the quantities in question concern the basic things that make up the world, so that there can be no clearer instance in which—to invoke an idea that once again fascinated Bergson—quality and quantity turn out to be the same thing. Though the Chain and the perspectives that flow from and are congealed in it are the main sources of the quasi-mathematical frame of the analysis that follows, I note with interest that Thomas Crump comments, in the context of his recent cross-cultural explorations of "numeracy," that "any cosmology belongs essentially to the world of applied mathematics" (1990:48).

The question will inevitably arise: Why carry out this separation into various schemata? One reason is that the view of cosmogony espoused here concurs with the point made by Lévi-Strauss, that the kind of temporality characteristic of mythological narrative has certain features that have to be taken into account, features that are different from those in which the ordinary "flow of life" is sometimes thought to be experienced. On one hand, myth seems to go on endlessly repeating the same thing on different levels; and on the other hand—and this is what concerns us here—it evinces a quality of evolving simultaneously on several levels (cf. Lévi-Strauss 1971). Assuming there is some mental reality to the schemata that I locate, it does not need pointing out that raising them to conscious awareness and analysis is not necessary in order for the myth to work—that is, to prove a captivating and compelling, not to mention in this case an extraordinarily aesthetically pleasing, account of the origin of the world. The ultimate intellectual reason for making the separation of levels stems from the belief that "poetics" has its rules, and therefore is subject to analysis, or in other words, that making such a separation of levels will facilitate an understanding of the cosmogonic formulation as object, including an understanding of why a given formulation can be pleasing.

The analysis is motivated in part precisely by the fact that the account is so intricate—leading to the question of how it is possible that the account be perceived as anything more than that which its narrative aligns itself against, namely, chaos and nonbeing. The schemata suggest different levels and modes of organization all going on simultaneously. The reason for the feeling or sense of satisfaction and of order within the diversity may stem from precisely a multiplicity of simultaneous schemes that—without necessarily being raised to consciousness; indeed for its success as a narrative it is no doubt preferable that they are not—are maintained beneath the diversity and detail. It could be argued that, as in the difference between a two-part and a four-part musical invention, the more themes that can be kept going simultaneously, the greater can be the sense of coherence and richness. Again, it appears that, when submitting in a sort of visceral way to the flow of either narrative or music, the mind is capable of subconsciously holding together more strands at one time than it is capable of doing consciously and analytically—the latter process being invariably and inevitably slow and laborious.

HOW MANY BEINGS OUGHT THE WORLD CONTAIN? FOUR COSMOGONIC SCHEMATA

The following is my summary of Te Rangikaheke's cosmogonic story:[1]

Rangi (Sky) and Papa (Earth) at first cling together, enclosing their children in darkness. The children multiply and seek for a way that they might grow. Some argue that the parents should be killed, while others argue that, rather, they should be separated, so that only one, the Earth, might remain a parent to them, while the other, the Sky, would become distant to them. They agree to separate the parents, with Tāwhiri (Wind) dissenting. Each of the children, in turn, attempts to separate the parents: Rongo (Kūmara [a cultivated Maori staple, something like sweet potato]), Tangaroa (Fish), Haumia (Fernroot), and Tū (Man). Finally, Tāne (Trees), by putting his head down and feet up, is able to push up the sky.

When the parents are indeed separated, then for the first time can be seen the myriad of beings hiding inside the hollows of the bosoms of Rangi and Papa. Tāwhiri, because he had not agreed to the separation, decides that he will fight against all the others; and so, when the Sky is pushed up, rather than remaining on the Earth Mother with the rest, he stays within the hollows of the Sky as it is pushed upwards. There, in consultation with the Sky, he raises up a brood of descendants to send in attack against his brothers—these descendants being various types of clouds and meteorological phenomena.

When the children of Tāwhiri have become numerous, they are sent out against the other sons of Sky and Earth. They attack Tāne (Trees), and snap him apart so that he falls to the ground to rot. They strike out against Tangaroa, who runs off to the sea. The descendants of Tangaroa, however, diverge—one group, the descendants of Ika-tere, going to the sea and becoming fish, the other, the descendants of Tū-te-wehiwehi, heading to the land and becoming lizards. In parting they exchange insults, the former telling the latter that they will be caught by fires in the fern, the latter telling the former that they will be served in baskets of cooked food. The one group cries "Us to the land," the other, "Us to the sea"; and hence there is a saying to that effect.

Tāwhiri and his brood turn to attack Rongo and Haumia, but the Earth Mother protects these by hiding them in the folds of her body.

Then Tāwhiri turns against Tū, who is vexed as a result of the fact that, in the gnawing of Tāwhiri and his brood, he alone has stood to fight. Tāne was broken up; Tangaroa ran to the sea; Rongo and Haumia ran to the land. Tū alone was brave in the face of Tāwhiri; they were equal to one another in fighting.

When the anger of Tāwhiri is assuaged, Tū himself turns against his brothers to seek vengeance against them for their failure to help him fight Tāwhiri. He makes nets to catch the children of Tangaroa, and throws them ashore. He goes after Rongo and Haumia; and even though the Earth Mother has hidden them in the folds of her body, he sees their topknots sticking up and spears them with a digging stick, throwing them on the land to be dried by the sun. He fears that Tāne will be able to raise up a brood to send against him; and so he attacks the children of Tāne (the birds) with snares. So Tū's brothers are all eaten by him, and are thus made *noa* [ordinary, no longer sacred] as a retribution for their sending him alone to fight Tāwhiri; all of them are killed and eaten, because Tū alone was brave enough to fight. When Tū has eaten and thus made *noa* his brothers, the *karakia* [traditional incantations] are separated from one another, and also Tū's various names.

The above summary is based on two different manuscripts that Te Rangi-kaheke wrote at approximately the same time. The two manuscripts contain a fair amount of overlap and no major contradictions. Grey presents transcriptions of both (which he calls 1 and 2) in the appendix to his *Ko Nga Moteatea*;

lines are occasionally left out, but other than this the transcriptions are fairly accurate. Curnow (1985:119ff.) has persuasively argued that there were originally two accounts and that the two accounts were intended for different audiences, the one (1, or MS 81) for Grey and the other (2, or MSS 43/44) for ancestors in Hawaii. Curnow has also suggested various ways in which the differences between the accounts reflect the different audiences—for instance, that in certain respects 2 seems to presume a greater general familiarity with the issues under consideration. Curnow does not note any major inconsistencies between the accounts. Treating the two manuscripts as containing a unitary account will, I hope, not introduce any great distortion. At the same time, the sources of the lines will be indicated according to the numbers that Grey assigned to the two accounts (1, 2) and by page references to Grey (*Ko Nga Moteatea*) and to the original manuscripts (GNZMMSS 43, 44, 81).

FIRST SCHEMA: THE ONE AND THE TWO
[1 → 2 / 2 → 1] → [INDEFINITELY MANY]

Numerous societies recognize a generative sexual dualism in humans, animals, plants, other sorts of objects, and/or in the cosmos or cosmic processes as a whole. The analysis here, however, begins not with that idea, but with one that is both more general and more specific. What is to be considered is the fact that a sexual duality is often thought of in terms of a more general question: Is the first "thing" really one or two? The idea of a sexual duality, regardless of the range of its application, does not necessarily implicate this more general question, nor would the more general question necessarily have to implicate the notion of sexual dualism. But the two frequently occur together, the duality of the sexes often providing the idiom in terms of which the general problem is envisaged and either solved or, perhaps more commonly, retained as an intriguing, useful, and, in some systems, unavoidable paradox.

While it is perhaps not in most cases a wise course to move directly from a particular instance to a level of comparative analysis, in this case the pattern has been so frequently recognized that more is to be gained by first noting its recurrent character in various mythologies of the world and then moving to the consideration of the particulars of this case, than by building, unnecessarily, from scratch.

The comparative religionist Mircea Eliade, in *The Two and the One* for instance, has written of a

> primordial Androgyne, the Ancestor of humanity, and the creation
> myths. In both cases the myths show that in the beginning, *in illo tempore*, there was an intact totality—and that this totality was divided or

broken in order that the World or humanity could be born. To the primordial androgyne, especially the spherical androgyne described by
Plato, corresponds, on the cosmic plane, the cosmological Egg or the
primordial anthropocosmic Giant.

A great number of creation-myths present the original state—
"Chaos"—as a compact and homogeneous mass in which no form could
be distinguished; or as an egg-like sphere in which Sky and Earth were
united, or as a giant man, etc. In all these myths Creation takes place by
the division of the egg into two parts, representing Sky and Earth—or by
the breaking up of the Giant, or by the fragmentation of the unitary
mass. (1965:114–15)

Lévi-Strauss has also written of the pattern, invoking some of the same concrete exemplifiers. But whereas Eliade emphasizes a primordial fragmentation, the passage from the one to the two, Lévi-Strauss, consonant with the
intellectually mediatory function that he consistently imputes to mythological
thought, emphasizes passage in the opposite direction:

> . . . some myths seem to be entirely devoted to the task of exhausting all
> the possible solutions to the problem of bridging the gap between *two*
> and *one*. For instance, a comparison between all the variants of the Zuni
> emergence myth provides us with a series of mediating devices, each of
> which generates the next one by a process of opposition and correlation:
> messiah > dioscuri > trickster > bisexual being > sibling pair >
> married couple > grandmother-grandchild > four-term group > triad
> In Cushing's version, this dialectic is associated with a change from a
> spatial dimension (mediation between Sky and Earth) to a temporal
> dimension (mediation between summer and winter, that is, between
> birth and death). (1967:223)

Eliade's examples are Old World; Lévi-Strauss's is from one of the areas
in the Americas, namely, the Southwest, in which mythologies tend to be
organized within encompassing cosmogonic frameworks.

Something like this schema occurs in the Arawa 2 cosmogony that is to be
considered here, as the declarative opening line of the account:

> E hoa mā, whakarongo mai, kotahi anō te tupuna o te tangata māori, ko
> Rangi-nui e tū nei, ko Papa-tūanuku, e takoto nei, ki ēnei kōrero.
> (Grey xxxi; MS 43:893)
>
>> Friends, listen! One indeed is the ancestor of the Maori people, Sky
>> standing here, and Earth lying here, according to this tradition.

The language itself is not difficult. The statement would seem to be either an
allusion to a former state in which two now-distinct things were one, or else
simply paradoxical; either way the statement suggests some mutually impli-

catory relation between the one and the two. This and other Maori cosmogonies picture the initial cosmic situation as that of Sky and Earth, male and female, at first locked together in a close embrace with their children between. The two are in the primordial state more like one, until rent apart by their children.

The occurrence of this ambiguity/paradox at the very beginning of the cosmology would in this case appear to be of particular significance. Patterns that are placed at the beginning of cosmogonies often set defining characteristics that in some sense are carried through the whole, particularly in those societies, such as Maori, where the *means* of totalizing—that is, of referring any "thing" or question to its largest possible context and ultimate ground—is to refer it to its originary event within an encompassing cosmogonic tale. In terms of structural significance, the paradox set at the beginning of this Arawa formulation can perhaps be seen as a logical schema that insures the permanent possibility of transition between two and one, and, more significantly, as a schema that insures the possibility of a dualism behind every seeming monistic formulation, and vice versa. There is another event that can be regarded as an instance of this schema; it is present in both texts in the particular way and logic in which Sky, the male parent, is separated from Earth, the female parent. They are separated into two, only to be reduced back to one. Or more precisely, the one is separated into two on the condition that, by the defining of a qualitatively different relation to each, the two is, for purposes of a given type of relation, reduced back to one. It occurs in 1 in the argument of Tāne-mahuta that the parents should be separated rather than killed:

> Ka mea atu a Tāne-mahuta, kauaka, engari, me wehewehe rāua, ki runga tētahi, ki raro tētahi, kia kotahi hei tangata kē ki a tātou, kia kotahi hei matua ki a tātou. (Grey iii; MS 81:53)

> Tāne-mahuta said, "No! Let's separate them instead, one above, one below, so that one will be a stranger to us, and so that one will be a parent to us."

The term with which Sky's (Rangi's) new place in the cosmos is described is of moment; it introduces the opposition of "parent" to "stranger." "*Kē*" is a modifier meaning "different," "of another kind"; "*tangata kē*," sometimes translated as "stranger," occurs frequently in narratives about later, historic times to designate someone from outside any particular geographical and tribal/kinship affiliation. It is perhaps not too much to read the text as suggesting that Sky (Rangi) and the son that follows him (Tāwhiri—Wind) form a second tribal entity (involving a kinship identity and territory) vis-à-vis that of the beings that remain on the earth, so that, along with everything else that it initiates, the great separation of sky and earth forms a kind of adumbration or allusion to the political reality of opposed tribal entities. The subsequent interaction of the beings of the sky and those of the earth conforms to the typical pattern that is recounted in tribal histories—namely, a series of ongoing skirmishes that, overall, results in a continuous dynamic standoff. Moreover, it embraces another characteristic of Maori tribalism: the difference between one tribe and another is often not based on absolute distinction between things related by kinship and things unrelated. Rather, in a cosmogonic model in which all things are ultimately related in one "gigantic 'kin' " (Johansen 1954:9), the relations between different groups are determined at least partly by the particular historical events that qualitatively shape the nature and origin of different tribes and their interrelationships, and influence the choice of which ancestral lines, among those available, are to be regarded as primary and socially defining.

Thus, in contrast with the occurrence of the schema of "the one and the two" in 2, which takes the form of a grand philosophical paradox, the occurrence in 1 is more specific, and begins to assess the practical implications for existence that stem from the primordial paradox, and more specifically, from the decision that is made about how to resolve it, namely, to accept disparity and opposition as part of the cosmos rather than to do away with its generative source.

A physical relation of proximity, incidentally, appears to be a significant criterion in the construction of cosmic ancestries. Within the Maori cosmic web of kinship, many of the assignations of parentage are roughly similar to those that are found, for instance, in the essentially morphologically inspired classifications of the Linnaean "tree," but there are also some differences in principle. One of these is evident in the fact that a certain kind of qualitative relationship—one of close proximity and dependence—can override morphology in the determination of parentage. This occurs in cases in which great swarms of miniscule beings habitually climb around on large ones, and flee to them for protection. In this case, irrespective of form, the miniscule ones can be said to be the "children" of the great ones. Many insects, for example, are descended from Haumia (Fernroot) or from specific plants they inhabit (e.g., Best 1977:778, 994); and birds are commonly said to be the children of Tāne (Trees). The point is that the quality of the ways in which the different things of the natural world interact with one another is as determinative of their "kinship" as is pure morphology. The system involves a poetic botanics or botanic poetics, since it is equally by a consistent ethnobotanical principle or by a poetic leap that Earth is properly called the parent of such elements as Kūmara, Fernroot, and Man.

The theme of separation of a Sky Father and an Earth Mother of course is common enough that it might be described as the "standard" Old World cosmogony.[2] A number of more specific parallels can also be found. For instance, in Hesiod's *Theogony* there is the battle of the children against the father, Heaven, in which the son, Cronos, who wins the battle for the children, is, like the Maori Tāne (in some versions), also the one who goes on to generate the human race. There are also some notable differences; for instance, in the Maori case the conflict is pictured as between the children on one side and the parents on the other, so that the primordial male and female retain an ongoing symmetrical desire for one another throughout, whereas in the *Theogony* the conflict is between the mother and children on one side and the father on the other. Nevertheless the final result in each case is a social entity of Earth and children opposed to Sky.

The question of whether any of the larger implications that will be suggested here in relation to Maori society are of any relevance to the social context of the *Theogony*, or in any other instances in which similar themes occur, would require a separate investigation. The schema of the "two and the one" need not necessarily have large structural implications on the level of cosmology. As in the familiar examples of the speech of Aristophanes in Plato's *Symposium* or the "Adam's rib" episode in Genesis, the schema may be directed to very specific topics, such as the nature/origin of sexual attraction, or a hierarchical relation between the sexes (see Dumont 1980:239). In the latter instance, which after all derives from a religion that sought its own definition in part by way of a contrast to what it portrayed as the fertility religions of its neighbors, sexual images tend to play a less patent role in defining the overall structure of the cosmos. In the Polynesian case, and many others, by contrast, cosmogenesis takes sexual generation as its main productive principle.

It is difficult to consider this reduction from two to explicitly one parent in the Arawa account without recalling the old theoretical problem of Maori, and more generally Polynesian, social structure, namely, its "cognatic" character. Perhaps we have in the sons' decision to send the father to the heavens to become a stranger (*tangata kē*) and to retain the mother as a parent (*matua*) the primordial indication that what we are dealing with is an "optative system."

While this interpretation is a bit coarse, I find it necessary to accept an optative theory *in some sense*. For there does not seem to be, in the Maori case, a set of rules of "descent" that are capable of, in themselves and as a closed system, assigning people unambiguously to particular social categories or groups. On the other hand, the notion of Firth (1963)—that it is individual practical choices regarding such matters as residence that effect, in each generation, the necessary reductions of two lines to one, making these systems "functionally equivalent" to unilineal systems—poses serious problems. Only if it were the case that a given individual's decision to live with and commit his energies to a certain group then limited his descendants to tracing descent through the side that he himself had opted for, would the notion of an optative system as formulated by Firth be of any great structural significance—because only in that case would the consequences of the decision necessarily ramify in time and in social structure. No doubt such choices are sometimes available, and do tend to influence the residence and the choice of ancestors that descendants would emphasize. But there is no proof that genealogy and residence of subsequent generations are permanently limited by such choices; and indeed there is much to suggest that at later points the other lines can be resurrected and emphasized (see Schwimmer 1978). To the extent that this revitalization is a possibility, the notion of an optative system, when thought of on the level at which Firth formulates it, recedes in significance, ultimately amounting to the platitude that a given person cannot be two places at once (which, in Polynesian societies, is a dubious platitude anyway).

While various options do seem to be built into the system, such instances of alternatives presented to individuals can perhaps be seen as one manifestation of a more general property of this system. At the very least, one should not ignore the manifestations of something like the same pattern in processes that are, rather, transgenerational, historical, sociopolitical, and indeed cosmological. Besides focusing on different (larger, sociological) loci, another way, already alluded to, in which this analysis will differ from the classical formulation of an optative system is that, in spirit with Maori cosmogony, it will assume less finality in the process of opting one way or another, and accord greater credence to the possibilities of retaining ambiguities and straddling alternatives.

One of these instances of straddling formulations is present, in a particularly intriguing way, in the Arawa cosmogonic account that is under consideration here. It is easily missed, for it does not even lie within the body of the narrative. While both texts (1, 2) recount the self-affirmation of the children in the separation of the two parents, and while both texts moreover explicitly describe the separation as a process of keeping one alone—the mother—as the parent (*matua*), nevertheless, in one of the texts (2), Te Rangikaheke has supplied titles for the various episodes; and the title that he has given to this episode as a whole is "The Sons of Sky" (*Tama a Rangi* [MS 43:893]). There are, then, two different formulations of the ancestry, and thus essential identity, of the original set of beings that make up the world, one declaring that the female is the parent, the other that the male is the parent. There is something very suggestive and focused in these alternative formulations. The identity that stems from the woman, Papa, is evident in part in the physical closeness of the sons to her; for it is the decision of most of the sons to live on Papa that accounts for their keeping her as the parent while sending Sky away to be a stranger. The rationale, on the other hand, behind the formulation that posits the identity of the original sons as deriving from (once Sky and Earth are separated) the distant outsider, Sky, is never spelled out, but merely alluded to in the title—though with no hint that it is anything less than obvious.

Something like the possibility of this sort of double or alternating formulation seems to run through much of Maori social thought. Probably the single biggest body of data relevant to the analysis of Maori social structure is that collected by Best in the Mataatua area, and particularly that comprised in the first part of *Tuhoe*, dealing with the older, premigration tribes of that area. Although it will be considered in detail at a later point, here one particularly significant and recurrent feature of Best's analysis will be pointed out: Throughout, Best pictures concrete social groups as somewhere in between two distinct formulations of their ancestral identity. Of the two formulations, one pictures a small unit that has a deep and long association with a particular tract of land (in many cases being grounded in autochthony). The other formulation is from the outside, the distance; it stems from a geographically, and sometimes cosmologically, remote source (in some cases Hawaiki) and overlays the first, bringing a number of the first type of formulation into a larger one.

Much of Best's discussion—indeed it is often his obsession—revolves around how particular concrete social units somehow straddle these two types of formulation. The pattern was nearly Best's undoing. The problem originates fundamentally in the fact that, for Best, the identity of Maori social groups ought to be proportional to their "blood" lines. They frequently took their names, however, from ancestors who accounted for less than half of their "blood." The central and recurrent case for Best is the Tūhoe tribe itself, a tribe that had incorporated, by intermarriage and conquest, a significant part of the aboriginal, premigration groups known as Ngā Pōtiki and Tini-o-Toi: ". . . the Tuhoe tribe is but the ancient Nga Potiki and Tini-o-Toi under a more modern name, albeit its members have inter-married with the Mātātua immigrants. Tuhoe-potiki, from whom the tribe derives its present name, was a great-grandson of Toroa, the principal chief of the Mātātua immigrants, but Tuhoe was three-quarter aboriginal in blood . . ." (Best 1977:210). Elsewhere Best writes more fully of the origin of this tribe:

> I have said mixed descendants, because intermarriages of migrants and the earlier people commenced with the arrival of the Mātātua canoe at Whakatane, i.e., several of the immigrants by that vessel married aborigines. Wairaka, daughter of Toroa (principle chief of Matatua) married an aboriginal, as also did her son Tamatea. . . . Taneatua also took to wife a woman of Nga Potiki.

These mixed descendants of the two people soon asserted themselves, and became the ruling people of the district, gradually extending their influence to more remote parts of the interior, as Rua-tahuna, Te Whaiti, etc., where the original people were still unmixed with the new comers. Such extension of influence was caused either by peaceful intermarriages or by such raids as those of Tawhaki, Tu-manawa-pohatu, Whare-pakau, etc. Hence the origin of an old saying of the Tuhoe people, viz., "*Na Toi raua ko Potiki te whenua, na Tuhoe te mana me te rangatiratanga.*" (The land is from Toi and Potiki, the prestige and rank from Tuhoe), thus admitting that they obtained their lands from their ancestors of the original people, but claiming that they derived their rank from the Mātātua immigrants, of whom Tuhoe-potiki was a (mixed) descendant. The *aho ariki*, or most revered line of descent of the Tuhoe people, is that from the original parents Heaven and Earth, through the Whaitiri line, including Tawhaki, Wahie-roa, and Toroa; and not through Toi, or Potiki, although the Tuhoe people are far more aboriginal in blood than they are Hawaikian (i.e., of the Mātātua migration). (1977:13)

Best expressed his consternation at a number of points, for example, in the following comment, which, in its relating of this particular derivation of tribal name to several other cases, indicates that he was aware that it was merely one instance of a more general pattern:

The principal location of Ngati-Rongo has always been at O-haua-te-rangi, in the Rua-tahuna district, until the last few years. As descendants of Rongo-karae they obtained their rights to those lands by inter-marriages with Nga Potiki. It has been shown that Rongo-karae was a restless, wandering person, like Tuhoe-potiki and Koura-kino, and his short stay at Rua-toki was but a slight incident in the history and development of the clan which bears his name. Why the names of these three aboriginal tourists should have been selected as clan names is past my comprehension. (1977:219)

The formulation was problematic for Best mainly because of the presuppositions about blood-proportionality that he brought to it. The indigenous formulations that Best reports seem centrally concerned not with such proportionalities, but rather with asserting the general idea of two qualitatively different contributions that the indigenous and immigrant sides bring to an essentially synthetic social formation. Quite apart from any proportion, the power to define larger-scale, overarching, incorporative sociopolitical structures appears to be regarded as part of the outside or immigrant contribution. The unsettled, wandering quality of such great ancestors leads Best to ask how such series of short stays at various places could be the basis for derivation of tribal names. But this roving, resettling quality—with the consequence of ancestors left in many places—is precisely the condition that creates the over-arching (even if "thin" in Best's terms) genealogies that form one potential source for the uniting of smaller groups within larger formations.

A further point can be made regarding the generality of such processes. It is widely acknowledged that the theme of an immigration figures centrally in Maori notions of history and political formation. But this theme is sometimes treated as if implying that the prior condition was viewed as a sort of steady state that was, with the migrations, once and forever radically transformed. Without going into details (there is a major study to be made here) Best's data on the early tribes stand in direct opposition to this view. There is very little by way of new political process introduced with the migrations. The premigra-tion tribes themselves are pictured as acting, within more circumscribed geographical domains, as indigenous and outside peoples toward one another. They are involved in major shifts, realignments, and expansive consolida-tions—but within which their prior identities are often at least partially retain-ed. Most noteworthy is the idea of an expansive consolidation known as Te Tini o Toi ("the Multitude of Toi"), stemming from various premigration groups related in varying ways to "the ubiquitous Toi" (see esp. Best 1977:15ff., 61ff.). Although the significance of the idea of the migration really cannot be overestimated, at the same time it is a mistake to miss the sociopolitical structural continuities that are pictured in the fascinating and copious data that Best collected on the early tribes. This material may be among the most useful that Best collected, and appears to be subject to a lesser degree than usual to his tendencies of repetition and incorporation of extraneous material from other sources. The possibility suggests itself that the significance of the idea of the migration lay not so much in the notion of a one-time radical transformation of process, but rather in the epitomization of processes that were seen as the sine qua non of political life more generally. The picture that emerges is one of identity conceived as lying somewhere along a continuum between two "ideal types," some groups leaning more one way, some more the other way, but with few ever seeming to cede either fully.

I will use the term "dual formulation," by which I thus refer to the co-existence of two different conceptions of the essential character and identity of a given concrete social unit. It is important that this notion of dual formula-tion not be confused with the notion of "dual organization." The classical notion of dual organization implies a single sòciological formulation (though it is a formulation that asserts that a given concrete social unit is composed of two symmetrical components). What I am referring to is the inverse of that: a case where a single concrete social unit has two different definitions or descriptions of its nature. Both notions actually occur in Lévi-Strauss's

(1967:129ff.) classic discussion of Radin's Winnebago data: First, there is the notion (though not all the data support it) that the main social unit is composed of two symmetrical subcomponents (i.e., "dual organization"). But then, beyond that, there are two different formulations (pictures, descriptions) of the nature of that main social unit (in this case, based on alternative views of how the two components are interrelated).

Another instance of dual formulation in the Maori case will be mentioned, though it too involves some jumping ahead. It appears to be a consistent feature of the various Maori cosmogonies that Sky and Earth's children, who are all male, form the source of the various main categories of things that live on the earth, as, for instance in the Arawa version, humans spring from Tū, sea creatures from Tangaroa, *kūmara* (perhaps more generally, cultivated foods) from Rongo, fernroot (perhaps wild foods) from Haumia. Here it will simply be noted that within the broader compass of Maori cosmogonic formulations, there coexist two different theories of the descent of the human species.

One of these theories (the Arawa account is an example) proposes a kind of direct descent from Tū, and the other (e.g., the Tūhoe and *Whare Wānanga* accounts) involves a long story of the procurement of the first human female by Tāne, and the production of the human species by his mating with her. Here the point is that, even on the level of cosmogony that deals with the origin of the major categories of earthly beings—as descendants of the first generation of the children of Sky and Earth—the ancestry of humans asserts itself in two different theories, both from males (inasmuch as the original children of Sky and Earth are all males), but one emphasizing a direct descent from one of the original males (Tū), and the other emphasizing the search, by Tāne (the name means "male"), for specifically a female element (*uha*) appropriate for the generation of the human species. In certain accounts (e.g., Tūhoe), Tāne mates with a number of different female elements; none of them is productive of the human species, but in these various matings Tāne inadvertently produces a great family of different natural species as his descendants before succeeding in generating man. Besides his roles as prolific and fertile genitor of numerous natural species and as genitor of man, Tāne also has a specific connection with trees and birds (it is this last role that is emphasized in the Arawa account). The forest, and particularly the trees teeming with bird life, tend to be regarded in Maori thought as the primary exemplar of the natural fertility and "plenitude" of living forms. All the roles of Tāne have in common this prodigious, fertilizing role.

The opposition of Tāne and Tū is one of the most interesting and significant within the original sons. They represent the two essential modes of self-affirmation and self-expansion (which is to say, tribal affirmation and expansion), procreation and conquest, activities which are in many different ways analogized in Maori mythology and proverb. Tāne fathers all; Tū conquers all. Each has an expansive cosmogonic role, one through creating encompassing genealogies, the other as conqueror in battle. One could almost see the story of Tū, in Te Rangikaheke's account, and the story of Tāne, in the Tūhoe account (Best 1977:763ff.), as competing or complementary stories— resting on the two different essential modes of expansion—of man's rise to superordinacy over the other beings that live on earth. In one case man's claim over nature is genealogical: Man (Tāne is, from the beginning of this account, specifically Male, searching for a human female), in trying to generate descendants for himself, fathers nature, and is thus its great ancestor. In the other (i.e., Arawa) case man's claim over nature is that of conquest: Man (Tū) defeats in battle the rest of nature.

The overall point suggested in these various examples is that this system tends toward dual formulation at every possible level; the tendency has been seen in the ancestry of the original sons of Sky and Earth, in the ancestry of man as a generic being by descent from this set of original sons, and in the ancestry of particular historical social groups, such as those studied historically by Best in the Mataatua area. Finally, the same tendency toward dual formulation, and even many of the specific contrasting values and axioms displayed in the two formulations, will be seen once again, and more encompassingly, in the grand contrast between two forms of cosmogonic recital found among the Maori—in the contrast between, on the one hand, cosmogonic prose narratives such as those we have been considering here and, on the other hand, cosmogonic genealogies, which we have yet to consider (in chapter 5).[3]

The primary focus is the "two and the one," by which I refer to the positing of this quantitative ambiguity as an underlying logical schema within cosmogony. The scheme can be manifested in a number of different concrete images. In addition to the bisexual or androgynous being mentioned above by both Lévi-Strauss and Eliade, Eliade mentions the cosmic egg, and Lévi-Strauss the brother-sister pair as exemplifiers. Various of these occur in different Polynesian cosmogonies (e.g., the brother-sister pair at pivotal positions in the Tikopian cosmogony [Firth 1961:22, 75]), so that this schema— as that which is constant behind these various operators—might be of a more general significance in Polynesia, and perhaps in any cosmogony whose essential "mode of production" is sexual.

In considering possible transformations of this schema within Polynesia, two of many possible "axes of transformation" come particularly to mind.

The first axis involves something like a contrast between "theory" and "practice," not so much in the form of possible contradictions between them, but rather of a possible selective implementation. One can perhaps think of Polynesia as possessing a large and for the most part shared inventory of mythological themes, most of which figure centrally in the symbolization of sociological relations, but only some of which, and with great variation amongst the different societies, occur as practices. Consider the following Tūhoe text:

> As for Te Pu and Te More, they were male and female. Te More is the lower, Te Pu is above. But these names are really one, the upper part is male, the lower part female. These two became united, and were of equal rank and importance. Such was the origin of sex, of male and female. These beings were not created, not made by hands. They became united and begat offspring. Originally Te Pu and Te More were brother and sister. They were the origin of the universe. (Best 1977:744–45)

In Hawaii, brother-sister marriage was a matter of chiefly practice; consistent with the kinship break between chiefs and commoners, the logic appears to have been to keep the chiefly lines from spreading—that is, to reduce continually that duality implied in sexual generation and thus, in certain instances, to approximate the ideal of a nonbifurcating line. In the Maori case, an inclusive, corporate ideology demanded an unrestricted branching so as to include all the members of a group as descendants from a common eponymous ancestor. But while brother-sister marriage does not appear to have ever been a practice, yet in the above text, the idea appears in the context of a skill for which the Maori are particularly noted, that is, as cosmogonists. The reason why it appears in this context is not difficult to discern: it is "good to think" certain problems of cosmogony. It affords the means, or at least reduces the difficulty, of accounting for the first thing, which, within this total system, ought in some respects to be one and in other respects would better be two. While Maori prose cosmogonies recount great disruptions and separations, the great cosmogonic genealogies tend to fill in disruptions with intermediary states. The above text is in fact a commentary on a cosmic genealogy, and as such it is remarkable. It contains four oppositions, of which two might be called the basic oppositions, one being spatial ("above" vs. "lower") and the other being sexual (male vs. female), and of which the other two constitute less abrupt (that is, more continuous) versions of the basic ones: "upper part" and "lower part," and "brother" and "sister." These oppositions account for the nature of the primordial cosmic elements, Te Pū (origin, source, root) and Te More (taproot), whose "names are really one." The passage between one and two can thus be mediated by pairs of things that are, in varying degrees, like one thing—such that as pairs they can form graduated series of mediations.

Principles of continuity will be considered in more detail at a later point (in the subsection "Fourth Schema: Metaphysical").

The other axis of transformation that initially comes to mind in considering the schema of "the two and the one" within Polynesia rests on an opposition of something like synthesis to analysis, operations which are arguably, even as abstractions, mutually implicatory. It will not be a matter of determining whether a given Polynesian society is primarily synthetic or analytic (undoubtedly all will be both, and on many levels) but rather a matter of considering the particular ways and the particular moments within the total system at which synthetic versus analytic applications are invoked. Even in the small parts of the Arawa account that have been considered thus far, the schema of "the two and the one" takes on synthetic and analytic applications.

One can find many other examples, for instance, the opposition, important through much of Polynesia, between "land" and "sea." In the Arawa account, (1, 2), following the primordial separation of Sky and Earth, the original set of sons themselves, in the face of Tāwhiri's attacks and in the context of disputes about where and how to live, separate from one another, to inhabit various regions of the earth (1):

> . . . ā haere kē tētahi, haere kē tētahi. (Grey v; MS 81:54)

> . . . one ran here, another somewhere else.

One of these instances—that of the separation of land and sea creatures—is singled out in the text (1) as paradigmatic of this episode of dispersion, in that a proverb is said to stem from it:

> Koia ēnei pepeha, tāua ki uta, tāua ki te wai. (Grey iv; MS 81:54)

> Hence these mottos, "Us to the land," "Us to the sea."

On the other hand, the opposition of land to sea occurs synthetically, for instance, in a kind of temporary, though highly significant, unity that is ritually created (or perhaps recaptured?) around particular issues in ceremonial gatherings, or *hui*. For, in the greetings that occur on the occasion of welcoming outside peoples to such meetings, the most common chant by the *tāngata whenua* (people of the land) is an invocation to haul the canoe of the incoming group, which is thus ritually from the sea. Within the system of a number of relatively balanced and autonomous tribal entities characteristic of Maori society, the ritual categories of "land" and "sea" are reversible, so that the land people in one context can be the sea people in another. But more important than the potential for reversal of political roles within the ritual is the fact that the ritual itself is synthetic, inverting a particular analytic cosmogonic moment.

In the process of political formation in the Mataatua area as recounted in Best's data, the opposition of land to sea occurs mainly synthetically. The synthesis is particularly exemplified in an oft-repeated proverb which, in juxtaposing the most famous indigenous and immigrant ancestors, pictures the contributions of each component:

> Na Toi raua ko Potiki te whenua, na Tuhoe te mana me te rangatiratanga.
> (Best 1977:13)

> The land is from Toi and Potiki, the prestige and rank from Tuhoe.
> (1977:13)

The emphasis is upon the combining and holding together of these two ancestries, and the particular qualities that each brings, within one political formation. The essentially synthetic nature of social formation tends to accompany all the instances of dual formulation, and the emphasis is upon retaining both ancestries and identities by the members of one concrete unit.[4]

But what are the two components? At least at certain points they clearly have something to do with the idea of an intrinsically generative sexual dualism. Is it ultimately, then, a sexual model? What is the relation to other oppositions like land to sea, or land people to sea people? The structural school of myth analysis has found numerous deficiencies in the earlier Jungian school, including the charge of a too-immediate linking of the meaning of symbolic schemata to particular unit contents. Nonetheless, it is at least partly because of the recurrent emphasis that Jung accorded to the theme of the one and the two (which he discussed most often in the guise of *coniunctio oppositorum*) that this notion has come to be a frequently discussed theme in later writers, even those of radically different persuasions. There is an interesting twist in the fact that one of the strongest cautionary notes regarding the identification of the schema with specialized content was voiced by Jung himself, for whom this schema provided the limiting case for his most central analytical concept:

> The male-female syzygy is only one among the possible pairs of opposites, albeit the most important one in practice and the commonest. It has numerous connections with other pairs which do not display any sex differences at all and can therefore be put into the sexual category only by main force. . . . When one carefully considers this accumulation of data, it begins to seem probable that an archetype in its quiescent, unprojected state has no exactly determinable form but is in itself an indefinite structure which can assume definite forms only in projection.
>
> This seems to contradict the concept of a "type." If I am not mistaken, it not only seems but actually *is* a contradiction. Empirically speaking, we are dealing all the time with "types," definite forms that can be named

and distinguished. But as soon as you divest these types of the phenom-
enology presented by the case material, and try to examine them in relation to other archetypal forms, they branch out into such far-reaching
ramifications in the history of symbols that one comes to the conclusion
that the basic psychic elements are infinitely varied and ever changing,
so as utterly to defy our powers of imagination. The empiricist must
therefore content himself with a theoretical "as if." (1977:70)

SECOND SCHEMA: THE SPACE-BETWEEN—
A REDUCTION OF THE CHAIN
6 → 5

The main point to be made in this section is that there is a specific moment
in the Arawa formulation that exemplifies the pattern pointed out in Lévi-
Strauss's cosmogonic analytic—indeed in some respects more convincingly
than in the examples that Lévi-Strauss gives. While the analytic of the Chain
inherently addresses totality, so that in purest form all possible things in the
universe might be implicated, in fact the pattern occurs commonly in application to the totality comprised in some more restricted sphere. Traditionally,
one of the objects to call forth the principles of plenitude, continuity, and gradation is the set of beings that compose the earthly biosphere. The object in Lévi-
Strauss's examples consists of the set of beings comprised in the human
"sociosphere," which, however, following the totemic hypothesis, is founded
upon analogy to the intellectual construction of the biosphere.

In the Arawa formulation, we encounter something like the Chain of Being
pattern—and moreover, its reduction—in what is therefore a predictable region.
For the pattern occurs in relation to the sons of Sky and Earth, who, *after being
reduced from six to five*, spread out to constitute the totality of the natural
world—the total set of beings that live between the sky and the underworld,
on the body of the Earth Mother.

The crucial being here is Tāwhiri. There was, as noted earlier, a previous
altercation among the children over whether the parents should be killed or
separated, which ended in the final agreement that the parents should be
separated; Tāwhiri alone does not accept the plan of separating the parents (1):

> Ka whakaae rātou tahi, ka tino aroha anō tētahi o rātou ki te mea i wehea
> ai rāua, tokorima i pai kia wehea, kotahi i aroha. (Grey iii; MS 81:53)

> They agreed, but one of them felt much pity because the parents would
> be separated; five approved of the separation, one felt pity.

Tāwhiri, in anger over the separation, decides to stay with the father during
the separation, so that the two of them can together plot how to avenge the
separation (2):

Te whakatikanga ake o Tāwhiri-mātea, anā piri ana mai i te ateatenga o
tōna matua tāne o Rangi-nui, ka tae atu ki reira, kātahi ka whakaarohia
nuitia e rāua tahi ko tōna matua tāne. . . . (Grey xxxii; MS 43:893)

Tāwhiri rose upward, clinging onto the bosom of his father Sky; and
when they arrived there they made momentous plans together. . . .

There are thus two essential cosmic reductions, belonging, I suggest, to
different schemata, one to a schema of "the two and the one," and the other
to the schema of the reduction of the Chain. But they are narratively aligned
in a single event: the raising up of Sky with his son Wind clinging to him, to
form a new tribe in opposition to that of Earth and her inhabitants.

The reduction from six to five happens to be numerically the same as in
the Ojibwa case, though there is perhaps no significance to this other than the
fact that many cosmogonies settle upon about this many as the number of basic
kinds of things in the world. Many cosmogonies evince a transition at about
this point. That is, working backwards, the various beings of the cosmos are
derived, often by sexual generation, as variations from a set of original basic
types. But the origin of the original types themselves seems often to require
some other principle. It is as if once the problem of the creation and fixing
of "difference" in the cosmos is satisfactorily solved with respect to large-scale
main differences of type (such as, for instance, things that live on land vs. in
the sea), then the smaller differences can be derived with little difficulty, often
in fact through processes of recombining the newly distinguished entities
(cf. Vernant 1982:106). It is to those relatively few but basic differences—those
that most forcefully illustrate the principle of difference—that traditional
cosmogonies frequently devote their first concern.

It was suggested above that the particular incident considered here supports
Lévi-Strauss's structural argument even more compellingly than do the
examples that he himself provides. For the main thrust of Lévi-Strauss's structural argument—that, through the deletion of one or some members of a continuum, the discreteness of the other members is insured by virtue of the greater
space afforded between them—is confirmed, in this case, in none other than
the tangible contents of the episode.

First of all, Tāwhiri, the being who might be interpreted, in the manner
of Lévi-Strauss, as constituting the member whose reduction affords the space
between the others, becomes, in this cosmos, precisely the space between the
others, that is, air—in the tangible and bellicose forms in which air affirms
itself as a positive being among beings, a warrior among warriors, that is, as
Wind.[5] The fact that Tāwhiri becomes specifically space in its bellicose and
concrete form is merely consistent with a general theme in this cosmogony,
in which all things are persons, namely, that any being who wishes to attain
a nondegraded claim to a presence in the cosmos must do so in a warrior spirit.

As will be discussed in the following section, Tū (Man) and Tāwhiri (more broadly, "the elements") are the only ones of the six original sons that attain this status, and it takes the form of a permanent standoff between them.

Tāwhiri tends to be the neglected one in studies of Maori cosmogony. But considered structurally within the context of cosmogony, Tāwhiri appears to maintain some of the most complex and totalizing roles, which, in ways that are admittedly somewhat speculative, I will suggest in the comments that follow. Plotting with Sky, Tāwhiri raises up a brood of children (the various forms of clouds and other meteorological phenomena) to attack the other original children in an attempt to avenge the separation of the parents. It is precisely the deleted member of the continuum, Tāwhiri, who, in these attacks, drives apart the members who have remained on earth. For it is specifically in the face of the attacks of Tāwhiri that the other five brothers fall into discord about the means of attaining secure existence, and come to partings of the ways, going off to occupy different "ecological niches" and live according to different customs. In consequence of Tāwhiri's attacks (2),

> Whatiwhati rawa a Tāne poro pū, ko Tangaroa, i oma ki te wai, Ko
> Rongo, ko Haumia-tiketike, i oma ki te whenua, ko Tū-matauenga, i tū
> tonu i te ateatenga o tōna whaea o Papa-tūanuku. (Grey xxxiii; MS 43:894)

> Tāne (Trees) was all broken up into pieces, Tangaroa (Fish) ran to the sea,
> Rongo (Kūmara), and Haumia-tiketike, ran to [hide in] the land, Tū (Man)
> alone still stood on the bosom of his mother, Papa-tūanuku.

But while the above passage summarizes the general result, the various episodes involved in Tāwhiri's revenge form one of the longest sections of this cosmogony, comprising many distinct, memorable incidents. As noted earlier, perhaps the most paradigmatic of the incidents is that of the separation of certain creatures to sea and land; this episode is given prominence in both of the two Arawa texts (1, 2), and occurs additionally in other, non-Arawa sources. In 1, Tāwhiri, directly after attacking the trees and breaking them up, turns to the sea:

> Ka whati a Tangaroa ki te wai, no reira aua tāngata i totohe ai, tātou ki
> uta, tātou ki te wai, tē rongo ētahi, tē rongo ētahi, wehea ake ētahi, he
> hapū anū, he hapū anō. Ko te hapū i a Tū-te-wanawana, i noho i uta, ko
> te hapū i a Punga, i haere ki te wai, ngā wehewehenga a Tāwhiri-mātea.
> (Grey iv; MS 81:54)

> Tangaroa was broken in the sea, so his children argued, "Let's go to the
> land! Let's go to the sea!" Some didn't hear the one, some didn't hear the
> other; they were separated into different *hapū*. The *hapū* of Tū-te-wanawana
> [lizards] lived upland, that of Punga ran to the sea. These are the separa-
> tions of Tāwhiri-mātea.

The most interesting phrase is the last one—"the separations of Tāwhiri-mātea"—which appears to summarize this and previous episodes. The phrase attributes to Tāwhiri authorship of the separations.

There is one other main point illustrated in the above passage which adds to the role of Tāwhiri as the great separator. For, in contrast with the episode in which Tāwhiri's attacks are the stimulus for the parting of the original five earthly brothers, the above separation constitutes specifically a "sub-speciation" in which fish and lizards branch off from the same parent, Tangaroa, so that lizards, who live on land, yet descend from the being who, in Maori and the rest of Polynesia, is associated with the sea. Since in Maori thought lizards tend to be feared and to be associated with various forms of potent magical/ritual spells, the situation also calls to mind the argument (associated particularly with Mary Douglas) that the exceptional status of "taboo" beings derives from their interstitial location within a classificatory scheme.

The interrelation of reduction and separation within cosmogony also occurs in a more "global" way. For the wrath of Tāwhiri has one other large effect, which ultimately is of great significance to the construction of the discrete identities of the various human tribes that will inhabit the land (2):

> No reira anō i ngaro ai tētahi wāhi o te whenua. No te putanga mai o te riri a Tāwhiri-mātea, i whawhai ra ki āna tuākana, ā ngaro ana te nuinga o Papa-tūanuku i te wai. (Grey xxxiv; MS 43:896)

> Thus part of the land was lost. In the bursting forth of the rage of Tāwhiri-matea, when he fought with his older brothers, most of Papa-tūanuku was lost to the sea.

The Maori genre of legends about the origin of distinctive features of landscape is rich and varied, and themes similar to the one above—the loss of most of Papa-tūanuku—show up in a number of different forms. In Best's data, for instance, occurs the story that even while Papa is protecting her children in the folds of her body, and while Hine-Moana (Ocean woman) is protecting the descendants of Tangaroa from Sun, who is trying to kill them, Ocean is making war on Earth. But various beings—Rock, Gravel, and Sand—protect Earth from the constant gnawing of Ocean (e.g., Best 1982:253). The overall picture is one of a delicately balanced contention among a host of different personal forces.

Various Maori artistic and speech genres give testimony to the significance of particular landmarks, especially rivers and mountains, that distinguish one tribal area from another. The most conspicuous example is afforded in a recurrent formula that defines a given region as a totality of conjoined natural and social entities, through a series of parallel phrases that list the proper names of natural and social beings. Though there are many variations the general form is something like:

> So-and-so is the river;
> So-and-so is the mountain;
> So-and-so is the man [a great chief of the region].

It is no doubt a variation on a more broadly Polynesian pattern of naming districts (see for instance the examples for Tahiti in Henry 1928:70ff.).

In all this, however, there is very little by way of praise of natural beauty in the abstract or merely in itself; natural beauty is intensely celebrated, but almost always in the recalling of personal/tribal/ancestral attachment to particular distinctive features of landscape. Hence a final way in which Tāwhiri is the great separator stems from his war against the land. For in eating away at the land, which is thus, as the Arawa tale recounts, reduced in quantity so that most of it is lost, he nevertheless creates the irregular, idiosyncratic *topoi* that necessitate and make possible a human organization that encompasses a diversity of kinds or tribes.

One also finds numerous allusions to the wind not as a source of separation, but precisely as a source of continuity between separate things, and particularly between separate tribal entities. The wind is a frequently invoked symbol in the greetings spoken at the time of ritual conjunction in intertribal *hui*. Shortland noted:

> The words *tou hau*, thy breeze, or the breeze blowing from the direction of your country, refer to an idea frequently to be met with in the poetry of this people—the imaginary connexion between two places established through means of the wind blowing from one to the other. . . .
> So prevalent is the influence of this poetic fancy among the New Zealanders, and so powerfully are their sympathies excited by the simple circumstance of the wind blowing from the country where an absent beloved person is staying, that a wife or lover may frequently be seen, on such occasions, seated with her face fully exposed to the breeze, while she gives vent to her affection in the peculiar wailing chant of the country, called *tangi*. (1856:192–93)

In the development of the cosmos, it is Tāwhiri who instigates and brings about many of the particular transitions from continuous to discrete, so that in a cosmic-historical sense he particularly stands in between and spans the transition between the two great epochs. But in the transformed cosmos, Tāwhiri, while the space-between, is yet full and self-affirming. The tentative suggestion offered here is that the fullest structural significance of Tāwhiri lies not in insuring difference/discreteness, or in insuring continuity, but, rather, precisely in mediating between the principles of discreteness and continuity.

The significance of Tāwhiri within the Maori cosmos may thus, on the level of comparative cosmology, have a distant cousin in the Western cosmological notion of "ether" (which had its origin in the idea of a layer of purer air, in the upper part of the sky, the abode of the gods). The concept of ether has a fascinating history; despite absence of direct empirical evidence (there is indirect empirical evidence for it, for instance, in the fact that the universe does not collapse), the concept was maintained into the twentieth century, apparently because of the reluctance of the mind, or at least of certain minds, to admit the idea of space in the sense of a true emptiness or absence. And thus there was the need for a principle and substance that mediates between discreteness and continuity—allowing space-between and thus affirming the possibility of difference and discreteness without surrendering a kind of ultimate contiguity, continuity, and cosmic fullness. But on the level of "the concrete" there is this difference between Tāwhiri in Maori cosmogony and "ether" in traditional Western cosmography: while, on a gross physicalist level, ether has no direct empirical verification, Tāwhiri can be tacitly perceived, as he swirls around, still attempting to avenge the original injury.

There is more to Tāwhiri; as the one between all the others, he is the one that is necessarily "in touch" with everyone at once. His role is, then, inherently the most totalizing of all the sons of Sky and Earth; and in fact he also plays perhaps the most significant structural role in establishing the hierarchy among the sons of Sky and Earth (which will be considered in the following section).

The pattern of reduction, it should be noted, is not confined to this first phase of cosmogony, in which the origins of the basic kinds of things that make up the cosmos are recounted. The pattern appears in various forms also in later phases, including the migrations from Hawaiki that constitute the starting point of Maori society. The way in which these migrations are described recalls some of the same patterns that are seen in the account of the sons of Sky. That is, the migration of a set of canoes (which come to symbolize the major tribal areas of Aotea [New Zealand]) is pictured as occurring within the context of strife among the sons of Toi (the name means "source"), the contentions leading ultimately to the dispersal of Toi's sons. The events thus in many respects recapitulate the earlier pattern of the filling of the various regions of the natural world in the original contention and dispersal of the sons of Sky. But, additionally, the voyages too implicate reductions of various sorts. Many of these might be considered in relation to the kind of pattern suggested for the story of the sons of Sky, that is, as transformations in the makeup of the Chain of

Being (in this case the human social totality). But the more prominent and important form of reduction, at least in this Arawa account, would seem to consist in the basic transformation effected by breaking the original series (of the sons of Toi) into two derivative series—those remaining in Hawaiki, and those making the voyage (2):

> Ka wehea i konei āna tama, kei Hawaiki ētahi, kei Aotea nei ētahi ōna uri. . . .
> Ka wehea hoki i konei, ki Hawaiki ētahi, i haere mai nei ētahi i runga i ngā waka i hoe mai nei ki Aotea nei. . . . (Grey liii; MS 44:916)

> His [Toi's] sons were separated here; some are at Hawaiki, and some of his descendants are in Aotea here. . . .
> They were separated here—some of them were left in Hawaiki, and some came here in canoes. . . .

There are also other ways in which the theme of reduction/impoverishment is present, some of them quite minor, such as the point, found in many mythologies, that the heroes of those times were physically larger than people now. Most notably, there is an incident having to do with the cargo from Hawaiki, the ritual-cultural center and homeland. The great *tohunga* of the Arawa canoe, Ngatoro-i-rangi, in revenge for the seduction of his wife by the captain of the Arawa, Tama-te-kapua, recites a *karakia* which draws the Arawa into a whirlpool, nearly causing it to sink. At the last minute, Ngatoro-i-rangi relents, and the canoe once again comes to the surface. But as a result of Tama-te-kapua's recklessness (2),

> . . . kua poto atu ngā utanga ki te wai; he ouou nei i toe iho ki te waka. (Grey lxii; MS 44:926)

> . . . most of the cargo had gone into the water; a few things only remained on the canoe.

These sorts of reductions and impoverishments are not necessarily the end of it. It could be that their *raison d'être* lies in part precisely in their calling forth a general ethic of antinegation.

THIRD SCHEMA: HIERARCHICALIZATION
[ORIGINAL PLURALITY] → 1 /
1 → [ORIGINAL PLURALITY]

The cosmogonic construction of hierarchy in this case appears as a transition—in the form of a sort of exchange—in which some of the self-unity of the superordinate being is bequeathed to the original plurality (the sons,

Sky, and Earth), so that its members become one in Tū, while some of the
plurality of the original set is imparted to the superordinate being, so that Tū
diversifies and becomes multifaceted according to the totality that he now
embraces. The two transitions—the unification of the plural and the pluraliza-
tion of the one—are presented directly adjacent to one another, as if they are
to be understood as the two parts of a single transition. The schema differs
from the others in that an intrinsically and necessarily reciprocal structure is
implied.

The chief characters in this event are Tū and, once again, Tāwhiri, that is,
Man and Wind, or, more broadly, Wind and his entire meteorological brood,
including various kinds of clouds and storms that Wind sends out against his
five brothers. The ascendancy of man is established in the fact that Man alone,
of the set of brothers who remain on earth, stands firm against "the elements,"
while the others run and hide. It would appear that Te Rangikaheke considered
this point—that "Tū-matauenga alone stood brave to fight Sky and Wind" (ko
Tū-matauenga anake i toa ki te whawhai ki a Rangi rāua ko Tāwhiri-mātea [1]
[Grey v; MS 81:54–55])—to be one of the most important in the account, in
that it is repeated, with slight variation, several times in each text (1, 2).

The changes in the cosmos that result from this often have a distinct quantitative dimension, for instance in the fact that, in Tū's eating of his earthly
brothers, the five become one. But, consistent with the general dynamic of
Maori cosmogony toward greater diversity, there is an equal emphasis on the
growth and differentiation of the superordinate being himself, as a characteristic of the hierarchical relation; for instance (1):

> Ka mate ōna tēina i a ia, kātahi ka wehewehea ōna ingoa, ko Tū-ka-
> riri, ko Tū-ka-nguha, ko Tū-kai-taua, ko Tū-whakaheke-tangata, ko Tū-
> mata-whāiti, ko Tū-matauenga.
>
> I whakaritea tonutia ōna ingoa ki a rātou ko āna [ōna?] tuākana, ā
> tokowhā ōna hoa, i kainga katoatia e ia, kotahi i tapu, ko Tāwhiri, ko
> tōna whakapakanga, i waiho tonu hei hoa whawhai mōna, i rite anō ki tāna
> riri tā tōna teina riri. (Grey v; MS 81:55)

> When his brothers were defeated by him, then his [Tū's] names were
> separated: Tū-ka-riri, Tū-ka-nguha, Tū-kai-taua, Tū-whakaheke-tangata,
> Tū-mata-whāiti, Tū-matauenga.
>
> His names were made equal in number to his brothers. Four of the
> partners were totally eaten by him; one remained tapu, that is Tāwhiri,
> who remained a sparring partner for him, the fierceness of his younger
> brother was equal to his own.

While the above text directly links Tū's defeat (eating and making noa) of
his brothers to the differentiation of Tū's name, the other text (2) links the same

defeat to the differentiating of the *karakia* with which Tū will control his brothers:

> Na reira i whakanoatia ai ōna tuākana, ā ka wehewehea i reira āna karakia, he karakia anō mo Tāne-mahuta, mo Tangaroa anō tōna, mo Rongo-mātane anō tōna, mo Haumia anō tōna, mo Tū-matauenga anō tōna. Ko te wāhi i rapu ai ia i ngā karakia nei, kia whakahokia iho ōna tuākana, hei kai māna. Ā he karakia anō mo Tāwhiri-mātea, he tūā mo te Rangi, he karakia anō mo Papa-tūanuku. . . . (Grey xxxiv; MS 43:895–96)

> So his older brothers were made *noa*, and thence his *karakia* were separated, a *karakia* for Tāne-mahuta, for Tangaroa, for Rongo-matane, for Haumia, for Tū-matauenga. The reason he sought for these *karakia* was in order to be able to cause his older brothers to return as food for him; and there was another *karakia* for Tāwhiri-matea, a *tūā* for the Sky, another *karakia* for Papa-tūanuku. . . .

The precise quantities that are implicated may not technically form perfect symmetries. For instance, in the first passage above, Tū firmly defeats, and eats, only four of his brothers, yet his name, at that point, is said to differentiate into six (the original and five new ones), thus equaling the entire set of original sons. In the second passage, the event of the making *noa* of the four is followed directly by the differentiating of *karakia* for all eight beings in the universe, including Tū himself. But even though Tū, in these episodes, unequivocally defeats only the four, in a lesser sense his relation to the other beings of the universe is of the same type. He is the ongoing sparring partner of Tāwhiri, and is the only one of the sons who had argued in favor of killing rather than separating Sky and Earth. Perhaps more important than the fact that the episodes may not present exact numerical symmetries, which may also reflect simply the homocentric orientation of this part of the story, is the fact that they do in a general way picture the construction of hierarchy as a reciprocal transition between two sets (that of the one, and that of the many). For it is precisely when the others—epitomized most clearly in the four—become one in Tū that Tū himself expands and differentiates, as if the two transformations are mutually implicating.

The construction of hierarchy here is ultimately two-staged. There is first the battle between the sky tribe and the earth tribe, in which man alone, of the inhabitants of the earth, refuses to be defeated. And then, there is a series of episodes in which Tū (Man), in anger over his earth brothers' failure to stand strong with him against Tāwhiri, turns on them, subduing them one by one by one and making them his food (Tāne—trees and birds; Rongo—kūmara; Haumia—fernroot; and Tangaroa—fish and lizards). This series of victories by man is sometimes regarded as the basis of his claim to primacy in the hierarchy of the various beings that inhabit the earth. But hierarchy—in its most culturally revealing ways—has already been established before this series of individual contentions between Tū and his earth-bound brothers. It is not just that Tū conquers his earthly brothers and thus is master of them, but that the prior cosmological battle (of all of them vs. Tāwhiri) results in a set of relationships that make it right that Tū should be the master of the other things of the earth; therefore he sets out to conquer them. The individual victories of Tū over his brothers, and his own consequent transition to a more highly faceted, "encompassing" nature, are merely, to borrow a phrase from Weber, the "inner-worldly" implementation and manifestation of a hierarchical relation that is already established cosmologically.

This double step—in the form of a double battle—is of immense interest in relation to the analysis of the concept of hierarchy and its symbolization. It perhaps suggests that the strongest formulations of hierarchy must necessarily make recourse outside of the things that are hierarchicalized; the scale or measure to which the members of the set must submit, itself must lie outside of their sphere. In this case Tāwhiri, who is independent, external, and totalizing (see previous schema), plays that role. At the same time, since in Maori cosmogony all things must come from a single source (Sky/Earth), Tāwhiri is initially not fit to serve as the measure, becoming so only after his main transition, that is, to the sky.

The issue is of course interesting to think of in terms of what Dumont sees as the main idea of *Homo Hierarchicus*, "the idea of hierarchy separated from power" (1980:xxxv). The question can be raised whether a hierarchy established fully from within—rather than through measurement against an external scale—could ever be other than a formulation of power (as opposed to value). What is particularly interesting about this Arawa episode in terms of Dumont's argument lies not in the fact that it pictures an instance of a formulation going outside of the inner-worldly practice of power in order to constitute hierarchy. Rather, what is interesting is that, within a formulation in which ability to demonstrate forcefulness in inner-worldly practice does figure explicitly in the establishing of hierarchy, it nevertheless seeks to constitute that practice cosmologically. Because man, *in practice, but initially on a cosmological plane* demonstrates himself to be braver and more steadfast in purpose than his earthly brothers, man's subsequent inner-worldly demonstration of power assumes the character of a cosmic act carried out in terms of a scheme of cosmic value.

The particular way in which hierarchy is established in this account serves also to illustrate the centrality of another fundamental Maori value, that of "*utu*" (return, balance, proper redressment). The main point here is that in this account the superordinate being achieves his status as such, not in the first instance by subduing the other members of his set, but rather by remaining, in the face of ongoing incursions, the only member of his set whose being does not fall under the shadow of an unavenged grievance. What is singled out consistently by Te Rangikaheke, in his accounting for Man's special place on the earth, is not the second, earthly battle and the string of victories that occur there, but rather the first, cosmological battle, in which Tū alone refuses to be conquered; it is then this difference in state that makes it right for Tū to become master of the others (2):

> Kātahi ka rapu a Tū i tētahi whakaaro māna kia tahuri ia ki te patu i ōna tuākana, no te kahakore ki te rapunga utu a Tāwhiri mo āna [ōna?] Mātua, ā koia anake i toa ki te whawhai. (Grey xxxiii; MS 43:894)

> Then Tū sought for some plan by which to turn and subdue his brothers on account of their weakness in the face of Tāwhiri's revenge over the parents, such that it had been he alone who had been brave enough to fight.

The principle of *utu* figures centrally also in the account of the origin of human society. For both texts go on to consider the origins of human society. The manuscript (2) that contains the episode that Te Rangikaheke entitled "The Sons of Sky" contains also a further episode that he entitled *"Tūpuna"* (Ancestors); and indeed the ancestors have a number of affinities with the sons of Sky. As already noted, the origin of the different human tribes of Aotea, just as the origin of the various species of the natural world, is pictured as beginning with the dispersal of a set of sons who, in difficult circumstances of intertribal feuding, are forced to leave Hawaiki.

Te Rangikaheke attempts to argue the preeminence of one of these groups in New Zealand—his own group, the Arawa. (No doubt any other tribal group would do the same, that is, posit itself as the center; versions of the migration stemming from other tribes will be considered at a later point, and it will be seen that this posit is indeed the case.) What is of interest here, however, is the particular form in which Te Rangikaheke attempts to make the argument regarding the social hierarchy. For as Tū, in the primordial event of the cosmic battle, was left as the only one of the sons not bearing an unredressed grievance, so the Arawa, Te Rangikaheke argues, was the only canoe strong enough to return to Hawaiki to avenge the expulsion—thus perhaps mitigating, for its descendants, the stigma that could stem from the inability to do so (2).

> Ko te Arawa anake te waka i whaikoha [= whaikaha?] ki te hoki atu ki Hawaiki whawhai ai, ki te rapu utu mo te pananga mai. . . . [The term that occurs in the preceding sentence is actually "whaikoha," but the

context and the fact that the sentence is repeated again, almost identical-
ly, with "whaikaha," suggest that the latter term is what the author had
in mind.] (Grey lxx; MS 44:934)

The Arawa was the only canoe strong enough to return to Hawaiki to
fight, to seek revenge for the expulsion hither. . . .

Put another way, the Arawa is the only canoe standing in a proper relationship of *utu* with the external cultural measure, Hawaiki, just as Tū (Man) is
the only one of the earthly sons of Sky and Earth to stand in a proper relationship of *utu* to the external natural standard of the elements (Wind and his brood).
The essential being of the other sons of Sky, and of the peoples of the other
canoes, in Te Rangikaheke's view, is constituted in their running and hiding.
So although hierarchy necessarily implicates success in cosmologically sanc-
tioned, inner-worldly force, the object of the inner-worldly force consists
essentially in maintaining a nondegraded existence. Hierarchy is constructed—
in regard to both the elemental relations of the things in the universe and the
social relations among migrating peoples—not in the first instance through
depiction of one's conquest of the others, but rather by reference to a differential ability to redress a grievance that has been perpetrated equally against all
the members of the set (cf. Schrempp 1985:25). The overall effect of the
analogies is, in a way, to naturalize society, but it is a naturalization to a nature
that, as noted previously, the earlier phases of the account are concerned
precisely to cosmologize and steep with values for man.

An Excursus

One who is engaging in the analysis of another society should of course
be willing to try the same methods and perspectives on the corresponding
phenomena in his own cultural tradition, in this case, traditional stories about
the origin of the universe. There are numerous anthropological precedents,
including some in Boas, who in his studies of North American Indian mythologies attempted to compare the general orientation with that of the traditional
Judaeo-Christian cosmogony. In more recent times there is an interest in
anthropological analyses of biblical myth. But besides the fact that such comparisons already have, to some extent, a place within anthropological method,
and, moreover, anthropology or not, one always engages in them anyway in
thinking about things produced in cultures other than one's own, there is the
fact that such comparisons are often instructive.

To revert to an earlier theme, it was noted that the part of Lévi-Strauss's
structural perspective that is oriented specifically toward cosmogonic myths
looms very small within his full corpus. While the methods and perspectives

that he developed have been applied within various kinds of data from different parts of the world, the interest that has been shown in developing this small cosmogonic part of his perspective has been correspondingly small.

It is no doubt just a quirk of fate that Edmund Leach's pioneering structural analysis of the Judaeo-Christian cosmogony ("Lévi-Strauss in the Garden of Eden" [1970]) happened to come out the year before the work that contained Lévi-Strauss's first explorations toward a specifically cosmogonic analytic (*Totemism*). The most glaring weakness of Leach's account corresponds to the precise point on which, as noted before, Lévi-Strauss's cosmogonic analytic offers something new in relation to his previous formulations on myth: a formal principle of totalization. While Leach sets up a vast panoply of the various transitions that take place within the Judaeo-Christian account, and, by representing them all on one big (and by now well-known) diagram, generates the effect of comprehending a totalizing view, nonetheless, the fact that it is all placed on the same diagram constitutes the only significant way in which a totalizing quality is represented.

However, the applicabilities to the Genesis account of Lévi-Strauss's cosmogonic analytic are numerous, the most significant being the use of various kinds of continua that have been turned into discrete series, to support and constitute other such transitions. As in other cases discussed by Lévi-Strauss, the establishing of temporal periodicity is a first order of business in some mythologies, since much else will rest upon it. In some of the American Indian accounts considered by Lévi-Strauss, the spatiotemporal periodicity implied in the act of running is used as the model for another level of periodicity—for instance, that of the seasons of the year. Moreover, in some North American Indian cases that will be considered at a later point, and in the case of the Genesis account, temporal periodicity—that is, the display of the possibility of a segmentation embodied in a temporal periodization—becomes the abstract model that is projected onto a being-continuum, in order to construct a theory of speciation, a chain of being.

But, the notion of, for instance, a culture hero/runner managing to establish the primordial temporal periodicity that can also serve as a model of qualitative speculation is a notion that, in the Judaeo-Christian cosmogony, is obviated in a way by a theology that posits a transcendent Creator who can create distinctions by mere willing. *And yet*, discrete time—day and night—is the first distinction the Creator formulates. (Here the concern will be only with the first of the two Creation accounts that occur in the Book of Genesis—that of the "P" tradition, Genesis 1:1–2:4a.) For the first form of discreteness, that of temporal periodicity, becomes the model for the discreteness of species, at least in the sense that they are created within it as if to maintain the difference between the different works of different days.

In regard to the totality of the Creation, there is this interesting situation: the temporal periodization projects a cycle of seven days or opportunities for creation of distinct things; *but only six are used.* Rather than a deletion, within this temporal cumulative progression the space is simply never filled. Moreover, it is as if the consequences of leaving an empty day ramify in the fact of, so to speak, an overcrowding that occurs on some of the days, particularly the third and fifth. As was recognized by Thomas Aquinas (who was thus no doubt the first to apply a structural perspective to biblical myth) in his distinction between "works of separation" and "works of ornamentation," the ("P") Creation account contains two different main paradigms, one pertaining to the general structure of the cosmos, where the key concept is invariably separation, and the other to families of living things, where the creation is indirect and the key phrase is "Let the earth/waters bring forth." There are four instances of each main paradigm. (The creation of man is part of the final instance of the "ornamentation" paradigm—the earth bringing forth mobile living things—but it also arguably constitutes a third paradigm.) The distinction between the two main paradigms seems to rest essentially upon reproductive versus nonreproductive things. The following is a summary of days and works:

1: —separation of light and dark (day and night)

2: —separation of waters above and waters below

3: —separation of land and sea

   —ornamentation of earth with vegetation

4: —separation of celestial light (greater/lesser; sun/moon)

5: —ornamentation of the sea with living things

   —ornamentation of the air with living things

6: —ornamentation of the land with living things

   —creation of man

The general pattern is for each work to get its own day; when the works do have to be bunched, it is in such a way as to minimize the possibility of conflation. On day three the two works combined are from different paradigms. On day five, while both works are of the "ornamentation" paradigm, nevertheless the creatures combined are those that can be assimilated to geographical realms whose separateness has been previously insured, so that the combination not only economizes, but in doing so it also reiterates a previous work. There are thus enough works that in certain arrangements they could fill up seven (or perhaps more) days. The fact that they are instead arranged in such a way that an entire major space can be left empty emphasizes a general point about the economy of the total order of things: when all is accounted for there must still be room left over. In this case, as in the Maori, however, the empty space is not in the end empty, but rather is developed—on a different level and therefore in a way that is not threatening to the enumerated order of the things of the earth—as a positive principle of totality. In the Judaeo-Christian cosmogony it takes the form of a space which summarizes all the others (Genesis 2:3): "And God blessed the seventh day, and sanctified it: because that in it he had rested from all his work which God created and made." Since the outlook of the "Priestly" redaction was specifically ritual/liturgical, it may well be that this part of the Genesis account presents a case of ritual (or in this case, a ritual calendrics) generating myth—in which case the schematic significance of the empty space within a segmented continuum belongs already and as much to the formulation of the temporal order as to the Chain of Being that is ensconced within it.

FOURTH SCHEMA: METAPHYSICAL
1 → [INDEFINITELY MANY]

Certain issues—indeed a certain general level of concern within the Arawa cosmogony (and Maori cosmogony more generally)—might be called metaphysical. Broadly, the focus here is upon formulations of the sort that would appear to transcend any specific region of being, and to address "being *qua* being" or "being as such." The problem of the "one and the many" thus seems to transcend not only any specific regions of being as envisioned in particular societies, but also particular societies themselves; it seems to be a recurrent if not universal concern of cosmology, one often worked out in terms of a transition from the one to the many.

Unity and Plurality
1 → [Indefinitely Many]

In this section I will argue that if Kant had found himself among the traditional Maori, he probably would not have added any new a priori categories to his tables. This of course marks a departure from what for some time has been the dominant theory of what Kant would have done in this situation, namely, that which was suggested several decades ago by J. Prytz Johansen: "If one could picture to oneself a person like KANT among the old Maoris—which indeed is difficult—one should not be surprised if to the fundamental categories of knowledge, time and space, he had added: kinship" (1954:9). At some level, the idea that "kinship" forms the most encompassing scheme is perfectly acceptable if not perfectly obvious. The idea forms one of the most time-honored notions in the anthropological study of Maori society. Elsdon Best's researches into cosmology led him to write of the Maori:

> Above all, he held the belief that all things, animate and inanimate, are descended from a common source, the primal parents, Rangi and Papa. This belief had a considerable effect on the native mind, for, when the Maori walked abroad, he was among his own kindred. The trees around him were, like himself, the offspring of Tane; the birds, insects, fish, stones, the very elements, were all kin of his, members of a different branch of the one great family. Many a time, when engaged in felling a tree in the forest, have I been accosted by passing natives with such a remark as: *"Kei te raweke koe i to tipuna i a Tane."* (You are meddling with your ancestor Tane). (1924b:128–29)

In similar spirit Johansen wrote: "The whole cosmos of the Maori unfolds itself as a gigantic 'kin,' in which heaven and earth are first parents of all beings and things, such as the sea, the sand on the beach, the wood, the birds, and man. Apparently he does not feel quite comfortable if he cannot—preferably in much detail—give an account of his kinship whether to the fish of the sea or to a traveller who is invited to enter as a guest" (1954:9).

But the kinship that is referred to in such passages does not necessarily have much to do with the kinship of technical anthropological literature. First of all we are talking about a set of relationships that constitute a general condition of the cosmos, and which are seen as human by derivation, rather than cosmological by extension. Secondly, inasmuch as there is a "kinship idiom" for constituting human groups, it does not conform to any of the standard anthropological paradigms, least of all the classic unilineal ones. So "kinship" in what follows is used in only a general sense—to refer to the fact that Maori have a cultural theory of the interrelation of the entire physical universe as a consequence of a generative sexual dualism through which it is thought to have come about. The particular issue that is raised, however, is whether there is any significant sense in which this kinship can be thought of as in itself imparting a definite form; or whether there is not some deeper and more abstract source for a particular notion of form, according to which this kinship itself is shaped, and in relation to which this kinship becomes the idiom for demonstrating that deeper notion's reality or concrete realization.

The point to be made here stems from a certain concept which is recurrent in the Arawa account, namely the idea of "separation" (*wehe*); it is the way in which that idea occurs and speculations about its larger significance in this scheme that constitute the basis for the critique that is offered here. The notion of separation serves to highlight the difference in general view characteristic

of the prose accounts vis-à-vis the genealogical account. As continuity, portrayed through myriad devices, constitutes an important general principle of
the genealogical cosmogonies (see chapter 5), discontinuity, in the explicit and
repeated notion of separation, forms the most recurrent and central theme of
the corresponding prose cosmogonic accounts. Michael Shirres (1979:23, 74),
in the context of a study of the concept of *tapu*, has called attention to the
process of separation, commenting that it is "the key notion" in the early parts
of this Arawa story. Each new coming-to-be is described two ways: *specifically*
as some event which, since the various entities of the cosmos are "all in the
family," leaves a genealogical trace and relation, and at the same time,
generically, as a "separation." Each of the two texts (1, 2), in a way, contains
two entire cosmogonic accounts—since either level alone would account for
the origin of everything in the cosmos, but under different descriptions.

Earlier I noted a pattern of "dual formulation," that is, the coexistence of
two different theories of ancestry and identity accounting for the origin and
nature of major entities at all the main levels of the cosmogony. The issue being raised now is not precisely the same. The notion of dual formulation was
suggested by the pattern of a coexistence of two different theories of the same
general level, such that, although the effort is toward retaining both, the two
could be seen as competing with one another. Now the issue is, rather, the
coexistence of two entirely different (and therefore noncompeting) types and
levels of explanation. Yet perhaps, despite this difference, the present pattern
and the earlier-discussed notion of dual formulation do display a compatibility
of "spirit," exemplified by what is common to them: the tendency for theoretical descriptions, in this cosmogonic tradition, to come in twos.

It is the recurrent, generic description, that of separation, that forms the
subject of this part of the metaphysical inquiry. In contrast with the particularist
descriptions, which are concerned to provide tangible and detailed accounts
of things, or the differences between things, in their particularities, this
"generic" level of description is concerned to integrate all the different kinds
of events under a description that can be common to all of them, even if abstract,
and which will reveal the consequences for being-in-general of all these different difference-generating events. This particular aspect of this cosmogonic
account stands to gain the least from a structural analysis, since, relative to
the other level—which might also be called the event level—of cosmogonic
formulation, that is what it already is. Reduced to its most general and encompassing process, cosmogenesis here amounts to progressive separation: *to the
fragmentation of a once-unitary being.*

The account of cosmogony through "separation" is all-inclusive. There are
a few instances in which the slight differences belonging to the various members

of a particular family, such as Tāwhiri's brood (e.g., the whole set of different types of clouds), come into being with no mention of the idea of separation. But in these cases the emphasis is clearly upon these entities acting in concert as a particular social totality. I have checked both texts (1, 2) carefully, and there is no coming-to-be of any major new entity, or new distinction between major types of entities, that (above and beyond any particularist descriptions) is not distinctly called a separation. To recap some of the main ones:

> —Na Tāne i tītoko, ka mawehe Rangi rāua ko Papa, nāna i tauwehe ai, ka heuea te pō, ka heuea te ao oi. (1) (Grey iv; MS 81:53)

> By Tāne propped up, Sky and Earth were separated; by him were night and day pulled asunder.

> —the sundry separations of Tāwhiri

> —the separation of Tū's names

> —the separation of Tū's *karakia*

Also, while I will not undertake a detailed analysis of the theme of separation beyond this first phase of cosmogony, the following at least should be added:

> —the separation of Toi's sons

The late Hawaiki period and the notion of ancestral separation appear as linked in some other tribal traditions as well, though not in the same form. Regarding one of the premigration place names, Best (1925:675), for instance, cites a Ngāti Awa authority:

> "*No Tane ma ka timata mai tenei ingoa a Mataora, No reira mai taua ingoa a Mataora, tae noa mai ki konei. No muri mai i a Mataora ka wehewehe nga iwi i raro i a Rangi*"—(This name Mataora obtained from the time of Tane and his contemporaries. From that time the name of Mataora has endured and is still known. After [the sojourn in] Mataora the peoples under Rangi separated). The same authority says: "*Te ingoa o te ao katoa, tae noa ki Hawaiki, ko Mataora*"—(The name of the whole world, including Hawaiki, was Mataora.)

The suggestion here is that the most fundamental and most encompassing structural frame of Maori cosmogony consists in the opposition of pure unity and pure plurality, held together and betokened by the universal application within it (spanning both spiritual and material worlds) of the idea of separation. Kinship may derive its form from this opposition and interrelation—not from anything that can be said to derive exclusively from within kinship as some sort of closed, self-adequate system. Whether indeed there is or is not a level of cross-culturally identical "facts of life," there are none that in themselves are capable of generating or defining a social form. This much should not be too difficult to accept, since even those fervently and fully committed to the notion of a cross-culturally valid study of kinship founded essentially on the biological facts of life nevertheless tend to admit that definite social form results only from these facts plus certain cultural rules—the most obvious being the unilineal rule—that reduce the possibilities generated through the facts of life. But, secondly, specifically in Polynesian studies, it is generally conceded that it is not even possible to find a set of such rules that, as a closed system, unambiguously produce definite social units. At the most there are only certain values—for instance, that a genealogical connection through an older brother is stronger than one through a younger brother, though even this principle is not without its ambiguities and inversions. The usual interpretation is that there is a built-in "flexibility" that allows other types of factors to enter in at particular points to make the final reduction from all that is possible.

But, if one accepts some version of the idea that there is a process that reduces possibilities to some definite specification of a social unit, there is still—and now in an even more glaring way—the problem of the genesis of social form as such. Namely: What, then, is the source of the particular idea of form *to which* that reduction of possibilities takes place?

Perhaps the source of the ruling idea of social form lies precisely in—or receives expression in—the opposition of pure unity to pure plurality. This notion provides the abstract ideal, or abstract guideline, of the form that, when all is said and done, kinship must resolve itself into, and serve to display in the concrete. In this sense, the form that must be displayed by kinship might have its source—as a pure idea of form—outside of kinship.

If this much can be accepted, then it would appear that the co-presence of two different levels of description of cosmogenesis—the one essentially this level of relation of oneness and plurality, the other a set of entities and events linked through a "web of kinship"—exists, not purely in consequence of the pleasure of proliferating different levels of explanation (though there may be that as well), but because the duality of explanation is central to the genesis of social form. The reason for the co-presence of the two levels, from this perspective, is precisely to produce an alignment or calibration of one to the other—that is, the alignment or calibration of the concrete idiom of "kinship" to the abstract notion of form, so that kinship learns, so to speak, what it is supposed to show.

Without necessarily discounting the possibility that there may be systems in the world that operate by positing a set of cultural rules (such as unilineal descent) that, in their consistent application, produce a definite social form, in the Maori case there appears to be rather a very loose and maximally inclusive notion of descent, and then a notion of form with its own origins. The latter acts, in the manifold political and historical processes, as guide for the former—as that which the "kinship" concrete should as far as possible attempt to realize.

This would not necessarily put Maori (Polynesian) systems in a category wholly different from a system that tries to construct social form through a set of rules of descent that fully and unambiguously specifies the makeup of social groups. That is, even in the latter system, the recognition of the necessity of creating reductive rules in order to achieve definite form, once more, though in a different way, indicates that the construction of those rules itself must be subject to some notion of form that lies outside of any facts of life. The differences would be, rather, that the Maori system postpones the reduction/resolution—preferring to maintain a duality and dialectic between an ideal notion of form and a maximally inclusive notion of descent for as long as possible—rather than immediately dispensing with the surfeit of possibilities. Further, to the extent that the reduction/resolution is achieved, it is by means of a hiding/backgrounding of the other possibilities, which are always there, however, to reemerge (cf. Schwimmer 1978). The pattern of resolution can be seen in the historical concrete in a number of instances, for example, in an account of the origin of a *hapū* (a descent unit which scholars have traditionally regarded as a subtribe) that has been provided by Eric Schwimmer. The ancestral founder of the *hapū* in question was Tautahi,

> . . . who (as in other cases found by myself, Elsdon Best and others) was a visiting stranger. All *hapuu* members were in fact his descendants either by one of his two local wives, or by his other wives. I showed also that the *hapuu* was not constituted until seven generations after this presumed visit, and that it took some generations after this until all those who could trace descent from Tautahi in fact chose to do so and call themselves Ngati Tautahi. What resulted was in fact a political formation which linked together the people of the whole of the Whangaruru peninsula, while excluding the people of the adjoining mainland. It joined together a number of older *hapuu*, four of whom were still resident of the peninsula at the time of investigation. Though these *hapuu* still existed as names, their members found it to be advantageous to emphasize for most purposes their affiliation to Ngati Tautahi, to use a common cemetery, respect a common *mana*. . . . (1978:214–15)

The argument that Kant probably would not have added another category has more behind it than merely this limiting conclusion about Maori kinship (i.e., the conclusion that Maori kinship is not merely constitutive, but is itself constituted according to some deeper notion of form; thus that kinship, while perhaps the single most pervasive concrete "idiom" of Maori cosmogony and cosmology, cannot as such be considered as a final and ineluctable category of thought). The argument that Kant would not have added a new category derives additionally—and this is more important—from the fact that one of the categories that belongs to Kant's original scheme in fact already provides a perfect characterization of the notion of form to which, I argue, the idiom of Maori kinship derives its shape, namely, the "*a priori* categories of quantity." This set of categories forms one of four triads (of quantity, of quality, of modality, and of relation) that in Kant's view form a total inventory of the pure concepts of the understanding. The triad of quantity is oneness, plurality (manyness), and allness or totality (*Einheit, Vielheit, Allheit/Totalitat*): ". . . in view of the fact that all *a priori* division of concepts must be by dichotomy, it is significant that in each class the number of the categories is always the same, namely, three. Further, it may be observed that the third category in each class always arises from the combination of the second category with the first. Thus *allness* or *totality* is just plurality considered as unity. . ." (1965:116).

The last point (allness/totality = manyness considered as oneness) can be advanced, tentatively, as identical with the logical framework implied in the "generic" level of Te Rangikaheke's cosmogony. What is it that is betokened by Te Rangikaheke's universal application of the concept of separation, if not a holding together of the conditions of oneness and plurality—such that the cosmos, by virtue of this holding together of its initial and final states, constitutes, in Kant's sense, a "totality"?

Besides this logical identity to a certain level of formulation within the Arawa cosmogony, Kant's formulation of the categories of quantity also provides a theoretical description of the way in which Maori social groups are most frequently named: by the combining of the plural term "Ngāi" or "Ngāti" (= "ngā āti," "the [plural] offspring") with a unitary term, the name of an eponymous ancestor, thereby creating a third, synthesized term (e.g., Ngāti Paraheka) that objectifies "manyness considered as oneness." Thus the constitution of social units is formally analogous to at least a certain level of formulation of the cosmos-at-large. Best notes that ". . . the Tuhoe tribe *are* Tuhoe solely because they are descendants of Tuhoe-potiki, and every member of the tribe is so descended" (1977:213).

There is a secondary pattern, in which this totality (constituted through a combining of singular and plural terms) is then put in relation with another type of singular term—the name of one of the eponymous ancestor's descendants—so that a given descendant then becomes identical with the same totality of which, in the primary formulation, he forms only one member of the plural term. It refers to a recurring grammatical pattern in which a tribal totality and a name of a particular member are in apposition. For example, a member of the Ngatiraukawa tribe says, "Warriors! Heretaunga will be conquered by *me*, by Ngatiraukawa" (cited in Johansen 1954:35; Johansen provides numerous examples of this pattern). It is taking Kant's formulation one step further, by using the totality—in Kant's view a necessarily combinatory term—as one of the two terms that compose a yet higher-level combination.

No—Kant, if he had found himself among the Maori, would not have added "kinship" to his table of categories; but it is possible that he would have seen in Maori kinship a confirmation of one of the sets of categories that he had posited (as far as we know) quite independently of any knowledge of the Maori. Certainly, however, Kant would have been directly aware of types of social formations—such as the notion of a "king" or "kingship"—that, though in slightly different form, nevertheless, similarly display in the concrete his a priori categories of quantity.

Speculation about the proper place for Kant in anthropological science constitutes a theme of considerable importance. One of the most significant influences of Kant was felt in Durkheim's attempt to replace pure a priorist reasoning with a "sociological epistemology," or, broadly, in the argument that the categories of the understanding have their origin in society. It might appear that the arguments presented above—and particularly the suggestion that in this case kinship seems to shape itself according to a Kantian category—would be directly opposed to Durkheim's thesis. In fact, however, no argument against Durkheimian sociological epistemology is intended, except perhaps insofar as the notion of kinship is concerned. That is, since the form found in kinship appears to derive from without, it is difficult to think of kinship acting as source or model for the categories of the understanding. The important point in the analysis above is that there are two levels of formulation—and that they are aligned, as different descriptions of the same process and system.

But while the emphasis has been upon the co-presence of the pattern of separation and a set of more particularistically inclined descriptions of cosmic events, it is important also to consider the pattern of separation in itself. From this perspective, the great issue that this cosmogony confronts is *the consequences for the cosmos of the introduction of the principle of separation*. It is very noticeable that the debate among the sons—firstly, over whether to change the situation at all, and, secondly, whether to change the situation by killing the parents or separating them—are set up as the first critical focus of the story. And as soon as the great decision is implemented, all being follows suit: the rest of the story can be seen as the playing out of the consequences of that first cosmic act. That is, the first great separation is achieved, and the cosmos rapidly goes to pieces.

Seeing it this way is not at all out of character with the emphasis accorded to the decision in the story, where it is presented as a momentous—that is, "cosmic"—decision:

> Na ko tēnā kupu, ko te nuia [nuinga?] ko te roanga, ko te nuinga ake o ā rātou whakaaro patu i ō rātou mātua, kia ora ai te tangata. (1) (Grey iii; MS 81:53)

> This phrase, "the greatness, the longness," refers to the magnitude of their idea to kill their parents, so that man might grow.

> Ā whakaaro ana aua tamariki i tā rātou whakaaro nui, kia patua ō rātou mātua. (2) (Grey xxxi; MS 43:893)

> Then those children thought their great thought, that their parents be killed.

It is also not out of character with certain patterns that are found in many other cosmogonies. Separation in the Arawa cosmogony has roughly the same "plot" significance as the first disobedience in the second ("J") Creation story in the Book of Genesis (the Garden of Eden story [2:4b–3:24]). Both stories revolve around a rebellion that introduces the *felix culpa* of that particular system. There is a momentous decision by which a new principle is allowed to enter into the cosmos and to change it utterly.

Since throughout this analysis quantitative indicators have been emphasized, it is worth noting a very interesting quantitative characteristic with respect to the implementing of these great founding decisions. It is as if it is just assumed that whatever principle enters through such focused events will fill up the cosmos. One can see this same pattern in different kinds of principles, for example, structural, moral, material. A great part of the overall concern of the composer of the "J" Genesis account appears to have been the moral nature of man and of the cosmos. In his cosmogonic formulation, once there is knowledge of good and evil, the world is suddenly and thereafter full of the opposition of GOOD AND EVIL—that is what the rest of the story is about. One can see the Arawa account as handling its own particular obsession in a similar way: the first separation is attained, and immediately the cosmos fills up with SEPARATION.

Examples of a similar, quantitative reasoning (or lack of quantitative reasoning), but in regard to a material principle, are afforded in many origin myths. For instance in the "earth-diver" myths of North America, if one of the animals can succeed in retrieving, from the bottom of the water that initially covers the surface of the earth, some, a handful, of earth—or in other words the principle of earth—then the cosmos will have EARTH aplenty, spreading out to its own limits.[6] The earth-diver myth might be seen as a particular development of a very widely spread cosmogonic *modus operandi*, in which the principles of things, once attained or achieved, spread out of themselves to seek their own proper extent; it is as if the utter disregard for quantitative precision in such moments throws the emphasis to the consideration of quality and of principle—and, in certain cases, of a recognition of an inherent futility in attempting to limit the scope of certain principles once they are given any kind of status at all.

Numerous other cultural contexts furnish themes that bear study in regard to the pattern of cosmogenesis through separation considered above. There is a type of *karakia* called a *wehe*; also, the term "*wehe*" and other terms dealing with connection or severance of physical interrelations occur prominently within *karakia* and other sorts of verbal and ritual formulations. The recurrent theme of separation seems to furnish a background against which ritual performances and political strategies emerge as attempts to recapture a lost unity.

As mentioned above, all the schemata are ultimately reversible in certain contexts. Of interest here is the possibility that *hui* (tribal or intertribal meetings) might be looked at as intimately related to the cosmogonic process analyzed above. The highly ritualized process of assemblage for *hui* might be viewed as an inversion of the process of cosmogony. It would seem to be precisely the underlying sense that the plurality of things derives from one thing that constitutes the condition for the possibility of these moments of assemblage (or reassemblage).

While these moments are marked by great affect, serious questions could be posed as to its source. In this case it would not seem to be the dissolution of structure, as suggested by Victor Turner, that permits the great display of affect. It is rather the bringing of structure to a particular kind of consummate expression—in the form of a background recognition that everything is ultimately from one thing and that therefore what is going on is a recapturing of a primordial reality—that constitutes the intellectual and "socio-logical" conditions for the possibility of the great affect characteristic of these occasions.

Certainly the way that these events are ritually organized supports this. In the Maori cosmogony, each separation, each new discontinuity, has its own specific place, time, and story. Reciprocally, discontinuity is overcome in *hui* one piece at a time. Each incoming group is acknowledged uniquely in building up the ritual totality; and it was stressed to me by Maori people that a successful greeting requires, not merely *general* sentiments, but also *specific* references to particular points of interrelation between the home and visiting parties (cf. Schrempp 1985:32; Salmond 1983). For each new incoming group there is a specific story or mythical allusion in the stock of tribal and intertribal lore. But at the same time the incorporation in each case takes the general form of a ritual conjunction of "land" and "sea," since the usual welcoming chant by the *tāngata whenua*, or land people, is an invocation to haul the canoe of any incoming group—inversely to the separation "Us to the land, Us to the sea" of the cosmogony. So, like the cosmogonic account considered above, the ritual of *hui* furnishes a double-level description, specific and generic, of its essential process.

The concrete contents of the ritual affirm that what is involved is not affect allowed by the dissolution of structure, but affect allowed by the bringing of the background structural character into prominence, in the recognition, through a history of separation, of the primordial interrelation of oneness and plurality. It would seem that the principles of Maori knowledge allow one to assume a priori that any two beings are related—so that the challenge in any case is not that of determining whether there is an interrelationship, but rather that of being able to adduce the historical/genealogical facts that define what that interrelationship is.

NEGATION AND AFFIRMATION

Philosophers have paid little attention to the idea of the nought. And yet it is often the hidden spring, the invisible mover of philosophical thinking.
                                        —Henri Bergson, *Creative Evolution*

Besides the term "*wehe*," one can note, in the Arawa account, the recurrence of the term "*tupu*." This term, whose minimal meaning is something like "to grow," has been analyzed in detail by Prytz Johansen (1954:40), who suggests the more philosophical "to unfold one's nature." Johansen emphasizes the broad range of applicability of this term—for instance, to disease, war and peace, thoughts and feelings—suggesting that in all these it takes on a meaning particular to that entity. "A name unfolds its nature (*tupu*) by spreading, . . . a grasp by being strong" (1954:40). "*Tupu* for man is his natural and characteristic unfolding of life, as firmness is to the pole and thriving to the plant" (1954:46). As the natural unfolding of the life of an individual it can be tantamount to "honor": "Life, strength, courage, honour, and repute thus are one in *tupu*" (1954:44). Johansen sees the term "*tupu*" as in basic opposition to another term, "*mate*," "to be insufficient" (1954:48), which has a similarly wide range of application. While Johansen does not particularly consider

cosmogonic contexts, he does note, "This unfolding is the essence of creation and must constantly be renewed by *karakias* (incantations)" (1954:41).

At one point Lévi-Strauss drew upon Johansen's analysis of *tupu* to suggest
that this term has some possible sociological implications, that is, implications
for organization of social units in Maori society. Schwimmer took exception
to Lévi-Strauss's suggestions regarding the sociological significance of *tupu*,
claiming that Lévi-Strauss was entirely correct when he wished to find some

> . . . Maori concept to account for group genesis and constitution. It is
> only for specific ethnographic reasons that I do not think the term *tupu*
> can carry this heavy conceptual burden. As I already indicated, this term
> does not really refer to much more than to the waxing and waning char-
> acteristic of the individual biological life cycle. Certainly, Prytz Johansen
> quotes some interesting metaphoric uses of the term, but they do not go
> beyond life forces found within individuals. It is more useful to look for
> more community centered concepts to account for Maori group genesis
> and constitution. (Schwimmer 1978:211)

Schwimmer's own research (some of which was considered earlier) into the
origin and nature of the fundamental Maori social unit of "*hapū*" led him to
suggest an emendation: "The terms *tupu* and *mate* are specifically attached
to individual biology; the genesis and constitution of the group cannot be
thought in those terms. I propose that the most useful concept for thinking about
them is that of *hapuu*, a term which in its primary meaning denotes 'pregnant' "
(1978:211).

Schwimmer's suggested emendation is interesting and curious in several
ways, most notably in the extent of the similarity between the two terms that
are here the object of dispute. Both *tupu* and *hapū* suggest the root *pū* which
in Polynesia recurs as a term that is linked, on the one hand, to the idea of natural growth stemming from a particular source or "root," and on the other hand,
to the form of human social groups. Both "*tupu*" and "*hapū*" are dynamic
terms that implicate a certain teleological view, of social groups or of whatever
object they may be applied to. One is reminded of the contours of being that
are sketched in the early phases of the cosmic genealogy, in which whatever
is—even nothing—has a certain career, runs a certain course from void to
fullness, and then gives way to something else (Chapter 5). Schwimmer's comments themselves were in fact prompted as a positive response to Lévi-Strauss's
comments (based to some extent on Johansen's analysis of the concept of *tupu*)
that the general character of Maori society and socio-logic is evolutionary.

While I have not so far found evidence that refutes the point made by
Schwimmer that social groups are not a main subject of which *tupu* is pre-

dicated, on the other hand, I do not see any justification for his claim that the primary meaning of "*tupu*" is individual life-cycles, and that other applications are metaphorical. In the Arawa cosmogony, "*tupu*" is one of the most recurrent terms and is used in a number of different ways. Its status in this cosmogonic account approaches that of the term "*wehe*" ("to separate") that was considered earlier. That is, one could take either term—"*wehe*" or "*tupu*"—and, merely by listing the statements that contain either of these terms, get a broad idea of the entire story; they are both pervasive and recurrent processes.

The following is, in rough outline, a summary of the main ways in which the term "*tupu*" occurs in this story. The first usage may be obvious to Polynesianists; the others are of particular interest to the topic of cosmogonic thought. There are numerous instances of each type of usage in this account; but because they are of particular interest to the issues raised by Schwimmer, several examples will be provided for second and third usages, whereas a single example will suffice for the others.

1. As a main term specifying ancestry.

   a. In nominalized form, it means "ancestor," for example:
      Kotahi anō te tupuna o te tangata Maori. . . . (2) (Grey xxxi; MS 43:893)

      One indeed was the ancestor of the Maori people. . . .

   b. In causative form, it means "to raise up descendants," for example:
      Kātahi ka whakatupuria ngā uri o Tāwhiri-mātea. . . . (2) (Grey xxxii; MS 43:893)

      Then the descendants of Tāwhiri-mātea were raised up. . . .

   c. In nominalized, causative form, it means "a [genealogical] generation": see the second example in type 2 below, that is, ". . . down to the generation of Māui-taha and his younger brothers." It can also apparently be used in a collective sense, where it perhaps suggests something like the entire "phenomenon of man," for example:
      Na tēnei anō te take o te whakatupuranga o te tangata. . . . (1) (Grey iii; MS 81:53)

      This is the source of the generation of man. . . .

(This usage shades into the usage that immediately follows.)

2. To refer to the growth of man *thought of generically*, for example:
   . . . ko tā rātou rapunga whakaoro [whakaaro?] hoki mō ō rātou mātua kia tupu ai te tangata. (1) (Grey iii; MS 81:53)

... their search for an idea concerning [what to do about] their parents, so that man might grow.

Ā ka tupu nei ngā uri o Tū-matauenga, ā nui haere, nui haere, ka tae ki te whakatupuranga i a Māui-taha rātou ko āna tēina. . . . (2) Grey xxxiv; MS 43:896)

The descendants of Tū-matauenga grew, increasing ever increasing, down to the generation of Māui-taha and his younger brothers. . . .

3. To refer to general conditions that may become pervasive in the world or cosmos, for example:
   Ka mahara ia kua whai uri ia, ā ka nui haere, ka whakatupu kino mai ki a ia. (1) (Grey v; MS 81:55)

He [Tū] was worried that he [Tāne—trees] would have descendants [birds], and that they would become numerous and perpetrate [*tupu*] harm against him.

Ka tupu nei te whawhai ā rātou i tō rātou nohoanga i Rarotonga, arā i Hawaiki, ka tupu nui haere, nui haere. . . . (1) (Grey vi; MS 81:56)

The fighting increased [*tupu*] among them while they were living in Rarotonga, that is, Hawaiki, and kept increasing [*tupu*]. . . .

Ka tupu te whakaaro i a Tāwhiri-mātea mō ana [ōna?] mātua, kei tupu te pai; tōna whakatikanga ake kei te whai anō i tōna matua, kia tahuri mai ki te whawhai ki ōna tuākana. (1) (Grey iv; MS 81:54)

The idea occurred to [*tupu*—lit., "grew"] Tāwhiri-mātea concerning their parents: that, lest peace should prevail [*tupu*], he would stay with his father (when his father was lifted up), so that he could then turn and fight his older brothers.

4. As in the previous example, in the idiom—which occurs a number of times in the two accounts (1, 2)—"ka tupu te whakaaro," lit., "the thought grew." How much should one make of this idiom? At the least there is a sort of narrative-suspense created by the sense of major new situations developing first as ideas or schemes, and then in their physical implementation.

On the basis of the pervasiveness of this term, one might say, in spirit with Johansen, that the real counterstate to the initial state of the cosmos—or, in other words, the opposite of *kore* (nothing)—is the state of *tupu*. As suggested in the example above, the term "*tupu*" is implicated in the statement that, of all that is proclaimed in this account, comes closest to expressing why the original condition was not satisfactory and why, therefore, the great cosmos-changing act—the separation of sky and earth—had to be carried out, namely: "so that man might grow" (kia tupu ai te tangata). It will be noted that most of the usages of the term "*tupu*" reflect specifically long time-scale, transgenerational processes; in this account at least there is no indication that the term is confined primarily to the span of individual life-cycles.

Such grand cosmogonic oppositions present a case in which the tension between the temporal and the atemporal can take the form of a balanced opposition. In the Maori case (but cf. also the previous summary of Lovejoy's studies) the basic, perduring, and in a way stable and timeless opposition that is set up as an opposition of possible general conditions of being, is precisely the opposition of the stable and inert to the dynamic and growing. It is perhaps the one special case of an opposition that is, at least in a sense, static, but which necessarily at the same time implicates a dynamism as one of its terms, that is, as the antithetical term, or perfect opposite, to the state of inertness that it posits as the first term, or the original condition.

The Ethic of Antinegation

Jean Smith (1974:23) notes: "For the Maori, a positive was most typically achieved through the negation of a negative."[7] According to the picture presented in Maori cosmogonic genealogies, the cosmos happens almost as an inevitable teleological process, in which, in a number of versions, concepts or metaphors of organic growth (e.g., the idea of roots or of gestation) figure centrally. But in the prose narrative view, cosmogony happens for one and only one reason: a rebellious self-affirmation, led by the great ancestors of man (Tāne and Tū), against the established order.

While there may be cosmogonies in the world that posit various forms of transition from void to plenitude in a purely disinterested intellectual spirit, and while indeed Maori cosmogony has something of this quality, the nothing here appears to be more than that. It is highly interwoven, not only with the other elements in this account, but also into the "fabric of life." The original situation demands a continuous response in the form of an adequate counter. The particular way in which the cosmos is set up lends itself to a certain "spirit," or attitude toward life and being.

The cosmic necessity for continuous affirmation is manifested not just in the systematic opposition of great cosmic terms (e.g., day/night, *ao/pō*) that are found recurrently in ritual and *karakia*, but more generally in a view of being which recognizes a general quality of what might be called cosmic resistance or cosmic inertia. This inertia shows itself particularly at the two most creative moments, namely the origins of the natural order of the cosmos, and the origins of Maori society. Sky and Earth must not only be propped apart as the first act, but they must also be continuously held apart, against their own desire to reunite (in a South Island account the rain is said to be the tears of Sky for Earth). In the Arawa version, the role of Tāne as trees is particularly emphasized; and one of his ongoing tasks as such is to hold the sky and earth apart continuously. The *Whare Wānanga* account, among others, contains the theme of the placing of posts which will insure the continuance of the separation (see Sahlins's [1987:54ff.] discussion of the symbolism of the posts). Then there is the series of stories of the feats of Māui, some of which consist of bringing about less radical but nevertheless necessary alterations of the cosmic order.

The theme of cosmic inertia once again obtrudes at the other great founding moment, that is, the origin of Maori society in the period of the migrations. Everything conspires against the transporting of culture and society to the new home. When the trees are cut down for hewing the canoes for the voyage, they go back up, until a suitable ritual remedy is found. There are a number of stories dealing with the problems of getting the central cultural and ritual goods—such as *kūmara*, ritual knowledge, and the gods themselves—to the new locale. The particularly recurrent patterns in these stories are the tendency of these goods of themselves to revert to their original home, and the overcoming of those tendencies through combinations of theft, the use of certain rituals that fix goods in new contexts, and appropriation of powers belonging to the female line. The last theme—the appropriation of the powers of the female line—is recurrent in cosmogonic situations that require some alteration of the cosmos in a way that will make it more suitable for human existence. The direct agents of these changes are usually male, but their success depends upon their gaining access to some power possessed by women. The archetypal incidents are Māui's cosmic feats such as setting the course of the sun aright. The feats are preceded by Māui's journey to his great ancestress in the underworld, to gain the tools and knowledge that are necessary for success. The original separation of Sky and Earth—in the form of the banishing of Sky—itself has something of this character: the sons depose the male cosmic parent and thus appropriate the female cosmic parent. A similar relation obtains in many of the stories of the transplanting of culture from Hawaiki to Aotea, and fixing it in place. In certain respects these accounts have the general character of the Māui stories: they recount a grand theft of cosmic things. Even so, as noted previously, there is a general sense that the goods make it to Aotea in only a limited and reduced way.

Cosmogonies pose at least two states or general conditions of being: one is the world as it is generally recognized in its present condition, and the other some previous state out of which the present condition developed. The idea of some previous, radically different phase of the cosmos is one of many types of alternate worlds or alternate realities that are pictured in mythologies; others are upperworlds, underworlds, and various theories about the societies that animals and fish live in when distant from interaction with humans. Often the temporally and spatially distant alternative worlds coincide, as, for instance, both the previous cosmic epoch and the ongoing underworld of the Maori are dominated by the concept of *Pō* (Night). Perhaps the oldest question in the study of mythology—a question which has inspired a number of different types of answers by anthropologists and psychologists—is: Why this imagining or portrayal of conditions alternative to those of the everyday world?

Without denying that there is a level and/or type of mythological thought that presents a view of the *necessity* of the world as it is, it is important, in the full scope, to recognize a type/level of mythology that imagines extreme alternatives (such as nonbeing) in order to give expression rather to the contingency of what is. In order for there to be human social life, it may be necessary that the world be a certain way. But below this lies the recognition that such conditions as may be necessitated by human social life are not necessarily cosmic givens, and should not be taken for granted. Far from being a necessity, in Te Rangikaheke's prose account the cosmos only just barely happens at all (five beings try, and only the last one succeeds in separating sky and earth), and thanks only to a specific effort by man's ancestors. Beneath the view of the dissatisfaction with, but proof of necessity of, the world as it is lies a more profound terror, envisaging, at least in fleeting moments, the possibility that the way the world is may not after all be necessary, and perhaps that neither is the world itself. But the downplaying of the necessity of the world at the same time constitutes an upgrading of the necessity of a human effort of creation. To the extent that the necessities of human life are not fully prepared by or freely given in the cosmos, they can be gained and maintained only through a continuous effort of affirmation and construction.

EVERYTHING AT ONCE
THE FOUR SCHEMATA, CONCLUDED

The main consideration left in regard to the schemata is the interrelation of the four. Within particular cultural contexts, no doubt all the schemata are subject to inversions. To take the most obvious example, the main way of thinking the unity of all that is, is through thinking back to the primordial undifferentiated state of the original parents. Although the tale tells of the fragmentation of being, Sky and Earth, Rangi and Papa, continue to serve as the main and most encompassing symbols of unity within this system.

But the schemata can also be considered simply as they are objectified in these particular texts (1, 2). Here they form, with respect to the basic directionality of cosmogony, an exhaustive set that might be described, approximately at least, through the logical terms of affirmation, negation/inversion, disjunction, and union. The metaphysical schema sets the basic direction of cosmogenesis, which is from nothing to oneness to plurality. The "reduction" schema negates or inverts that basic directionality at particular moments to institute a fixity in certain relations. While founded on an ambiguity, the schema of "the one and the two" occurs mainly as the means of getting from one state to the other—*either* in the differentiation of one into two *or* the reduction of two to one. And the hierarchical schema differs from all the others in demanding a formulation that unites, reciprocally, *both* directionalities (expansive and reductive). These interrelations could be examined further; here it is enough to note that the pattern exhibited in their interrelation indicates great logic and economy. This cosmogony embodies a set of tools that are not only interesting and diversified in themselves, but are also complete and economical in their constitution of a "kit."

The last point suggests something that is true in general about this cosmogony, and which might be affirmed against a characteristic that has been more commonly called to attention in mythologies. That is, it is frequently pointed out, by Lévi-Strauss and others, that myths can exhibit a great extravagance in the sense of endlessly repeating the same patterns in different codes or concrete contents. Examples of this tendency can be found in the Arawa account considered here. But the contrary characteristic—that of economy—must be noted as well. In this example, for instance, the hierarchical schema, rather than, so to speak, starting from scratch, uses the metaphysical schema, to constitute half of itself. The pattern of separation runs through everything; the hierarchical schema takes excerpts from this pattern—for instance, the separation of the *karakia*—and simply joins these excerpts to a reciprocal pattern that is based on the opposite operation, that of conjoining, to constitute a schema that is thoroughly reciprocal or bi-directional. Numerous other examples of this sort of economy can be found. On the whole this cosmogony is impressive, less for a proliferation of the same schema through different kinds of contents, than for the number and complexity of schemata that it is able to maintain within the limits set by its physical brevity and its small inventory of concrete contents (characters, motifs, and so on). Provided that I am indeed justified in separating these various schemata, then it is perhaps possible to state, in a formal or semiformal way, one of the reasons for the poetic elegance that is often commented about in this account: the relatively limited and nonextravagant contents are formulated in such a way that they simultaneously support several main conceptual patterns, each of which constitutes a distinctive source of coherence.

Chapter Four

Other Variants

The *Whare Wānanga* Transformation

Among European scholars, two Maori cosmogonic accounts are particularly well-known—that published by Grey, which we have already considered, and an account published by S. Percy Smith under the title of *The Lore of the Whare-wānanga*. Smith gives the following account of the origin of the latter materials:

> In the late fifties of last century there was a large gathering of Maoris in the Wairarapa District, East Coast of New Zealand, the object being to discuss some political affairs; and on the conclusion of the business it was suggested by some of the people that the learned men there present should explain to the assembled tribes how and when New Zealand was first peopled by the Maori race. After three of the priests had consented to do so, one—Te Matorohanga—was appointed to lecture on the subject, the other two to assist by recalling matters that the lecturer might omit, and also to supplement the story from their own knowledge. It was also decided that the lectures should be written down, a work that was undertaken by two young men named H. T. Whatahoro and Aporo Te Kumeroa, who had been educated at the Mission schools.
>
> Much matter was written down at that time; but it was amplified subsequently by the old priest named above, and by one of his confreres named Nepia Pohuhu, when H. T. Whatahoro spent some years, off and on, in recording to the dictation of these old men, the ancient beliefs and the history of their branch of the Maori people. (1913:i)

Though Smith claims that the material he is presenting has the approval of "the most learned men left of the Ngati-Kahu-ngunu tribe" (1913:ii), the many recopyings and modifications of the original manuscripts present a set of complex problems regarding authorship. While some work has been done on this matter (see Biggs and Simmons 1970), it seems safest, for the moment, to stay with a generic and pragmatic designation for this text, i.e. *Whare Wānanga* account. This account seems in general to be more influenced by Christian scriptures and doctrines than does the Arawa account considered in the previous chapter; and, additionally, Percy Smith's translations contain further attempts to align the Maori concepts with Western ones (e.g., Maori Raro-henga with Hades). But the final verdict on the degree and nature of Christian influence is not yet in. Moreover, there is a possibility, too little explored at this point, that lies between retention of "indigenous" doctrines and "syncretism." That is, one can picture mythological texts as particular concretizations of a vast pool of ideas, only some of which became recorded "texts." It is quite possible that in some of the historically late Maori cosmogonic texts, the composers were moved to create an account that maximized similarities with Christian ideas—not by borrowing from Christianity so much as by accentuating those indigenous ideas that most approximated Christian ones. I suspect that the *Whare Wānanga* account was influenced in some way by the encounter with Christianity, and I will call attention to the ways in which this account parallels Christian ideas; yet in the end there is virtually no element that one can assign with certainty to borrowing from Christianity. The following discussion is not intended to make any addition to the work of disentangling sources, but is concerned rather with attempting to characterize and understand some of the forms of transformation that are evident in the materials that Smith has presented. Smith's volume presents the Maori account first, and then an English translation (in which, however, many of the episodes are related in an order that differs from the Maori account); both the Maori text and the English translations will be presented in the following analysis. Parenthetical and bracketed commentaries are Smith's, except where used to indicate spelling errors; I have not attempted to improve on Smith's frequently inconsistent punctuation and word division.

I propose to show, first, that the first two schemata take, in the *Whare Wānanga* account, forms that are chiasmatically inverse to their forms in the Arawa account, and that the two inversions are structurally interrelated. In the case of the third and fourth schemata, transformation in the form of historical syncretism will be considered in addition to the more logical form of transformation that predominates in the analysis of the first two schemata.

First Schema: The Two and the One

This schema takes, in the *Whare Wānanga* case, a form inverse to that in the Arawa case. Rather than the assertion of an original unity that is separated into a duality, the first scenario is that of a primal mating of Sky and Earth, which are originally separate (at a later point they are again separated by the children, much as in the Arawa case). The original scenario in the *Whare Wānanga* case is as follows:

> Ko Rangi-nui e tu iho nei ka hiahia ki a Papa-tua-nuku e tiraha ake ana te puku ki runga; ka hiahia iho ia hei wahine māna. Ka heke iho a Rangi ki a Papa. I taua wa te maramatanga he maramatanga po-kutikuti, kakarauri nei te ahua; kaore hoki he ra, he marama, he whetu, he kapua, he ao, he kohu ranei, he kotaotao wai ranei (19)

> The Rangi-nui [great sky], which stands above, felt a desire towards Papa-tua-nuku [the earth], whose belly was turned up [towards him]; he desired her as a wife. So Rangi came down to Papa. In that period the amount of light was nil; absolute and complete darkness [*po-kutikuti kakarauri*] prevailed; there was no sun, no moon, no stars, no clouds, no light, no mist—no ripples stirred the surface of ocean; no breath of air, a complete and absolute stillness. (117)

In contrast with the Arawa account, the entire treatment of the relation of Sky and Earth in the *Whare Wānanga* account is synthetically oriented. This pattern will emerge more fully in the many specific forms considered in the analysis of the next ("reduction") schema; but it is also worth noting that the generally synthetic character of all beings is also *directly* affirmed at one point in the account:

> Na kia marama ano koe: He wahi nga mea katoa no Papa raua ko Rangi-nui; kaore he mea e taea te ki, no Papa anake, a no Rangi-nui anake. . . . (50)

> This, also, must be clearly understood: Everything is a part [*wahi*] of the Heavens and the Earth; there is nothing of which it can be said, it is of the Earth alone or of Heaven alone. . . . (172)

The question can be raised, whether this particular inversion can perhaps be looked at as a possibility built directly into this very widely distributed opening cosmogonic theme of Sky and Earth as primal parents, since Maori does not seem to be the only case in which *both* forms—the original separation, and the original joining—occur (cf. O'Flaherty 1985). The *Whare Wānanga* account also poses a double theory of man's relation to the original sons of Sky and Earth. On the one hand, the main line of the story recounts the construction, by Tāne and his brothers, of the first human female, Tāne's mating with her, and the procreation of the first humans. But Tū-matauenga also figures centrally as an ally of Tāne in the setting up of the world order; and at one point the proverb is quoted:

He uri toa no Tu-mata-uenga. (45)

A warrior, descendant of Tu-mata-uenga. (152)

The implications of the inversion of the first schema, however, are to be found in the other schemata, particularly the second, and so I proceed directly to it.

Second Schema: A Reduction of the Chain
70 → 69 [68?]

While the inversion of the first schema can be stated tersely, the particular way in which the *Whare Wānanga* reduction constitutes an inversion of the Arawa reduction (inversion inherently presupposing features that remain constant as well as features that are reversed) requires a rather lengthy exposition.

Consistent with the idea embodied in many versions of Maori cosmogony that the appropriation of the world by man is necessarily an aggressive appropriation, the original sons of Sky and Earth in the *Whare Wānanga* account are specifically designated a "*hokowhitu*," a term that is used commonly in tribal histories to mean a large group, very frequently a war party. In this account there are seventy sons of Sky and Earth; it projects a more finely partitioned original totality than does the Arawa account.

The following are excerpts from S. Percy Smith's fairly accurate translation of one part of the story; the immediate focus will be upon the character of Whakarū:

Ko Whakaru-au-moko e kai ana tenei tamaiti a Papa i tona u. Ka wehea nei a Rangi raua ko Papa i tona whanau, ko ta raua tamaiti whakamutunga tenei. I muri iho i te wehenga i a Rangi raua ko Papa, ka titiro a Tāne raua ko Paia ki te nui o te aroha o Papa ki a Rangi, kaore e ata tau ana; ko te mahi a nga waewae he hokai tonu, huri atu, huri mai te tinana. Ka whakaaro a Tāne raua ko Paia me etahi o a raua tuakana, kia hurihia te aroaro o to ratou hakui ki raro ki Te Muriwai-hou ki Rarohenga, kia mutu ai te kite o Papa i a Ranginui. Ka ki atu a Paia ki a Tāne, "Kei te kainga au e te aroha ki to taua taina, ki a Whakaru-au-moko. Me tango mai ra to taua taina i te poho o tona hakui ki a taua noho ai." Ka mea atu a Tāne, "Kaore e taea e taua; waiho atu he whakawerawera i te poho o to tatou hakui." Ka rite te whakaae o ratou katoa kia hurihuri te aroaro o Papa-tua-nuku ki raro. Ka karanga a Paia ki nga tuakana, "Kati! Ka pena koutou me hoatu he ahi mo to tatou taina." Ka whakaae a Tamakaka, ka hoatu te ahi-komau ki to ratou taina, i makaia ki roto ki te hou-ama, katahi ka hurihia to ratou hakui me to ratou taina ki Rarohenga. (53)

The youngest child of the Sky-father and Earth-mother was Whakaru-au-moko (70) who, when the Earth was turned over was a child at the

breast; it was their last child. After the separation of Rangi and Papa,
Tāne and Paia saw the great love the Earth-mother bore to the Sky-
father; she could not rest in quiet; she continually turned from side to
side. So Tāne, Paia and some other gods, thought it best to turn the face
of their mother downwards to Te Muriwai-hou, to Raro-henga (Hades),
so she might no longer see Rangi-nui, her Heavenly husband. Paia said
unto Tāne, "I am consumed with love for our younger brother, Whakaru-
au-moko (70), let us take him from the breast of his mother and retain
him with us." Tāne replied, "We cannot do that; leave him to warm and
comfort the breast of our Mother-Earth." It was then agreed by all the
gods that Papa should be turned over with her front or face downwards.
Paia, seeing this agreement in opinion of the other gods, said, "If such
is your determination, let us [at least] give unto our younger brother some
fire." To this Tama-kaka (63) consented, and gave some *ahi-komau* (volcanic-
fire . . .) to their youngest brother; it was placed in the *houama* [other-
wise called the *whau*, or cork-wood, *Entelea arborescens*] and then their
mother and young brother were turned over to Raro-henga (Hades). (147)

The narrator offers a detailed explanation of the *ahi-komau*. The term refers
to a technique of setting up a long-smoldering fire for the hearth, one which
will remain burning while an individual is away for extended periods of time;
this technique thus metaphorically accounts for the origin of the long-
smoldering fires underneath the earth. The account goes on to tell of Whiro,
another denizen of the underworld:

Kia mate a Whiro-te-tipua me ona hoa i Te Paerangi, ka heke i te ara i
Taheke-roa ki Te Muriwai, ki Raro-henga; ka tae ki te kainga i a
Whakaru-au-moko raua ko Hine-nui-te-po, ki nga kainga i kiia ake ra.
Ka tipu te whakaaro i a Whiro ki a Whakaru-au-moko, kia kotahi ta raua
whakaaro ki te takitaki i te mate o to raua hakui me to raua hakoro. Ka
whakaae a Whakaru-au-moko; ka mea a Whiro kia tikina mai ki runga
nei ki te Ao-tu-roa pakanga ai ki a Tāne me ona tuakana. Ka ki atu a
Whakaru-au-moko, "No runga koutou; haere ki runga ta koutou pakanga.
No raro nei au, hei raro nei au whakatipu i taku pakanga." Ka ui atu a
Whiro, "Kei whea hei rakau mau?" Ka ki atu a Whakaru-au-moko,
"Maku e tiki i roto i a Puna-te-waro; kei reira te Ahi-komau."

Koia tenei te putake o te puia, o te rū, o Hine-tuoi, e ngaoko nei i te
whenua me te moana—o reira mai taua pakanga tae mai ki naia nei. Ka
kiia i konei te ingoa tuatoru o te Ahi-komau, ko "Te Ahi-tahito" ko te
"Ahi-tipua" a Whakaru-au-moko e horo nei i te whenua, i te kohatu i te
rakau, i te tangata me nga mea katoa na Tāne ratou ko ona tuakana i hanga.

Ka ea te mate o nga matua i Te Rangi-tau-ngawha, i wehea ra a Rangi
raua ko Papa. (55)

When Whiro-te-tipua (6) was defeated in the series of battles known
as Te Paerangi . . . , he departed [from the presence of the other

gods] and descended by way of Taheke-roa to Muri-wai-hou, to Rarohenga (Hades), and then arrived at the dwelling place of Whakaru-au-moko (70) and his wife Hine-nui-te-po [former name Hine-titama], to the places mentioned above. Now the thought grew in Whiro and Whakaru-au-moko, that they should have but one object in common to avenge the illtreatment of their mother (the Earth) and their father (the Sky). Whakaru-au-moko consented to this proposition, and then Whiro proposed they should operate above in the Ao-tu-roa [the world of light, this ordinary world] and make war on Tāne (68) and his elder brethren. Whakaru-au-moko replied to him, "Ye are all from above; carry on your warfare above. I am from below, and here I will engender my warfare." Whiro asked, "Where will you find weapons?" The other replied, "I will make use of Puna-te-waro [volcanic forces, earthquakes, eruptions, hot-springs]; for in it is contained the *ahi komau* [volcanic fires]."

Hence is the origin of the eruptions, the earthquakes, of Hine-tuoi [emblematical for hot-springs], which agitate both land and sea—even from those times of ancient strife down to the present. And, now was given the third name to the 'Ahi-komau' (first), the 'Ahi-tawhito' (second), the 'Ahi-tipua' (third) of Whakaru-au-moko, which cause the landslips, and the fall of rocks and trees, of man, of all things, which Tāne and his brethren had made.

And thus it is that the illtreatment at Rangi-tau-ngawha [the name for the separation of Heaven and Earth] when Rangi was separated from Papa, is constantly avenged. (149)

The parallels between this story and the earlier-recounted one of Tāwhiri in the Arawa case are of course numerous and obvious, and the relation between them could be represented in the form of a chiasmatic inversion. The protagonist in each case is the youngest son, with the implication of a special *aroha* for the parents that is related to that close dependence. As *"tāwhiri"* may imply "a forceful swirling around" *"whakaru"* means "to cause to shake." While Tāwhiri clings to the father's bosom as he is raised up, Whakaru is nursing at the mother's breast when she is turned over to face downward. In relation to Man and his brothers who remained on the surface of the Earth, the one becomes the threat from the upper periphery of the cosmos, the other from the lower periphery. To the attacks of these two, respectively, the two accounts attribute the present impoverished-but-differentiated topography of the earth. The theme as it occurs in the Arawa account has already been discussed. The section quoted above from the *Whare Wānanga* account notes:

Ka hurihia nei a Papa raua ko tana potiki ki Raro-henga; koia i takoto tutangatanga ai a Papa i a ia e takoto nei. . . . (54)

So Papa and her youngest child were capsized over to Rarohenga; hence, is the broken up appearance of the Earth at the present time. . . . (148)

The theme is mentioned at another point as well, that is, in a comment that Whakarū was one of the gods who

> . . . whakarere ke kia kino te takoto o nga mania o nga pakihi, o nga wai o te whenua katoa. (13)

> . . . changed [the surface of the earth] and caused the present ill condition of the plains and rivers. (106)

Thus both Tāwhiri and Whakarū become threats whose source is beyond the reach and the ability of man to subjugate. These two, Tāwhiri and Whakarū, are left as repositories of particularly strong cosmic powers, the one as the source of storms, the other as source of earthquakes and volcanoes. Even though both are male, as are all the original children, their cosmic powers are related to the genders of their cosmic domains, since, within Polynesia in general, sky and meteorological phenomena tend to have male associations, whereas earth, the underworld, and volcanic fire tend to have female associations. Both are outside of the human space of being and of human control. Each is the only one of his brothers whom Man cannot subdue, and in relation to whom Man achieves a standoff at best. In the Arawa account, after Man had conquered all his other brothers, Tāwhiri

> . . . i waiho tonu hei hoa whawhai mōna, i rite anō ki tāna riri tā tōna teina riri. (Grey v; MS 81:55)

> . . . still remained as a sparring partner for him, because his younger brother's fierceness was equal to his own.

The episode of Whakarū and Whiro concludes with the note that:

> . . . kaore ano i mau te rongo o te pakanga o Whakaru-au-moko raua ko Whiro. (55)

> . . . peace has never been made in the wars of Whakaru-au-moko (70) and Whiro [against mankind]. (149)

The Development of the Sky

The sky in the *Whare Wānanga* account is developed precisely as a *finely* graded continuum, that is, a series of slightly differing regions with various sorts of spiritual inhabitants acting as messengers between the levels, the uppermost, or twelfth, heaven being the home of the high god Io. Whether or not the high god Io is a postcontact phenomenon, the multitiered heaven is a Polynesian conception.

> Ko aua rangi nei, ngahuru-ma-rua e haerea ana e nga Apa-atua o aua rangi. Kotahi te rangi e kore e taea a aua Apa nei, ko Te Toi-o-nga-rangi, tetahi o nga ingoa ko Tikitiki-o-rangi; koia nei te rangi tapu o aua rangi

katoa; i a Io anake taua rangi, me nga Apa-whatukura, me nga Apa-marei-kura o tera rangi. Ko nga Marei-kura me nga Whatu-kura e tomotomo ana i nga rangi nga-huru-ma-tahi nei, tae mai ki a Tua-nuku nei. Ma Io rawa te karere ki tetahi o nga Apa o nga rangi nahuru-ma-rua, katahi ano ka tapokotia a Tikitiki-o-rangi. E kore e tapoko noa. (18)

Those twelve Heavens are where the Apa-atua [the messenger-gods, or perhaps, the company of gods] of each Heaven move too [*sic*] and fro. There is only one Heaven that cannot be attained by these Apa—the Toi-o-nga-rangi, or, otherwise, Tikitiki-o-rangi; this is the most sacred of all the Heavens, and Io alone, with the Apa-Whatu-kura [the company of male guardians, or gods] and Apa-Marei-kura [the company of female guardians, or godesses (*sic*)] of that Heaven dwell there. The Marei-kuras and the Whatu-kuras have the entrée to all the eleven Heavens, and even down to the earth. It is only when Io sends his messengers to one of the Apas of the twelve Heavens that they are allowed into Tikitiki-o-nga-rangi. They never enter it without permission. (116)

This arrangement of the heavens in a way that allows passage between the uppermost heaven and earth is critical to a central part of the story, that is, a journey by Tāne from the earth to the uppermost heaven to gain from the high god Io the knowledge necessary for controlling the world successfully (the nature of the journey will be considered in the following—"hierarchical"—schema).

It was noted in the analysis of the Arawa account that Tāwhiri in general had a double cosmological role: as the space-between, Tāwhiri is in the position to insure both continuity and discreteness, and may be said to mediate between the two principles. But while in the Arawa account the differentiating character of Tāwhiri (summed up in the phrase "the separations of Tāwhiri") is to the fore, in the *Whare Wānanga* account his role is precisely reversed: it is the continuity-engendering capacity that is stressed. The Tāwhiri who, along with his family, is, in the Arawa account, the archenemy of Man and the other beings living on the Earth Mother, waging continuous war on them and driving them apart, emerges, in the *Whare Wānanga* account, as the critical helper who, in the corporate effort by the denizens of earth to gain the knowledge for controlling the cosmos, carries Tāne through the various layers to reach the uppermost heaven. The narrator lists the names of a number of winds, and comments:

Koia nei te whanau a Tawhiri-matea, nana nei a Tāne i kawe ki Te Pu-motomoto o Tawhiri-rangi. (26)

These then were the families of Tawhiri-matea, who carried Tāne to the Pu-motomoto [the entrance] of Tawhiri-rangi [guard-house to the up-permost heaven]. (128)

The generally peaceful relation between the family of Tāwhiri in the Sky and Tāne and other fellows on earth is reaffirmed in other ways as well, for instance, in long episodes in which Tāne takes charge of the arrangement of celestial bodies in the sky, and in other comments on the functions of Tāwhiri which indicate no sense of emnity between the family of Tāwhiri and the inhabitants of the earth. Most notable, however, is the fact that, while Tāwhiri in the Arawa account, as the last born, is the one opposed to the separation and committed to avenging it, the avenging role, in the *Whare Wānanga* account, falls, as noted earlier, to Whakarū; and Tāwhiri, in the *Whare Wānanga* account, is specifically mentioned (121, 22) as one of those agreeing to the separation of the parents. While the theme of the pining of Sky for Earth is present, there is no indication of hostility for the Sky Father toward his children that was characteristic of the Arawa account.

The Relation of Earth and Sky

In the Arawa case, Earth is *matua* (parent) and Sky is a *tangata kē* (person from another tribe), and the relation between the inhabitants of the earth and those of the sky (both Sky himself and his Tāwhiri along with the latter's brood) can be described quite tersely: an all-out, ongoing war. The relation of earth and sky, in other words, is constructed as one of firmly opposed terms. By contrast, in the *Whare Wānanga* case, the fine graduation into levels, the filling of these with messengers capable of moving between different levels, the reversal of the character of Tāwhiri from differentiation to continuity, the fact that the knowledge for controlling the earth is eventually obtained from the sky through a peaceful visit, and the general statement noted earlier that all things are both earth and sky, all point to a view of the relationship of sky and earth that, in direct contrast with the Arawa account, maximizes continuity and interpenetration; and this view is consistent in turn with the picturing of the first situation as one of opposed entities in need of synthesis (the two and the one) vis-à-vis a unitary entity in need of analysis (the one and the two).

It is, furthermore, possible to account for why the element that is deleted from the original earthly continuum must, in the *Whare Wānanga* cosmos, be removed specifically to the underworld rather than to the sky, as in the Arawa case. Namely: because sky and earth are, in the *Whare Wānanga* cosmos, continuous; a removal of the deleted element to the sky could not constitute a real reduction.[1] That is why—structurally speaking—the deleted element in this cosmos must go in the opposite direction. The general development of these two cosmogonies, Arawa and *Whare Wānanga*, bears all this out: the war that man, in the Arawa account, fights unceasingly with the sky, is the same war that man, in the *Whare Wānanga* account, fights unceasingly with the underworld.

In this way, the inversion of the first two schemata (one and two → two and one; reduction by removal to above → reduction by removal to below) are fused as one total cosmological transformation.

The Power of Tāwhiri and Whakarū

It was noted that in the Arawa account, the element that has been removed from the original continuum has a special role with respect to the totality from which it is removed, that is, it becomes "the measure of all things," the central principle in the establishing of hierarchy among the remaining members of the set. The reflection of this Arawa upperworld scheme in the *Whare Wānanga* underworld scheme embraces a hierarchy-creating capacity as well. The underworld in general is a repository of special powers; there is a series of legends recounting how the demigod Māui and also other human ancestors attempt to capture these powers mainly by theft and deception. Some of these legends, such as the accounts of the gaining of controlled fire, cloaks, and the art of weaving, have to do with the origins of society and culture, and thus in a general way have to do with the hierarchical relation of man to the rest of nature. The hierarchy-creating power that is most closely associated specifically with Whakarū, however, has to do with the origins of hierarchy in the human social world, for Whakarū is the origin of the chiefly art of tattooing (his full name is Whakarū-au-moko, "*moko*" being the term for tattoo). The hierarchy-creating potential of Tāwhiri in the Arawa account is most directly focused upon the superordinacy of man over the rest of nature, but inasmuch as chiefs tend to be associated with the sky and celestial phenomena, it might be said to pose a general analogy to the formulation of hierarchy in the human social order.

While the hierarchy-creating potential of Whakarū emerges more directly in the human social order, nevertheless the means by which he contributes to the creation of human social distinction is analogous to his distinction-creating role in nature: through earthquakes and volcanoes he brings about the large-scale geographical topography; as the source of tattoos he brings about the small-scale physiognomical topographies that constitute a central mark of human social differentiation (see Hiroa 1958:298 on the ridge style of tatooing characteristic of the Maori).

I offer some further suggestions on the special hierarchy-creating potential accorded in the Arawa account to Tāwhiri and in the *Whare Wānanga* account to Whakarū, based on extrapolations from a comment that Lévi-Strauss makes about the nature of a certain kind of power in relation to continua. The details of the case concern an association that he finds in South America between rainbows and certain fish poisons, and need not concern us in their particulars; the general comment, once again, is:

> It is as if South American thought, being resolutely pessimistic in inspira-
> tion and diatonic in orientation, invested chromaticism with a primordial
> maleficence of such a kind that long intervals, which are necessary in
> culture for it to exist and in nature for it to be "thinkable" to men, can
> only be the result of the self-destruction of a primeval continuity, whose
> power is still to be felt at those rare points where it has survived its own
> self-destructiveness: either to the advantage of men, in the form of poisons
> they have learned to handle; or to their disadvantage, in the form of the
> rainbow over which they have no control. (1970:280)

From this comment, one can extrapolate to a view that accounts for the
power that is accorded to such elements, and which moreover contributes to
an understanding of why many societies are disposed to picture an initial
general condition of being that might be described as one great interstice, whose
loss is regarded with mixed emotions. Such phenomena may be powerful,
rather, by virtue of the particular way in which they are able to pose or recall
the totality. By virtue of the overthrowing of some particular opposition, they
provoke the mind to a chain of thought that can end only in the oneness of being as reality, and classification as artifice. If such objects sometimes become
agents of particular sorceries, perhaps this is by virtue of their power to focus
and reflect back the generalized sorcery residing in any act of categorizing.
While through most of her treatment in *Purity and Danger*, Mary Douglas tends
simply to present the power lying in margins as a sort of self-evident truth,
it is interesting to note that her formulation, too, in the end, points to a
cosmological source, so that it is not margins per se that are powerful, but the
totality which is glimpsed in a particular way, in the margins. After citing Eliade
regarding the notion of water as a symbol of dissolution of form (e.g., in the
theme of a flood or primeval ocean), Douglas goes on to say: "The danger
which is risked by boundary transgression is power. Those vulnerable margins
and those attacking forces which threaten to destroy good order represent the
powers inhering in the cosmos" (1970:190–91).

To account for the special powers of elements like Tāwhiri (in the Arawa
account) and Whakarū (in the *Whare Wānanga* account), one might simply
add to Lévi-Strauss's comment, that, besides surviving in various elements
which escape the original breakup to inhabit various peripheral regions of the
cosmos (e.g., rainbows and various poisons), the power of the original continuum also survives in the various "linch-pins" like Whakarū and Tāwhiri
(and Hine-nui-te-Pō [see below]), so that, as implicit in the discussion of the
Arawa material earlier, the deletion in certain cases might provide the means
not only of breaking up the continuum, but also, simultaneously, of constituting
a source of transcendence with respect to the discrete entities created in the

breakup. In good Durkheimian fashion, the transcendence of the transcendent turns out to be none other than just this special capacity to stand for the totality *as such.*

Third Schema: Hierarchical

In the analysis that follows, the possibility of certain syncretisms will be considered. As noted earlier, there is a kind of syncretism that consists, not so much in taking in new elements, as in calling to the fore those elements in one's own traditional stock that find the most confirmation in the new external doctrine. This is why it is possible to say at the same time that, on one hand, there is a probable Christian influence, and, on the other hand, it is next to impossible to isolate elements that are definitively and solely Christian in origin. Syncretisms will be suggested here; but their precise nature—that is, whether they are direct incorporations or, rather, some more general form of influence—will necessarily be left open.

While the construction of hierarchy in the Arawa account is multifaceted and complex, the schema singled out for critical attention was that of man's achieving superordinacy over the rest of nature; this ascendancy was affirmed with the presentation of two transitions directly adjacent to one another—when man conquered and ate the others, then man's own name separated into diverse names, and the *karakia* by which man controls the other beings also separated—as if they are two parts of a single transition. While no such terse formula characterizes the ascent of man as recounted in the *Whare Wānanga* account, some of these same elements are nevertheless still present. It has also been noted that the Arawa account, in which Tū is man's ancestor, and the Tūhoe account, in which Tāne is man's ancestor, present two theories, consistent with the respective characters of the two primordial beings, of man's superordinacy over the rest of nature; in the one case, it is by virtue of conquest, in the other by virtue of procreation (so that man is the great ancestor of nature).

The *Whare Wānanga* account presents a third main model of man's ascendancy over nature, one that is similar to the idea that informs the Garden of Eden story from Genesis, namely, that man's ascendancy over nature derives from his divine appointment as caretaker of the garden. Among the works of Sky is that of clothing Earth:

> Na, ka moea e Rangi-nui a Papa-tuanuku i konei, hei wahine māna. Ka
> hikaia e Rangi-nui ko nga otaota hei taupaki mo te aroaro o Papa, mo
> nga keke, mo te upoko, mo te tinana; i muri o tenei ko nga rakau-riki hei
> tupuni mo raua ko te wahine. I muri o tenei ko te rakau tu i te wao nui,
> ka tangi te ahuru i konei ki a Papa, katahi ka mahana, ka kau-awhiawhi

mai te mahana. Katahi ka makaia ko te aitanga-pepeke, ko te aitanga-
pekepeke-tua, hei whakatau mo roto i te otaota, i te huru-puia i te wao-
tu-rangi. (19)

And so Rangi-nui dwelt with Papa-tua-nuku as his wife; and then he
set [hikaia-whakato, to set, plant] plants to cover the nakedness of Papa;
for her armpits, her head, and the body; and after that the smaller trees
to clothe them both, for the body of the earth was naked. Subsequently
he placed the upstanding trees of the forest, and now Papa felt a great
warmth, which was all-embracing. After this were placed the insects of
all kinds, the aitanga-pekepeketua [the ancestors of the tuatara, great
lizard], appropriate to the recesses of the smaller vegitation [sic], the
clumps of smaller trees, and the wao-tu-rangi, the great forests [whose
heads reach the skies]. (117)

Consistent with the fact that in this account it is Tāne rather than Tū who
attains ascendancy over nature and becomes ancestor of man, the conquest and
eating of the other primordial beings are absent; but it should be noted that
in this account the two processes which Te Rangikaheke's two accounts link
respectively to the conquest and eating—the differentiating of names and the
differentiating of the various karakia—are both linked to Tāne's acquiring
of special forms of knowledge. At the summit of the heavens, Tāne receives
seven new names (129); thus we again have a pattern of the superordinate being's names diversifying. The acquiring of spells to control nature is the goal
of the journey, and is tantamount to man's ascendancy over nature. As in the
Arawa account, this ascendance is directly associated with the acquiring of
the karakia, one of the three baskets of knowledge being

te kete uruuru-rangi, o nga karakia katoa a te tangata. (28)

the kete-uruuru-rangi (or tipua), of all prayers, incantations, ritual, used
by mankind. (130)

Hine-ūtama (Hine-nui-te-Pō) and Whiro

The Arawa account deals centrally with two upperworld beings, Sky and
his son Wind, both of whom are developed as the archenemies of Man and
the other denizens of the earth. The Whare Wānanga account, in addition to
Whakarū, deals centrally with two other inhabitants of the underworld, Hine-
ūtama, who, upon moving from earth to the underworld, becomes Hine-nui-
te-Pō (Great Woman of the Night), where her cosmological role is closely
associated with the dead. According to some interpretations she is the source
of death, and to others merely the claimer of the souls of the dead. Hine-ūtama
is the daughter of Tāne and Hine-hau-One (Woman Made of Sand), the first

human female, who was constructed by Tāne for the procreation of humans.
Tāne then takes Hine-tītama as wife, Hine-tītama not knowing that Tāne is her
father. Hine-tītama's journey to the underworld is precipitated by shame, upon
the discovery of her incestuous relationship. There is an exchange between
Hine-tītama and the guardian at the door to the underworld, Te Kū-watawata:

> . . . "Tukua atu au ki te angi!" Ka ki atu a Te Ku-watawata, "Hoki atu!
> Kei muri i a koe te Ao-marama me te toiora." Ka mea atu a Hine,
> "Tukua atu au ki te angi o Te Muri-wai-hou, hei kapu mai i te toiora o
> aku tamariki i te Ao-tu-roa nei."
>
> Koia tenei te take i ora ai te wairua i hoki mai ai ki te ao nei haere ai.
> Ka whakaae a Te Ku-watawata ki te tuku i a Hine-titama kia haere ki
> Rarohenga. Katahi a Hine ka tahuri ki muri i a ia, ka kite i a Tāne, e
> tangi haere mai ana. Ka karanga atu a Hine, "Tāne e! E hoki ki ta taua
> whanau, ka motuhia e au te aho o te ao ki a koe, ko te aho o te Pō ki
> au." (38)

> . . . "Let me pass on to the descent" [into Hades]. Te Ku-watawata
> answered, "Thou art leaving behind thee the world of light and life!"
> Hine-titama then said, "Let me proceed to the descent to Muri-wai-hou
> in order that I may ever catch the living spirits of my children now in the
> 'everlasting light' [a name for this world]."
>
> Now, hence arises the fact that the spirits return to this world. . . . So
> Te Ku-watawata allowed Hine-titama to pass on to Hades, and as she did
> so she turned round and beheld her husband, Tāne, approaching, shedding
> tears as he came along. Hine called out to him, "Tāne e! Return to our
> family, for I have cut off the *aho o te ao* [the cord of the world] to you
> [and your descendants], whilst the cord of Hades remains with me
> [forever]." (145)

There is a further comment on the significance of the cord:

> Me whakaatu ake e au i konei: Te kupu a Hine i ki atu ra ki a Tane,
> "ko te aho o te ao ki a koe, ko te aho o te po ki a ia," tona tikanga, ko te
> ora o nga mea katoa i te ao ki a Tāne, ko te mate o nga mea katoa i te ao
> me riro i a ia ki te po. (39)

> Let me explain here: The words used by Hine to Tāne, i.e., "the cord
> of the world remains with you, the cord of Hades with me"; its meaning
> is, the life of everything in the world is with Tāne, but the death of all
> things in the world remain with her. (146)

Cords and their cutting, particularly the umbilicus, form one of the most central
Polynesian symbols of continuity and separation; the cutting of the cord here

affirms the general suggestion made above that, by contrast to the continuity of earth and sky, the relation of underworld and earth is one of discontinuity.

Thus, analogously to the removal to the underworld of one member (Whakarū) of the original series of beings (the children of Sky and Earth) who make up the natural world, so here, with the event of Hine-tītama's departure, there is the removal of one of the initial series of humans, the children of Tāne and Hine-hau-One. The figure who is removed in order to insure against conflation, departs, according to the story, because of incest—which is a kind of improper sociological conflation. Finally, the removed becomes the remover; Hine-tītama's chief cosmological role becomes that of continuously reducing the human stock through death. Hine-nui-te-Pō and Whakarū, who in this account are said to become husband and wife, generate the underworld family of various types of volcanic phenomena.

There are, to be sure, legends of visitations to the underworld, but these are fundamentally treacherous and defined by a sense of general hostility between the two realms. A common theme in accounts of the acquiring by upperworld beings of the arts of the underworld is the incident, analogous to Hine-tītama's cutting of the cord and sending Tāne back, of the subsequent closing off of the underworld to any further passage (e.g., see Smith 1913:182–93; Best 1982:226ff.; Biggs, Lane, and Cullen 1980:54ff.)

The account discusses one other of the first seventy sons to move to the underworld, a being called Whiro or "Whiro-te-tipua" (the term *"tipua"* designating some sort of malevolent or demon-like spirit). His story forms one instance of the very widely spread mythological theme of battles between the gods, ending in the expulsion of some to the underworld.

> Engari enei whawhai he whawhai atua na ratou whakaatua ki a ratou ano.
>   Ko te mutunga o tenei pakanga, ko Whiro-te-tipua i hinga; ko te take tena i heke ai ia ki Raro-henga—koia i kiia ai ko Taheke-roa taua matenga; ko te tino ingoa nui o taua matenga ko te Paerangi. Ka oti atu a Whiro ki Te Muri-wai-hou, ki Raro-henga; ara, ki Te Reinga e kiia ana. (31)

> But these battles were fought as gods between gods.
>   The end of it was that Whiro-te-tipua was defeated, and that was the reason he descended to Raro-henga [Hades]—hence is that fatal descent of his named Taheke-roa [the eternal fall]. The true [or general] name of this [series of] battles is Te Pae-rangi. Whiro disappeared for ever into Te Muri-wai-hou, to Raro-henga; that is, to the place called Te Reinga. (134)

But that is *not* the end of it; to return to a part of the large passage cited earlier,

> Ka tipu te whakaaro i a Whiro ki a Whakaru-au-moko, kia kotahi ta raua
> whakaaro ki te takitaki i te mate o to raua hakui me to raua hakoro. Ka
> whakaae a Whakaru-au-moko; ka mea a Whiro kia tikina mai ki runga
> nei ki te Ao-tu-roa pakanga ai ki a Tāne me ona tuakana. Ka ki atu a
> Whakaru-au-moko, "No runga koutou; haere ki runga ta koutou pakanga.
> No raro nei au, hei raro nei au whakatipu i taku pakanga." (55)

> Now the thought grew in Whiro and Whakaru-au-moko, that they should
> have but one object in common to avenge the illtreatment of their mother
> (the Earth) and their father (the Sky). Whakaru-au-moko consented to
> this proposition, and then Whiro proposed they should operate above in
> the Ao-tu-roa [the world of light, this ordinary world] and make war on
> Tāne (68) and his elder brethren. Whakaru-au-moko replied to him, "Ye
> are all from above; carry on your warfare above. I am from below, and
> here I will engender my warfare." (149)

It is evident from the language that the situation here takes the form of the
highly recurrent paradigm (discussed earlier) in which two beings part to live
in different realms, thus becoming different species, as a result precisely of
their inability—despite their agreement on general goal—to achieve accord
regarding *modus operandi*. The implication of this general paradigm at this
point is one more confirmation of the general thesis that the relation of underworld and upperworld seems to be one of maximized discontinuity, concretized
especially in the stories of the two original gods/sons who—together with Hine-
Tītama—play out a scenario of the creation of the underworld through the
reduction of the upperworld.

Fourth Schema: Metaphysical

The concern of the metaphysical schema, in the analysis of the Arawa
material, lay in certain formulations which appeared to have as their object
being as such; the main focus was upon a recurrent notion of separation
through which all the particular events of diversification were integrated
into a single paradigm of a progressive division of being. The hierarchical
schema and the metaphysical schema were closely interrelated; among other
things, the metaphysical schema, in posing a general model of the once unity
of all being, served as one possible source of any unification of a more restricted scope. Indeed the formulation of the hierarchical relation of man to
the rest of nature was seen to consist in a joining of the separation model as
it applied to man (Tū's names and *karakia*) with a reciprocal pattern of conjunction of the diverse subordinate elements into one (among other things,
Tū's eating of them).

As the hierarchical and metaphysical schemata were closely interrelated in the Arawa case, so they are also in the *Whare Wānanga* account. The source of the unity of all being in this account lies not, or not primarily, in an ongoing separation, but in an all-powerful high-god, Io, who is the source of all life and being, whose embracing character is expressed in, among other things, a plurality of names, such as Io-nui (Io-great), Io-roa (Io-long), Io-matua (Io-parent), distinguished by epithets not unlike those that figure in cosmic genealogies.

> Enei ingoa katoa, he take katoa. Ko Io he ingoa poto tera nona; ko
> Io-nui, koia te atua nui o nga atua katoa; ko Io-matua, koia te matua o
> nga mea katoa, te ora o nga mea katoa, Ko Io-te-wānanga, koia te wānanga
> o nga mea katoa. . . . (16)

> Each of these names has a cause, a reason. Io is his name in short.
> Io-nui, he is the god of all other gods; Io-matua, he is the parent of all
> things, the life and being of all things; Io-te-wānanga, he is the *wānanga*
> of all things. . . . (111)

Tāne's receiving of new names upon the ascent to heaven is a taking on of a metaphysical character analogous to that of the high-god; it was already noted that the diversification of names in the process of man's ascendancy over nature was central in the Arawa formulation. One more point of comparison can be made. In the Arawa account, the primal separation—of sky and earth—was found to be merely the opening instance of a schema based upon separation as its unifying principle. In the *Whare Wānanga* account there is an analogous primordial separation, and then a few other instances (e.g., in the battle, the winners from the defeated). But, up to the point of Tāne's visiting the uppermost heaven, there is nothing that quite matches the consistent pattern posed in the Arawa account. However, with Tāne's taking on of the metaphysical character of the encompassing high-god, "separation" ("*wehe*" is here translated as "separated" and as "distributed") occurs:

> Na, i konei ka tahuri a Tane-matua ratou ko nga tuakana me te taina
> ki te wehewehe i nga Pou-tiri-ao, o ia mahi, o ia mahi, ki tana wahi tu ai
> o taua whanau, tokorua, tokotoru ki te kauwhanga o Papa-tuankuku, o
> Rangi hoki, tae noa ki te moana—pera katoa te ahua o te whakahaere; ka
> wehewehea nga taonga o nga kete e toru o te wānanga. (30)

> Now, at this period the attention of Tāne-matua (68) and his elder
> and younger brethren was turned to the separation of the Pou-tiri-ao . . .
> to their different spheres of action in their separate places, by twos and
> threes, to each plane of the Earth, the Heavens, and even the Ocean.
> Thus was the work directed; and the valuable contents of the three
> "baskets" were distributed. . . . (133)

In the Arawa case the interrelation of unity and plurality through separation originates in the progressive separation of being itself; in the *Whare
Wānanga* account, it is present, rather, in the division of the divine knowledge
that overlays all things and holds them in unison.

The sons of Sky and Earth appear in Maori ethnography more generally
both as the great ancestors of the various realms of the cosmos and as the focal
gods or spiritual principles of those realms, who can be addressed through
various types of incantations. While neither aspect is totally absent from either
account, the former dominates the Arawa account and the latter—in line with,
but not necessarily only a result of, the Judaeo-Christian metaphysics that
seems to have influenced it—dominates in the *Whare Wānanga* account. Tāne
and his brothers assign the various Pou-tiri-ao, or guardians, to the various
realms of the cosmos.

While it is not totally clear what the nature of these guardian-beings is, it
is interesting to note the occurrence of the term "*pou*," or "post," in their title,
the notion of a post, or the action of setting up a post, being recurrent both
in cosmogonic accounts (posts are set up to insure that Sky and Earth are held
apart) and in the accounts of the voyages (posts are set up to mark land claims),
so that the designating of these spiritual beings as "posts" resonates with a
wider idiom related to the fixing of cosmologico-political borders. "*Tiri*" can
mean "apportion," so the sense may be of posts that apportion the *ao*, or world
of social life, which is typically contrasted with the *pō*. After the knowledge
and these Pou-tiri-ao are separated, the sense seems to be that the children of
Sky and Earth, or the children's children, are then themselves separated, being
parceled out to the various regions of earth and sky:

> . . . kaore he mea kotahi o te whanau a Rangi raua ko Papa i kore he
> putanga ki te Ao-turoa. Kua korerotia te wehenga i taua whanau ki nga
> Pou-tiri-ao o nga Rangi-tuhaha ngahuru-ma-tahi me o ratou Kauwhanga
> tae mai ki a Papa-tuanuku-matua-te-kore. (56)

> . . . there was not one of the family of Rangi and Papa that had not off-
> spring in the "everlasting world." The division of that family into the
> Pou-tiri-ao [guardian-spirits] of the conjoint Heavens, eleven in number,
> with their special spheres of action, even down to Papa-tua-nuku-matua-
> te-kore [the Parentless Earth-mother] has been explained. (162)

So the origin of the various regions of the cosmos still contains—though
in some more roundabout way—the model of the separation of the set of original
sons, even though the central focus is the origin of a system of spiritual
guardianship of the realms of the cosmos, as contrasted with the origin of the
types of physical beings in themselves that compose the various regions.

The World as Error and Approximation

Here I return to the Tūhoe account of Tāne that was mentioned earlier, from which a section of Best's summary will here be quoted:

> Tane sought long for woman. He found the female element in divers forms, but these forms were not human. He found one Apunga and begat shrubs and small birds. He found Mumuhanga and begat the *totara* (a forest tree). He found Tu-kapua and begat the *tawai*, *kahikawaka*, and other trees. He found Hine-wao-riki and begat the *kahika* and *matai* trees. He found Mango-nui and begat the *tawa* and *hinau* trees. He found Ruru-tangi-akau and begat the *ake* and *kahikatoa* trees. He found Rere-noa, who bore the *rata* as well as all climbing, parasitic and epiphytic plants. He found Te Pu-whakahara, who produced the *maire* and *puriri* trees. He found Punga and begat the *kotukutuku* and *patate* trees, also all insects. He found Tutoro-whenua, who bore Haumia (the starchy rhizomes of a fern, *Pteris aquilina* var. *esculenta*). (1977:765; cf. Best 1976:119ff.)

While this pattern will not be considered in great detail in this study, nevertheless an important general point is to be made with respect to the "metaphysical" concern of this study. It was noted that this account provides a means of man's claim to superordinacy over the rest of nature, or (varying with different accounts) at least over a large and centrally important sector, here, forest life, by making the great ancestor, who is identified particularly with man and who specifically has the intention of generating man, also the ancestor of the natural world. There is no reason to assume other than that this aspect of the account is essentially indigenous in inspiration.

Within the present context of concern with metaphysical schemata, another aspect of the Tūhoe formulation will be brought into focus, the fact that the generation of these other forms of nature are, as Mauss has at one point observed of this account, seemingly "errors," that is, forms generated as offshoots in the process of attempting some other goal. They are experiments along the road to humanity. A similar theme is to be found in many of the world's Creation accounts, including that of Genesis:

> And the Lord God said, It is not good that the man should be alone; I will make him an help meet for him.
> And out of the ground the Lord God formed every beast of the field, and every fowl of the air; and brought them unto Adam to see what he would call them: and whatsoever Adam called every living creature, that was the name thereof.
> And Adam gave names to all cattle, and to the fowl of the air, and to every beast of the field; but for Adam there was not found an help meet for him. (Genesis 2:18–20)

It is this incident that leads to the biblical schema of the "two and the one"; that is, because of the lack of success in the attempts at a separate creation of a helpmate, the creator god ends up making the helpmate for Adam out of Adam—the rib episode. This event, incidentally, also brings to focus the difference in general orientation of the two sources that appear to have been placed adjacently to form the Genesis account: the one, distant, transcendent, majesterial, liturgically precise and systematic; the other positing a much more intimate and naive deity, who, like Tāne, and also like many trickster or trickster-like figures, does not completely understand his own powers and limitations, and creates as much through accident and experiment as through omniscience and design.

On the other hand, Mauss's comment on this theme was made specifically in the context of a comparison of this and other Maori themes (including the separation of sky and earth) that are also found in the classical mythologies, such as Egyptian mythology and Hesiod. Regarding Maori, Mauss says, "All the great themes of the great ancient cosmogonies have found their logical place; thus the myth of the errors of the gods who engender—as in Hesiod—animals instead of men" (1968:189, my translation).

The theme of unintentional or erroneous creation is geographically very widespread, so that it is not at all clear that this element is syncretic. Moreover the sexual/procreative naivete displayed by Tāne in his dealings with the various female elements found in his roamings of the Earth Mother is mirrored by a similar naivete on a small scale, that is, with respect to the topography of the first human female in his attempts to generate humanity. He attempts to mate with the various bodily orifices, and while eventually successful in procreating humanity, produces, by virtue of the prior experiments, the exuvia belonging to the various orifices. The account provides an explanation of these problematic, interstitial bodily substances—namely, that, on the level of the human bodily organism, they too are failed attempts at humanity.

With respect to the present metaphysical concerns, the following point can be made about this theme as it occurs in Maori and perhaps more broadly: it might be seen as betokening a metaphysic that, although quite different from that which appears in the Arawa case (and in a reduced way in the *Whare Wānanga* case), nevertheless achieves the same structural condition, that is, the interrelation of unity and plurality. The unity of the varied is found, in these Tūhoe cases, in a theory that a series of different phenomena are yet all approximations of a given particular idea—as one possible strategy of positing the relation between the one and the many. They are accorded a form of unity by some idea or intention lying behind them; but it is a form of unity that also imposes a hierarchy, in the sense that one among the beings is a fulfillment of that of which the others are mere approximations. This scheme, in the Maori case, introduces a triple hierarchical impetus: first, in the sense just noted, that man is the maximal fulfilling of some idea; secondly, in the sense that, since Tāne from the first appears to be man in some sense (so that it is Man seeking to generate man), Man is thus the great ancestor of nature, and by virtue of that holds a special position with respect to nature; and thirdly, following the general folkloric pattern that it is necessarily the final attempt that works, the man that is generated by Man is in the genealogical position of younger brother to, or usuper of, nature—a theme that brings us back to the Arawa account of the ascendancy of man as Tū. The most fundamental significance of the perspective of the world as error and approximation would seem to lie, as in the theme of separation, not in affording an account of the unity of the world, or an account of the variety of the world, but rather in the positing of an interrelation between the two conditions.

A SOUTH ISLAND TRANSFORMATION

This section will deal with a set of texts which stem from the South Island, and which, though having much in common with the Arawa and *Whare Wānanga* variants, contain distinctive elements as well. The analysis here will focus most centrally upon an account for which the manuscript source is known; the other accounts are all more problematic as to origin.

The manuscript in question is attributed to Matiaha, a chief of the Moeraki area of the South Island. Harlow (van Ballekom and Harlow 1987) identifies Matiaha as Matiaha Tiramōrehu, and provides some biographical details. The manuscript is now located in the manuscript collection of the National Library of Australia (MS 4017). It is dated 1849, the same year in which Te Rangikaheke is thought to have written the Arawa account considered earlier. Large sections of this manuscript appear in transcription and translation in John White's *The Ancient History of the Maori*, though broken up to conform to the various topical chapter divisions that White utilizes (someone, presumably Elsdon Best, has written on the manuscript some notes that include cross-references to White).

Relative to the Arawa and *Whare Wānanga* versions, the most distinguishing feature of Matiaha's account is the theme of a prior union of Papa-tūanuku (Earth) and Tangaroa (a primordial being connected especially with the sea, who, in the Arawa and *Whare Wānanga* accounts is, rather, one of the original sons of Rangi and Papa). While Tangaroa is away, Papa-tūanuku lives with Rangi, and from this union there are several children. Upon Tangaroa'a return, Rangi and Tangaroa fight; Rangi is speared in both buttocks by Tangaroa, who, however, then departs and leaves Papa-tūanuku as wife for Rangi.

There is one other important difference in the Matiaha account. Unlike the Arawa and *Whare Wānanga* accounts, in which Rangi and Papa form the generative pair from which derive all the beings of the cosmos, in Matiaha's account Papa-tūanuku is only one of several wives of Rangi, and from each of the different unions derive different sets of descendants.

The analysis here will be concerned with the first part of the Matiaha manuscript, from the opening account of the different descendants of Rangi and his various wives and the fight between Tangaroa and Rangi over Papa-tūanuku as wife, through the account of the separation of Rangi and Papa as led by Tāne. In the manuscript account these elements are arranged as a continuous story; this section of the manuscript however has been split into two accounts by John White, as indicated in the table. In the discussion that follows, texts will be designated as follows: "MM" refers to the Matiaha manuscript, which is written in Maori; "WM" refers to White's Maori transcription in *Ancient History of the Maori* (1887); and "WE" refers to White's English translation, also in *Ancient History*. Because of the length of the relevant passage, I have included only the English translation; the Maori text can, however, be found in two transcriptions—that of White and that of van Ballekom and Harlow (1987).[2]

The Matiaha Account as Transcribed and Translated by White

Genealogies of Rangi, flowing directly into story of Tangaroa and Rangi's duel, flowing directly into ⟶	Story of separation of Sky and Earth
MATIAHA MS (MM)[a]	
P. 1 (top) through p. 4, 2nd line from bottom, ". . . Taneitewaiora"	P. 4, 2nd line from bottom, beginning "Na konei i piri tonu," through p. 8, line 1, ". . . Ko Parawhenuamea"
WHITE TRANSCRIPTION (WM)[b]	
P. 17, beginning "Keia te Po te timatanga . . . ," through p. 20, end of 1st paragraph, ". . . Tane-i-te-wai-ora"	P. 39, "Na konei i piri tonu . . . " through p. 42, end of 2nd paragraph, ". . . Ko Para-whenua-mea . . ."
WHITE TRANSLATION (WE)[b]	
P. 18, beginning "The atua (god) began his chant of creation . . . ," through p. 23, ". . . or water of life)."	P. 46, "Raki, though speared by Takaroa, . . ." through p. 49, end of 2nd paragraph, ". . . covering for Raki"

[a] Pagination has been added for reference; MS is unpaginated.

[b] The part that White has placed before the beginning of the genealogy is found in the MS at a much later point—p. 20.

In the excerpt from White's translation which follows, I have reconnected the narrative at the point where White had broken it apart.

Now, Raki had no right to Papa-tu-a-nuku—she was the wife of Taka(Tanga)-roa. She went to live with Raki when Taka-roa had gone away with the placenta of his child. On his return, he found she had been living with Raki for some time, and had given birth to Rehua, and Tane, and the other children we have mentioned. Raki and Taka-roa proceeded to the sea-beach, where they fought with spears. Raki was pierced by Taka-roa with a *huata* (a barbed spear) through both thighs, but he was not killed. The offspring he had by Papa-tu-a-nuku after this were a weak or sickly family. The names of these were Whanau-tu-oi (born lean), Whanau-takoto (born lying down), Tane-kupapa-eo (Tane who lies flat on the flat rocks), Tane-tuturi (Tane who kneels), Tane-pepeke (Tane who draws his legs up), Te-oi (the shaker, or trembler), Upoko-nui (big head), Upoko-roa (long head), Upoko-whaka-ahu (the large head), Tane-i-te-wai-ora (Tane at the living water, or water of life).

Raki, though speared by Takaroa, still adhered to the top of Papa; and Raki said to Tane and his younger brothers, "Come and kill me, that men may live."

Tane said, "O old man! how shall we kill you?"

Raki said, "O young man! lift me up above, that I may stand separate; that your mother may lie apart from me, that light may grow on you all."

Then Tane said to Raki, "O old man! Rehua shall carry you."

Raki answered Tane and his younger brothers, "O young men! do not let me be carried by your elder brothers only, lest my eyes become dim. Rather all of you carry me above, that I may be elevated, that light may dawn on you."

Tane said to him, "Yes, O old man! Your plan is right—that light may grow into day."

Raki said to Tane, "It is right, O Tane! that I be taken and killed (separated from my wife), that I may become a teacher to you and your younger brothers, and show you how to kill. If I die, then will light and day be in the world."

Tane was pleased with the reasons why his father wished them to kill him; and hence Tane said to another branch of the offspring of Raki—to Te Kore-tua-tahi (the first broken), and even to the Kore-tua-a-ngahuru (the tenth broken), and to Te Kore-au-iho (the broken tending downwards) and to Te Kore-au-ake (broken tending upwards), and to the Makore-kore-te-po (broken of night), and to the Makore-te-ao (broken of the light), and Kore-a-te-ao-tu-roa (broken of the longstanding world), and to the Makore-a-te-ao-marama (broken of the world of light)—"Tread on Papa, tread her down; and prop up Rangi, lift him up above—to Tu-moremore (the bald, or open space), to Tu-haha (stand breathing)—that the eyes of Raki, who is standing here, may be satisfied. Behold Te-Huinga (the assembly), Pu-tahi (the first, or origin), Taketake (the root, or foundation), and Rehua." Now, this was the origin of the heaven. It was made by Tane and admired by him, and he uttered the words of his prayer to aid Rehua to carry their father above. It was at this time that Tane hid some of Te-Kore (the broken or imperfect beings) in the Maunga-nui-o-te-whenua (great mountain of the earth), in which they remained for ever.

Tane now took Raki on to his back; but he could put Raki no higher.

Raki said to Tane, "You two, you and your younger brother (Paia) carry me."

Then Paia prayed his prayer, and said,—

> Carry Raki on the back,
> Carry Papa.
> Strengthen, O big back of Paia,
> Sprained with the leap at Hua-rau
> (the many hundreds).

Now, Raki was raised with the aid of this prayer, and spoke words of *poroporoaki* (farewell) to Papa, and said, "O Papa! O! You remain here. This will be the (token) of my love to you: in the eighth month I will weep for you." Hence the origin of the dew, this being the tears of Raki weeping for Papa. Raki again said to Papa, "O old woman! live where you are. In winter I will sigh for you." This is the origin of ice. Then Papa spoke words of farewell to Raki, and said, "O old man! go, O Raki! and in summer I also will lament for you." Hence the origin of mist, or the love of Papa for Raki.

When the two had ended their words of farewell, Paia uplifted Raki, and Tane placed his *toko* (pole), called Toko-maunga (prop of the mountain), between Papa and Raki. Paia did likewise with his *toko*. The name of the *toko* of Paia was Rua-tipua (tupua) (pit of the god); and whilst in the act of propping up Raki, Paia repeated this prayer:—

> The prop of whom?
> The prop of Rua-tipua (god's pit).
> The prop of whom?
> The prop of Rua-tahito (tawhito)
> (ancient pit),
> To prop the gentle slope,
> To ward off the
> Blast of the south.
> The prop ascended up—
> The prop of this heaven.

Again Paia prayed, and said,—

> Prop the big cloud,
> The long cloud,

> The thick cloud,
> The door of Raki(Rangi)-riri
> > (fountain of fish),
> The gathering of Raki(Rangi)-ora
> > (heaven of life).
> O Rongo! come forth.

Then Raki floated upwards, and a shout of approval was uttered by those above, who said,—

> O Tu of the long face,
> Lift up the mountain.

Such were the words shouted by the innumerable men (beings) from above in approval of the acts of Tane and Paia; but that burst of applause was mostly in recognition of Tane's having disconnected the heaven, and propped up its sides, and made them stable. He had stuffed up the cracks and chinks, so that when Raki was complete and furnished, light arose and day began.

Tane saw that Raki had no covering by which he could appear seemly. He went to fetch, and obtained, the *rahuikura* of Ao-kehu (sacred red), and fastened it on Raki; but it did not suit him, as at night it was not seen—only in the light of day was it seen; so that he swept it off, and Raki again became naked. Then he went to the Kores he had hidden in Maunga-nui-o-te-whenua (great mountain of the land), and drew forth Riaki (lift up), and Hapai (carry), and Te Tihi (the pinnacle), and Te Amo (carry in a litter), and Katari (Nga-teri) (vibrate), and Te Mania (the slide), and Paheke (the slippery), and Tu-horo (stood on the slip), and Ta-wharu-wharu (sag down), and Tapokopoko (sink in), and Awa (river), and Tipu-nui-a-uta (great growth on shore), and Para-whenua-mea (scum of the flood). . . .

First Schema: the One and the Two

As noted earlier, one of the most distinctive elements in the Matiaha formulation is the additional element of the previous union of Papa-tūanuku with Tangaroa, and the subsequent contest over the woman by Tangaroa (Sea) and Rangi (Sky). Both the Te Rangikaheke and the Matiaha formulations place a central emphasis upon the origin of both of two oppositions, that of land to sea and that of land to sky. In both cases, the origins of the two oppositions are causally linked in the sense that the origin of the one contains the precipitating cause of the origin of the other. One way of viewing the relation of Te Rangikaheke's and Matiaha's formulations is in light of the different organization of these two central oppositions vis-à-vis one another. Te Rangikaheke's account treats the separation of Sky and Earth (as primordial male and female) as more fundamental, with the separation of land and sea opening up at a later

point as an opposition between various of the first series of children. In
Matiaha's account it is, by contrast, the opposition of land to sea (in the union
and subsequent parting of Papa and Tangaroa) that occurs first. Yet, in
Matiaha's account, the two oppositions are placed at the same level, that is,
they are both pictured as the relation of primordial male and primordial female.
The *ménage à trois* character of the Matiaha formulation in fact admirably
reflects a general condition of the Maori categorial system, in which two of
the most central categorial oppositions (land/sea; land/sky) share one of their
terms. The two oppositions based on three terms constitute a three-dimensional
world, originating in the separation first of land and sea (note that Tangaroa
and Rangi go to the seaside—or dividing line between land and sea—to fight
their duel), and then of land and sky. It was noted that in the Arawa account
the special interrelation of sky and earth takes the form of a separation of an
original monad into a male and female part, while in the *Whare Wānanga*
account it takes the form of a primordial mating of the two. The Matiaha account formulates this relation in a third way. White has rendered this section
as follows:

> Na konei i piri tonu ai a Raki ki runga ki a Papa, a na konei a Raki i ki
> atu ai ki a Tane ratou ko ona taina (teina), kia tikina mai aia kia patua,
> kia ora ai ka (nga) tangata. (WM:39; cf. MM:4-5)

> Raki, though speared by Takaroa, still adhered to the top of Papa; and
> Raki said to Tane and his younger brothers, "Come and kill me, that
> men may live." (WE:46)

The phrase "though speared by Takaroa" is not in the original manuscript.
White had to supply it because it was at a point just prior to this that he had,
in conformity with his own topical chapter arrangements, split the account into
two stories—that of the duel of Tangaroa and Rangi, and that of the separation
of Rangi and Papa. By virtue of restoring the continuity between these events,
and based on certain grammatical indicators (e.g., the "*ai*" particle after the
verb generally indicates the action to be a consequence of something previous),
I suggest that Rangi's clinging to Papa is not a condition that arises "despite"
his having been speared, but precisely as a result of it. A more likely translation of the passage would be:

> As a result of this [being speared] Sky continued to cling to Earth; and
> he therefore said to Tāne and his younger brothers that they should raise
> him up, that man might grow.

Note the similarity of the theme "that man might grow" to the Arawa text.
    While the other South Island texts are in varying degrees questionable,

nevertheless it should be noted that several of these confirm this interpretation, explicitly citing the spearing as the cause of the unseparated conditions of sky and earth. The great archetypal separation, of sky and earth, is thus accompanied by the transition from immobility to mobility—or at least there is that hint in the fact that the raising of the sky is pictured as an attempt to terminate the constricted condition that is imposed by a primordial lameness.

Despite the fact that Maori cosmogony in general is not set out in the form of a "great race," we nevertheless are brought back to the concern with motion and forms of mobility (and its defects) with which, in the context of Lévi-Straussian theory, we opened our investigation. The theme of the lameness of the original inhabitants of the earth here figures in two different ways. On the one hand, it is used to account for the original unseparated condition of sky and earth. That is, as a result of the spearing, Sky cannot stand up and can only lie prostrate on Earth. The inhabitable world seems to be dependent upon the opposition of (Earth) lying to (Sky) standing, or, in other words, upon a three-dimensional universe. On the other hand, the theme is present in the motif of a sickly family (described in part as various deformities of the legs) that is generated by Rangi after the spearing.

The theme of a transition from immobility to mobility is, once again, developed more explicitly in some of the other variants. The relation of mobility to discreteness or separation is inverse to that discussed by Lévi-Strauss in the context of North American material. There, following Lévi-Strauss's argument, the possibility of separate things emerges as a consequence of a primordial motion, whereas in the present case, the possibility of mobility arises in consequence of a primordial separation.

Second Schema: Reduction

It will be noted that the above account includes a subplot concerning Rehua (the term in some contexts refers to the star Antares) and other beings who carry Sky upward. Both the Maori of the original manuscript and White's translation are quite terse, and the episode is a little unclear. But it appears that a certain part of the children carry up Sky and remain above themselves (as heavenly bodies?). At a later point in the manuscript, Tāne goes up to the sky to visit his brother Rehua. Furthermore, the long genealogical recital that begins the entire Matiaha account also distinguishes two different groups of children of Rangi and Papa-tūanuku (see WM:19, paragraphs 1–3; WE:21, last two paragraphs). One traces descendants from the older brother Rehua, and ends with the comment:

> Ko te aitanga tenei a Raki i whakawairua, i noho tonu atu ki runga ki nga raki (rangi) katoa. (WM:19; cf. MM:2)

These offspring of Raki were spirits, and stayed in all the heavens.
(WE:21)

One might also note a similarity to a statement about the progeny of Rangi and Heke-heke-i-papa:

Ko te aitanga tenei a Raki raua ko Heke-heke-i-papa i tumou tonu atu ki runga ki te Raki. (WM:18; cf. MM:3)

These of the issue of Raki and Hekeheke-i-papa remained up above. (WE:20)

The other group of descendants of Rangi and Papa-tūanuku, who apparently stay on earth, contains Tāne, Roko (Rongo) Rū, and Tū, among others. Of the six sons of Sky and Earth given in the Arawa account, three (Tāne, Rongo, and Tū) are thus given as sons of Rangi and Papa in the Matiaha formulation. Two others, Tāwhiri and Haumia, are given as children of Rangi's other wives; and the final one, Tangaroa, is present as the contending husband. Some of Sky's children—Tū, for example—are given as descending from more than one of his marriages; but this pattern is by now nothing new. The overall point is that the form taken by the genealogy in distinguishing certain groups of descendants as living in the sky from others on the ground would lend support to the notion that there is at least one sense of reduction in the idea of a breakup of the original family into two spheres. The idea of the members splitting up to live in two main places might be compared to the theme of the breakup of the family of Toi to occupy two different places, Hawaiki and Aotea, as formulated in the Arawa account considered earlier. There is, moreover, in a later part of the manuscript, an account of a cosmic battle that eventuates in the driving of certain elements to the underworld, though it does not contain the story of Whakarū that was focused upon in the *Whare Wānanga* account (MM:22ff.; White has incorporated this story at another point in his work—see WM:29ff.; WE:36ff.).

But while there thus may be a general sense of reduction of the earthly sphere in the story of the separation of sky and earth and in the later cosmic battle, there is a particular, curious event, occurring in direct connection to the raising of the sky, that is of even more immediate interest to this notion of reduction. The first part of the episode of the raising of the sky is concluded with the comment:

E hoa ma ko te timatanga tenei i hanga ai te Raki e Tane. Ko te kupu inoi hoki tenei a Tane ki te kaha o Rehua hei whakawaha i to ratou matua ki runga. Otira na konei i huna ai etahi o nga Kore e Tane ki roto kia Maunga-nui-a-te-whenua, oti rawa atu aua Kore ki reira, a nga (ka) whakawaha a Raki e Tane; a kihai hoki i rewa ki runga. (WM:40; cf. MM:5-6)

Now, this was the origin of the heaven. It was made by Tane and admired
by him, and he uttered the words of his prayer to aid Rehua to carry
their father above. It was at this time that Tane hid some of Te-Kore (the
broken or imperfect beings) in the Maunga-nui-o-te-whenua (great
mountain of the earth), in which they remained for ever. (WE:47)

A more exact translation of the first part of this passage would be:

Friends, this was the beginning of the construction of the Sky by Tāne.
Here were uttered the prayerful words of Tāne to give strength to Rehua
in carrying up their parent above.

The Kore (lit., "nothing") referred to here are presumably those that are
referred to just previously in the same account, the first group of which are
simply a series of ten Kore, designated as "the first Nothing" through "the
tenth Nothing." In the manuscript, all ten are written out; the series thus corresponds to one of the series utilized by Te Rangikaheke to construct the
cosmogonic genealogy that will be considered at a later point.

It is not clear precisely what these Kore are. White inserts the explanation
that they are "the broken or imperfect beings," suggesting that the reference
is to the sickly family that is generated by Rangi after his being speared; and
the account says that they are one of the branches of Rangi's offspring. Whether
the reference is specifically to the sickly family, or merely to a general type
of entity that Maori cosmogonic genealogies typically posit in accounting for
the transition from nothing to being, the episode suggests a fascinating parallel
to the Bororo solution to the problem of the surplus of being. Unlike the extravagant Tikopian solution (reduction from unlimited amount to four) and
unlike the pragmatic Ojibwan solution (which also appears to be the Arawa
and *Whare Wānanga* solution—namely, the reduction of a series by one member), we have in the Bororo case—and perhaps in the South Island too—what
might be called the penurious solution. It is implicitly hierarchical, and consists of the insuring of the discreteness of the more significant categories of
a set by suppressing the insignificant, fractional members. The analogy between the South Island account and the Bororo one of course constitutes a bit
of a leap; but it provides a plausible account for what must be otherwise left
as merely a curious little event. It will be noted that the hiding of these various
Kore occurs precisely at the point at which Lévi-Strauss's theory predicts it
should. Tāne causes the sky and earth to be separated, thus initiating the
archetypal transition from continuous to discrete; this event is followed immediately with, "It was at this time that Tāne hid some of Te-Kore. . . ."

But this reduction of being also turns out to be a conservation of being. For,
as in the *Whare Wānanga* account, Tāne here takes upon himself the task of

ornamenting the sky. And for this purpose, some of these elements of (problematic? fractional? interstitial?) being are taken back out of hiding. They undergo a secondary removal when they are used for ornamentation of the sky—as if these elements, problematic and perhaps inadequate to serve as things-in-themselves, nevertheless can serve as a reserve adequate for supplying the finishing touches for things that can stand as things-in-themselves.

Thus, even though this solution is somewhat different from the Arawa and *Whare Wānanga* solutions, nevertheless there is a consistency in that (in contradistinction to the pattern that Lévi-Strauss has noticed) the removed elements are not lost, but are, in different ways, accorded a positive presence in the cosmic scheme. Note that in all cases the removed elements are placed away from the surface of the earth—Tāwhiri, in the Arawa account, above in the sky; Rū, in the *Whare Wānanga* account, below in the underworld; and here, the Kore are put first below, under the mountain, and then moved above, to the sky. In each case the earthly inventory is reduced. The cosmological role accorded to the removed elements in this case is not, on the surface of things, as immediately central as that accorded to Tāwhiri and Whakarū in the Arawa and *Whare Wānanga* accounts, respectively. On the other hand, various celestial phenomena, such as stars, do in general figure significantly in the conduct of life in traditional Maori society (e.g., the timing of the agricultural cycle). Thus it cannot necessarily be concluded that the ultimate cosmic role of these "nothings" is an insignificant one.

Third and Fourth Schemata:
Hierarchical and Metaphysical

There is no definite scheme in Matiaha'a account that provides the basis for hierarchy in a manner as direct and focused as in Te Rangikaheke's. There are several manifestations of hierarchy; these tend to be linked to the patterns that have been considered as "metaphysical"; and the two schemata will for present purposes be treated as one.

The preeminence of Tāne in this account is manifested in his taking charge in the separation of heaven and earth, the ornamentation of the heavens, and, at a somewhat later point, a cosmic battle in which some of the defeated members are cast down below—much of this similar in broad framework to the *Whare Wānanga* account.

Additionally, there is the theme, noted earlier in the Tūhoe account, of the errors of the gods. In the present case, the theme is intertwined with the quest for a suitable ornamentation for the sky. The use of various Kore for this purpose was itself the second main attempt at outfitting the sky, and, like the first attempt, it also was not totally satisfactory. White breaks off the account after the incident of the Kore. But in the manuscript account, this incident is then followed by Tāne's wandering about, settling with various females—with the explicit implication that the various beings thus produced are possible candidates for the ornamentation of the sky. The Tūhoe and Matiaha accounts thus both interrelate the conditions of unity and plurality through a schema of unsuccessful creation, such that being, or at least a sector of being, is united in the unitary idea that lies behind it. The Arawa and *Whare Wānanga* accounts, on the other hand, achieve something like the same interrelation by picturing the coming to be of variation as a progressive separation. The fact that these accounts emphasize one or the other schema (i.e., that the schemata are in complementary distribution) might be taken as an initial confirmation of the suggestion that they are functionally equivalent schemes.

Both of these methods of interrelating unity and plurality are aligned with genealogies, so that the relation that the method asserts in the abstract is expressed in the concrete through a set of diverse offspring stemming from a given ancestor.

It might be noted that the very long genealogy of Rangi and his diverse wives that opens the Matiaha account is, though lacking the element of erroneous creation, similar in form to the encompassing lines that stem from Tāne in the Tūhoe account, and also from the immigrant voyaging chiefs in the Tūhoe account. Rangi's usurpation of Papa from Tangaroa can be seen as an event in the process of the general expansion of the tribe of Sky. Since the central cosmic role of Sky is ultimately usurped by Tāne, there is a perspective from which it emerges as a matter of little consequence for the final order of the cosmos, whether it is Rangi or Tāne, or both as in the present account, who is placed at the apex of these world-encompassing genealogies.

A number of other texts resemble in broad outline, and often in specific detail as well, the account that has been considered here. These include an account that occurs—each time a little differently—in the handwritten and published papers of the South Island missionary J. F. H. Wohlers (1874; 1895:129ff.; GNZMMSS 55; MS Ml., 234), an account given by Shortland (1882:10–24), and a number of the other accounts found in White's *Ancient History of the Maori*. The degree of homogeneity among them is notable—and perhaps a bit suspicious. Bruce Biggs (1976) for instance has argued that parts of White's material, those parts attributed to the Ngāti-Hau and Ngāti-Kahungunu, are reworkings of material from Wohlers. For the moment the caution must be added that it is uncertain who is producing all the variants; the unanimity of this group of texts may turn out to be partly a reflection of different scholars having access to the same material.

Chapter Five

Antinomy and Cosmology:
Kant Among the Maori

There has always existed in the world, and there will always continue to exist, some kind of metaphysics, and with it the dialectic that is natural to pure reason.

—Immanuel Kant, *Critique of Pure Reason*

THE COSMOGONIC RECITAL of the Maori, as of many other Polynesian peoples, takes two distinct forms: one, that of a prose narrative depicting the decisions and feats of various founding heroes, and the other, that of a cosmic genealogy that terminates in all the beings that presently make up the universe.[1] The notion that genealogy is a principal idiom of cosmology—one that is no less integral to Maori cosmology than prose-narrative representations—is a recognition that must be achieved over against a long-standing tendency of European scholars to neglect the genealogical form in favor of the prose form. Many of the main European collectors (including those perhaps most widely known outside of New Zealand, George Grey and S. Percy Smith) dismissed with scant commentary the cosmogonic genealogies that even now can be found in their archival collections. This would seemingly be because of an apparently less significant role of genealogy *as cosmogony* in the Judaeo-Christian scriptures (though some scholarship argues that the attitude toward genealogy in the Judaeo-Christian scriptures has been similarly one of scholarly neglect, a notion which suggests that the real defect, vis-à-vis the Maori, is the attenuated genealogical orientation of "modern" European society). To restore the notion of cosmology, in European scholarship on the Maori, as an enterprise intrinsically involving a dialectic of two forms would be no small task. For the problem lies only in part in the one-sidedness of the scholarly tradition; the other, and greater, difficulty lies in the condensed form of genealogies themselves. In this chapter I make one possible beginning at a theoretical understanding of the relationship between one of the narratives and its corresponding genealogical form—specifically, the Arawa account of Te Rangikaheke, with which I began my discussion of the narrative accounts. If chapters 3 and 4 dealt with "Maori cosmological narratives," the present chapter deals with "Maori cosmology."

The theoretical vehicle that I bring to my exploration of this dualism of form is the doctrine of "the antinomy of pure reason," a set of arguments formulated by Immanuel Kant to show that reason engaged in cosmology necessarily ends up "divided against itself," that is, compelled by both members of a number of pairs of contradictory propositions. The idea of this exploration was suggested by the fact that many of the contrasts that emerge in the two Maori cosmogonic forms align, at least roughly, with those that Kant has encompassed in the "antinomies."

There are several motives for this exploration. First, there is the obvious one: to see whether Kant's analysis might be useful in attempting to understand this characteristic of Maori cosmological thought. Secondly, every study of one society by a member of another society involves, at least implicitly, a process of comparison. The dualism of Maori cosmology is the kind of cultural phenomenon that a Western observer could easily highlight as a sort of exotic species of thought—and I admit to being so inclined at times. The value of Kant here lies in the perspective he presents for thinking about the Maori practice in relation to the Western cosmological tradition. In the Kantian view the dualism of Maori cosmology might not be very interesting in itself, since a dualistic tendency is seen as of the essence of reason so engaged. What might be interesting, and worth pursuing, is, rather, the differences in the ways in which a dualistic tendency is developed and deployed in various cultural traditions.

Thirdly, this exploration takes us directly to some crucial issues in the development of Western academic anthropology, specifically, the relationship of anthropological theory, in its formative phase, to Kantian and neo-Kantian epistemology. Emile Durkheim in particular absorbed much of Kant in constructing his sociological perspective. But it is as if Durkheim decided to restrict his interests to the first half of the *Critique of Pure Reason* only, the "Transcendental Analytic," or the section that sets out the "*a priori* categories of the understanding." The "antinomy of pure reason" is set out as part of the "Transcendental Dialectic," the second of the two main divisions of the *Critique*. Durkheim's failure to deal with this second part raises a number of questions, and also invites speculations concerning what Durkheim might have had to say regarding the sociological character of cosmology had he pursued the "Dialectic"; and I will in fact offer some comments on this issue.

Finally, there is a proximate stimulus to the Kantian perspective in the comment, already noted in a previous context, with which J. Prytz Johansen, one of the greatest European scholars of Maori society, opens his discussion of "The Kinship Group": "If one could picture to oneself a person like KANT among the old Maoris—which indeed is difficult—one should not be surprised if to the fundamental categories of knowledge, time and space, he had added: kinship" (1954:9). The statement appears to be intended as a kind of metaphorical assertion of the centrality of kinship in Maori thought; indeed Johansen goes on: "The whole cosmos of the Maori unfolds itself as a gigantic 'kin,' in which heaven and earth are first parents of all beings and things, such as the sea, the sand on the beach, the wood, the birds, and man. Apparently he does not feel quite comfortable if he cannot—preferably in much detail—give an account of his kinship whether to the fish of the sea or to a traveller who is invited to enter as a guest" (1954:9).

But I find this statement, when considered literally, to be even more intriguing than when read metaphorically—though in need of a rearrangement of priorities. Kant would not have altered his categories in recognition of kinship, but perhaps would have attempted to alter prevailing notions about kinship in light of his categories—thus producing a sociological version of his so-called Copernican revolution. There is a point in his analysis of cosmology at which Kant, who in fact is extremely deft at concrete imagery, invokes genealogy in the midst of a rumination on the problem of the infinite regresses into which certain categories, such as "cause," might lead: "Can we say that the regress is *in infinitum*, or only that it is indeterminately far extended (*in indefinitum*)? Can we, for instance, ascend from the men now living, through the series of their ancestors, *in infinitum*; or can we only say that, so far as we have gone back, we have never met with an empirical ground for regarding the series as limited at any point . . . ?" (1965:452). One can surmise that the Maori strategy of formulating cosmogony as genealogy is a practice that would not go unappreciated by Kant.

Before proceeding, it is necessary to comment on the nature of my use of Kantian theory, which in some respects is rather selective. There is, first of all, the issue of what is meant by the "antinomies," for Kant presents this doctrine in several different forms. The *Prolegomena to Any Future Metaphysics* (1983:80) contains a particularly terse, summarizing statement:

1
Thesis
The world has, as to time and space, a beginning (limit).
Antithesis
The world is, as to time and space, infinite.

2
Thesis
Everything in the world is constituted out of the simple.
Antithesis
There is nothing simple, but everything is composite.
3
Thesis
There are in the world causes through freedom.
Antithesis
There is no freedom, but all is nature.
4
Thesis
In the series of world-causes there is some necessary being.
Antithesis
There is nothing necessary in the world, but in this series all is contingent.

This summary is accompanied by the comment:

> Here is the most singular phenomenon of human reason, no other
> instance of which can be shown in its any other use. If we, as is com-
> monly done, represent to ourselves the appearances of the sensible world
> as things in themselves, if we assume the principles of their combination
> as principles universally valid of things in themselves and not merely of
> experience, as is usually, nay, without our *Critique*, unavoidably done,
> there arises an unexpected conflict which never can be removed in the
> common dogmatic way; because the thesis, as well as the antithesis, can
> be shown by equally clear, evident, and irresistible proofs—for I pledge
> myself as to the correctness of all these proofs—and reason therefore
> sees that it is divided against itself, a state at which the sceptic rejoices,
> but which must make the critical philosopher pause and feel ill at ease.
> (1983:80–81)

Thus, the antinomies as presented in the *Prolegomena* are four pairs of contradictory propositions, accompanied by a promise that there are forceful
arguments supporting each thesis and antithesis.

The full arguments themselves are found in the *Critique of Pure Reason*,
where the antinomies are set out within a more elaborated architectonic. The
fact that there are four antinomies follows from the general plan of the *Critique*, in which the "categories" are organized under four headings: quantity,
quality, relation, and modality. The four antitheses each present a potentially
infinite series or regress, and the four theses each present an idea that terminates that particular series or regress (the idea of a border in time and space
terminates the seriation belonging to space and time; the idea of an indivisible substance terminates the idea of qualitative decomposability; the idea of

a first cause terminates the regress of causes). And Kant (1965:396ff.) presents, arranged in columns directly adjacent to one another, pairs of detailed arguments that purport to prove both the thesis and the antithesis of each antinomy. It is to these sets of arguments that critical discussions of the antinomies most frequently gravitate.

But at yet other points in the *Critique* (1965:300ff.), Kant develops something like a *generic* characterization of cosmological antinomy, a characterization that suggests a common structure to the four antinomies that are specifically developed into full arguments. In this generic characterization, cosmological antinomy emerges as a conflict between the fact that certain categories lead by their nature into infinite series or regresses of "conditions," on one hand, and, on the other, to a "principle of reason" amounting to the fact that, presented with such series, reason attempts to bring them to completion—attempts to ascend the series of conditions to an "unconditioned." While there would seem already to be a tug-of-war merely in the conflict between seriation and completeness, Kant tends to picture the conflict, rather, as lying in the fact that the "unconditioned" can be thought in two equally compelling ways. It can be envisioned either in the form of a terminating condition or in the idea of an infinite series itself thought of, precisely because infinite, as unconditioned by any further term. Because it is the most abstract, this generic characterization of cosmological antinomy would seem to hold out the most cross-cultural potential, and the discussion that follows takes its main inspiration from it.

Closely related to the issue of what one draws out as constituting "the antinomies" is a basic methodological issue: What kind and degree of intellectual similarity or universality must be presupposed to exist interculturally in order to make this particular, admittedly far-flung, comparison? It is clear that Kant envisioned the antinomies within an architectonic that included all other aspects of his epistemology. Therefore, one might reasonably ask whether, in order to make a valid comparison, one must not also show that the Maori espouse, for example, a conceptualization of time and space similar to Kant's own.[2] There are three main points to be made regarding the requirements of cross-cultural comparison, all of them important in clarifying the attitude toward Kantian epistemology that is adopted here.

The first point is that the parameters of what one could compare would be relative to what one takes as constituting the antinomies, as discussed above. If one takes as the antinomies the sets of detailed arguments themselves, one is led to ask whether the more technical concepts, "substance" or "necessary being" and so on, have analogues in non-Western cultures. This would be a legitimate investigation, and, to some extent I will explore such possibilities, even as far as setting up my analysis in terms of the particular categories which Kant invokes to present his doctrine. But, since I am particularly focusing on the more generic characterization of cosmological antinomy, the "bottom line" of what I am suggesting as common to Maori cosmogony and Kantian philosophy is just the kind of structural conflict suggested above. This kind of conflict could be induced by any category of the type that, in carrying the subject from one object to another, carries itself over as a category (as, for example, "cause" carries one over from an object to an anterior object, and in the process carries itself over as a category applicable to the anterior object as well). Kant's "Transcendental Dialectic" is strongly imbued with a concern that is too easily lost sight of in the study of categorial systems, namely that categories, or at least some of them, lead us beyond, and have consequences for the nature of consciousness that are larger than, any specific empirical application of them—or even of the sum of their empirical applications.

The second point is that Kant seems to have considered a conscious knowledge of the principles of "transcendental idealism" as a prerequisite for a theoretical resolution of the antinomies, but *not* as a prerequisite for what one might refer to as their basic manifestation. For accompanying Kant's formulations of the antinomies are recurrent allusions to the tradition of Western metaphysics as a kind of *locus classicus* of the antinomy of pure reason concretely manifesting itself. Specifically, for two millenia metaphysics has haggled over such issues and failed to settle them. Thus, to the several forms, noted above, that the antinomies take as a philosophical doctrines, it is quite clear that the antinomies are yet one thing more to Kant, namely, a historical generalization aimed at a set of tangible data. It is worth noting that the "world of impossible contradictions" that Lovejoy (1960:331) reveals in his historical study of the Chain of Being confirms and adds flesh to the historical generalization implicit in Kant's philosophical doctrine; for example, the great antinomies of unity/diversity and of freedom/determinism, which Lovejoy characterizes as focal points of controversy in the Middle Ages, are at least loosely reminiscent of the Kantian second and third antinomies.[3] Kant clearly saw "the antinomy of pure reason" as a generalization abstract enough to hold of metaphysics in general despite the variety of distinct doctrines about the nature of time and space that are contained in this tradition, and despite the fact that such doctrines were, in Kant's view, based upon fundamental misunderstandings of the nature of time and space. There is every indication that Kant thought of antinomy as a universal characteristic of pure reason, though the universality that is implied is potential only. The claim is less that the antinomies will be manifested everywhere, than that anyone who should attempt to settle cosmological questions will find the resources of reason such that it can generate equally compelling proofs in opposed directions. And therefore, any claim to have solved such issues will amount to arbitrary dogmatism.

Now, the Maori appear to have maximally invested themselves in cosmology: they have adopted cosmology as the privileged idiom of their self-definition, sense of values, and political/social theory. If any society can be expected to have exhausted the possibilities of this concern, it would be this one. Given the Maori predilection for cosmology, given the universalist inclinations of Kantian epistemology, and given finally the fact that Kant himself clearly was willing to use the "antinomy of pure reason," not merely as a disembodied philosophical doctrine, but also as a historical generalization about the basic character of attempts to do cosmology, the project of considering Kant's theory in relation to Maori society does not strike me as radically un-Kantian.

But this brings us to the third issue: To what extent must one be a Kantian, in the sense of accepting the central tenets of "transcendental idealism," in order to espouse the antinomies as an analytical tool? In the overall scheme of the *Critique of Pure Reason*, one of the purposes of the antinomies is to show that there are conflicts that cannot be laid to rest *unless* one adopts the central tenets of transcendental idealism, especially the famed phenomenon/noumenon distinction. But I would argue that one can separate the antinomies, as more or less descriptive statements about certain properties of cosmological thought, from Kant's use of them as a support for transcendental idealism. Indeed some such distinction would seem necessary to Kant's strategy itself, since transcendental idealism is posed as a means of resolving an old and perennial problem of metaphysics. In various other ways Kant provides the basis for distinguishing between antinomies as problem and transcendental idealism as solution. For example, he finds in Zeno of Elea an early recognition of the divided nature of cosmological thought (1965:446ff.). Kant finds his intellectual ancestor in Zeno; the general form of the antinomies (and especially the "mathematical" antinomies) suggests the genuineness of this attribution. But there is one particular point in Kant's attribution that must be greeted with a bit of skepticism. Specifically, in a rhetorical flourish Kant (1965:446ff.) attempts to imbue Zeno's formulations retrospectively with the spirit of transcendental idealism. Kant is here clearly adding his own twist to Zeno. There is no evidence that Zeno independently ennunciated "transcendental idealism"; and to the extent that Zeno is taken as having adumbrated the "antinomy of pure reason," the tradition of Zeno can be taken only as an articulation of the problem as distinct from Kant's specific attempt at solution.

Kant's attempt to lay the antinomies to rest takes the form not of a decision in favor of either of the poles of any of the antinomies, but rather of a general claim that the problem itself turns out, in light of transcendental idealism, as wrongly conceived. His notions of the proper way of conceiving of the antinomies ramify through his entire philosophical system. My concern in this analysis, however, is not with Kant's proffered resolution, but rather with his characterization of the problem. For the antinomies display in a sophisticated and wide-ranging way certain problems faced in the cosmological endeavor, and perhaps intrinsic to it. Kant's formulation might be examined ethnographically—here, as a first step, in terms of its adequacy as an abstract descriptive characterization of the dualism of Maori cosmology. But the question of whether transcendental idealism provides a resolution, or the only possible resolution, of the antinomies—let alone whether it makes any sense at all as a philosophical system—is not the issue here. I take as my purpose merely an initial exploration of what seems to be a parallel insight, occurring within two cultural/intellectual traditions, about the basic nature of cosmology.

Finally, it should be noted that, in anthropology at least, the term "cosmology" has the character of being, on one hand, one of the most frequently invoked analytical terms, and, on the other hand, one of the least critically examined. What do we mean by this concept? In the context of this exploration, we might ask whether our tacit use of "cosmology" does not itself involve antithetical tendencies: on the one hand, the recognition that there are categories that pull the subject beyond the bounds of sensible experience, and, on the other, some blind disposition to seek completion, in the form of either ultimate boundaries or some *final* statement of their impossibility.

THE THIRD ANTINOMY

For the following discussion I will focus upon the prose and genealogical accounts written by Te Rangikaheke, the Arawa chief whose prose narrative cosmogony was discussed in chapter 3. In the analysis that follows I use the method of citation used in chapter 3 (see pp. 56 and 60); for passages from chapter 3 that are repeated in chapter 5, I will give only my English translation, and not repeat the original Maori text. With respect to the issues involved in the third antinomy, this formulation can be taken as fairly typical of Maori cosmogony in general.

In Kant's *Prolegomena*, the thesis of the third antinomy is, "There are in the world causes through freedom." The antithesis is, "There is no freedom, but all is nature." In the more complex statement of the *Critique* (1965:409), this antinomy is posed as:

Thesis	*Antithesis*
Causality in accordance with laws of nature is not the only causality from which the appearances of the world can one and all be derived. To explain these appearances it is necessary to assume that there is also another causality, that of freedom.	There is no freedom, everything in the world takes place solely in accordance with laws of nature.

It is this antinomy which gave rise to my project and which is the main focus of my argument. For the most immediately noticeable difference in the two Maori cosmogonic forms lies in the respective ways in which they portray the motive force of cosmogenesis. Earlier I called attention to Kant's own figurative use of the principle of one of the two forms of Maori cosmology, namely genealogy. By happy coincidence it turns out that Kant would also have appreciated the idiom of the other, that is, the prose form of Maori cosmogony. For as part of the "freedom" pole of the third antinomy, Kant presents the following argument:

> If, for instance, I at this moment arise from my chair, in complete freedom, without being necessarily determined thereto by the influence of natural causes, a new series, with all its natural consequences *in infinitum*, has its absolute beginning in this event, although as regards time this event is only the continuation of a preceding series. For this resolution and act of mine do not form part of the succession of purely natural effects, and are not a mere continuation of them. (1965:414)

It so happens that the cosmos-creating decision of the Maori prose cosmogony is also a decision to stand up. In Te Rangikaheke's account, the universe is created by the success of one of the sons of Sky and Earth in first pushing the pair apart, thus creating the space of being (the analysis that follows depends upon the reader's familiarity with this account, summarized in chapter 3, pp. 58-59). There are certain variations in different Maori tribal accounts, but one of the more consistent motifs in these accounts—and in fact in numerous accounts of this story found in other parts of the world as well—is the concern with posture, and specifically with the ability to extend legs straightly and move about in a functional way. In some Maori accounts the failures are portrayed as a sickly family whose names bear epithets suggesting difficulties in standing and walking. As Lévi-Strauss has repeatedly pointed out, walking posture and its defects (e.g., limping) constitute a recurrent cosmogonic theme, one often intricately connected with a theory of man's place in nature (a notion that scientific evolutionism has also found to be of some merit).[4] One could also go on at great length concerning the implications of the idea of "standing" for the Maori. Tū (lit., "stand") is the Maori god of war, and in this capacity, the term connotes steadfastness and bravery. Tū is also one of the original group of cosmological beings, and in some accounts, including the present one, he is the progenitor of humanity, his particular resoluteness eventuating in human superordinacy over the rest of nature. One can of course make too much of Kant's invocation of a decision to stand up as an epitomizing example of "freedom"; imagining him crumpled up over his manuscript and looking forward to his famous daily walk, we can understand why this particular example of freedom should have leapt to mind. But in the Maori case one cannot overestimate its significance. It carries the weight of the decisiveness and resolution that shape the cosmos and engender the particular species-character of humans.

And even beyond the singular event of the decision to stand, the Maori prose account is permeated by a sense of contingency: what happened might not have, and in two different ways. First, what actually happened reflects a decision that was made regarding two alternatives that were considered (the debate and the attempt to establish consensus over whether to kill or separate the parents). And second, the course that was decided upon might have failed, and almost did fail, in the execution. The contingency is highlighted by the fact that only the final possible effort succeeds. The very terminology of the prose account is a terminology of "will," involving concepts such as "thinking," "having an idea," "deciding," "making plans," "agreeing/disagreeing," "standing firm," and so on.[5]

The same general emphasis on willfulness as the necessary motive force of cosmogenesis continues throughout the subsequent phases of the prose cosmogony. The various children of Sky and Earth are, in their initial condition, pictured as nondescript, as being no particular kind of thing. But once Sky and Earth are separated, there is a scramble to develop life-strategies, and the development of the myriad forms of the natural world takes the form of a series of debates concerning such strategies, the various beings ultimately insulting one another on their respective views, and going off to live in divergent ways. The parting of ways between land animals and fish is a particularly famous event, but there are many others. One account tells of the parting of mosquitos and sand flies—for the mosquitos want to attack man by night, and the sand flies by day.[6] The coming into being of the entire biosphere is constituted in a spirit in which species character follows species commitment and act. Yet it must be noted that there is a paradoxical character to the "spontaneity" of will, specifically, in that the exercise of will produces its own, though only very general, kind of regularity. That is, differentiation of forms of life through spontaneously emerging choices of ways of life creates a general paradigm of cosmogenesis within the prose cosmogony (cf. Valeri, 1991).

Following this initial diversification in ways of life, there is a phase of cosmogenesis dominated by a sort of demigod-trickster figure, Māui, who carries out such deeds as fishing up the land, snaring and slowing the sun so that its course is appropriate for human life, and stealing fire for human use. Māui is perhaps the quintessentially willful being, and his famous deeds are once again presented as self-assertions against the parent (his mother, in a recapitulation of the original cosmic situation, keeps Māui in a dark, stopped-up room from which he must initially extricate himself before going to work on the specific details of the world). Following Māui, the next great era is the human era, specifically migrations to New Zealand and the establishing of land claims. The heroes in this era are navigators of great prowess and cleverness. In both of these phases there is a recurrent theme of success through craft and deception. This theme of deceitfulness among founders is in fact found in many mythologies, and has brought forth a number of interpretations, psychoanalytic and otherwise. What is of interest here is not any immorality of theft, but the amorality of it—placing the processes of cosmogenesis outside of what can be accounted for through the regularity of law, whether natural or social.

Now, on the other side of the third antinomy, Kant has in mind processes that work by virtue of regular and consistent laws of nature and devoid of "spontaneity of will." In the other Maori portrayal, the "genealogical" account, cosmogenesis takes the form of a regular and overarching process, expressed in two main ways: through consistent allusions, in the elements used to construct the genealogy, to organic processes of growth or gestation; and through repeating mathematical patterns. Particularly common in the first way are terms designating types of roots and root fibers.[7] The mathematical pattern is the more dominant in the account considered here. The first cosmic sequence is:

Ko te pō, ko te pō, ko te pō tuatahi, ko te pō tuarua, ko te pō tuatoru, ko te pō tuawhā, tuarima, tuaono, tuawhitu, tuawaru, tuaiwa, tuangahuru, tuarau, tuamano, tuatani. (Grey xlix; MS 44:915)

The night, the night, the first night, the second night, the third night, the fourth night, fifth, sixth, seventh, eighth, ninth, tenth, hundredth, thousandth, indefinitely-manyeth.

Night is followed by nothing, then searching, seeking, pursuing, sky, earth, and cloud.[8] Each of these elements, except cloud, is presented with essentially the same series of numerical epithets as night. For sky there is also a " qualitative" series of epithets connoting spatial extent and degrees of lightness and darkness:

Ko Rangi-nui, ko Rangi-roa, Rangi-poto, Rangi-pōuri, Rangi-potango, Rangi-whētuma, Rangi-whēkere, Rangi-pakakina, Rangi-pakarea, Rangi-kāhiwahiwa, Rangi-kānapanapa. (Grey 1; MS 44:915)

Big Sky, Long Sky, Short Sky, Dark Sky, Very Dark Sky, Lowering Sky, Dark Colored Sky, Glowing Sky, Gloomy Sky, Intensely Dark Sky, Gleaming Sky.

Cloud appears with only a qualitative series (similar to that attached to sky). Then there is the statement, "The coming out into the bright light, into the day light," and the genealogy continues, eventually leading to Māui and then human ancestors of the Maori tribes.

It is important to note, then, that the genealogy does not merely list in order of procreation the beings who appear in the prose account; rather it casts these as a distinctive model of cosmogenesis, one based on a regular and patterned unfolding. The sequence of epithets in the above example contains a series of four models of increase, each more powerful than the last. First, there is mere repetition (the night, the night); then an arithmetic sequence (one through ten), then an exponential sequence (ten, hundred, thousand), and then finally the use of a term ("*tini*") that connotes "the innumerable." The Maori genealogical portrayals of cosmogenesis have often elicited the discourse of natural sciences from Western scholars, especially in the characterization of the essential process as one of evolution. This seems to me a fair assessment, provided that one limits the claim to genealogy insofar as it is used by the Maori as an idiom for cosmology (I make no claims about the nature of Maori genealogy outside of its use in accounts of cosmogony).

However, while it does seem to be the case that the genealogical cosmogonies locate the motive force of cosmogenesis in the continuity of an overall process, it is not quite accurate to claim that there is no reference to the vocabulary of "will." This particular genealogy, and many others, contains terms such as "searching," "seeking," "pursuing"; these terms appear to be allusions to the dissatisfaction of the children with the original state of affairs as recounted in the prose account. What is noteworthy in the genealogical accounts, however, is that, rather than emphasizing major disruption, such terms are taken up within the patterned regularity and repetitiveness that constitute the overall process. Terms such as "the searching" here take a grammatical form roughly analogous to a gerund, or a nominalized verb—that is, an action thought of as a thing.

These last observations present the occasion for posing a broader and at this point rather impressionistic comment: if something like the valences of the Kantian third antinomy are manifest in the Maori dual (i.e., prose vs. genealogical) representation of cosmogenesis, they are manifested not so much in the genealogical account as "natural process" and the prose account as "will," but rather in the form of the genealogical account as the recasting of will as natural process, and in the prose account as the recasting of natural process as will. As an example of this latter direction (i.e., the recasting of natural process as will), I call attention to the fact that some of the very rhythms that underlie the regularity of the genealogical account—that is, seasonal cycles of plant and fish life—become, in the course of the prose account, subject to human will. This happens when Tū, ancestor of humanity, conquers and eats his brothers (who are ancestors of the other natural species), and thereby renders them *noa* (no longer sacred). Tū as a result receives a *karakia* (incantation, spell) that permits control of each of the other beings:

> So his older brothers were made *noa*, and thence his *karakia* were
> separated, a *karakia* for Tāne-mahuta, for Tangaroa, for Rongo-matane,
> for Haumia, for Tū-matauenga. The reason he sought for these *karakia*,
> was in order to be able to cause his older brothers to return as food for
> him. . . . (trans. of Grey xxxiv; MS 43:895–96)

Unlike the situation that Kant thought he saw in Western metaphysics, here we seem to have a self-aware dialectic, in which each formulation is responsive to the other, subordinating the same elements under a different framing attitude regarding the "cause" of the cosmos. This self-awareness is evident most obviously in the fact that the prose and genealogical accounts focus on the same "people" (especially Sky and Earth and their brood), but in many other minor ways as well.[9]

Many of the best sources on traditional cosmogonic recital, including the one considered here, are manuscripts written by Maori people in the mid-nineteenth century. While it is more difficult to infer whether there were contexts which favored one form or the other, one can at least infer from these sources that a knowledge of both forms and the practice of alternating between them were widespread.

THE FIRST AND SECOND ANTINOMIES

As noted at the outset, a contrast in modes of motive force of cosmogenesis distinguishes the two main Maori formulations of cosmogenesis, and the contrast seems to be similar to that depicted by Kant in the third antinomy; this has been the main focus of my presentation. Kant calls the third and fourth antinomies "dynamical," since they have to do with the propulsive force of origination and therefore of "dependency of existence" within the cosmos. I will not here deal specifically with the fourth antinomy—which opposes the idea of a "necessary being" to the idea of the contingency of all things—

because it is somewhat redundant with the third. This seeming redundancy of the third and fourth—that is, the "dynamical"—antinomies is not, however, the case with respect to the first and second antinomies, which deal with extension and divisibility, and are termed mathematical. The first antinomy can be divided into the spatial and temporal dimensions; and then the first and second, or "mathematical," antinomies can be displayed in their main features through the following arrangement:

The universe is limited:

—as to extent in space

—as to extent in time

—as to extent of qualitative divisibility

   versus

The universe is infinite:

—as to extent in space

—as to extent in time

—as to extent of qualitative divisibility

These various mathematical axes are useful in characterizing the differences between the Maori prose and genealogical cosmogonies, for along each axis the two forms do seem to pose an antinomy. The antinomies posed are not always rigorously characterizable as between the finite and the infinite, as in the Kantian formulation; in some instances the contrast would seem to be more properly characterized as between the finite and the indefinite. [10] Nonetheless, I will briefly consider the Maori material in relation to the various mathematical axes—partly because there would seem to be at least some limited analogies with the concerns of the Kantian antinomies, and partly because the mathematical axes form, in any case, a useful grid through which to explore the phenomenon of cosmological antinomy more broadly.

If the motive force of the Maori prose cosmogenesis is "will," the cosmic problem to which it is applied is the finitude of space; the cosmos-initiating act is that of wresting some space by propping sky and earth apart. The product of this effort seems to be a "closed" universe, with earth as lower and sky as upper barrier. In some accounts the celestial bodies are said to be attached to the front of Sky's body facing downward toward Earth; and most of the accounts suggest that the space of being must be in an ongoing way held open, that is, that Sky and Earth must be propped apart against their own desire to unite.

Space in the genealogical account is more difficult to comment upon; the most notable characteristic vis-à-vis the prose account is the less focused concern on spacial finitude. As noted earlier there are some terms ("searching," "seeking") that would seem to be allusions to the original enclosed condition. Yet this spatial concern certainly is not the crux of the account. This theme is, rather, absorbed as one set of elements in a larger configuration of patterned expansiveness. And within that longer stream there is a set of epithets that seem to engage the idea of space in the form of a free adducing of varying spatial characteristics ("Big Sky, Long Sky, Short Sky"). One can say minimally that there is a contrast between a universe that is spatially finite—in which spatial finitude is indeed its single most salient characteristic—and one that does not appear to be so defined.

But there is another approach to the spatial character of the two accounts, an approach that is both simpler and more attentive to the *modus operandi* of the two accounts. For there are certain images that spatially define the cosmos in the two accounts. In the prose account, the image is of male and female seeking to unite sexually, and the space of the cosmos is the distance between them. The very single central image that is chosen as the image of the cosmos is thus an image laden with the range of human desires and strategies. The alternative images chosen for the cosmos, in the genealogical account, present a more ordered or patterned character, the main images being that of an open numerical series and that of organic growth, such as a spreading plant.[11] The different spatial images belonging to the two accounts suggest a contrast of the finitely extensible with the indefinitely extensible. As noted earlier, the prose and genealogical accounts mutually incorporate and subordinate one another's claims. Both the principle of expansion and the principle of containment are present in both the prose and genealogical accounts. In the prose account expansion is subordinated to containment: the supreme achievement is a mere contingent holding open of the cosmos against its implosive tendency. In the genealogical account, containment is subordinated to expansion—the original containment being recast as merely one set of elements in a pattern of ongoing expansion, modeled on organic growth, or, in some cases, on an open, compounding numerical series.

The two accounts also differ in the way that they construct the cosmos temporally. While there may be in the prose cosmogony a vague sense of the timeless existence of sky and earth, the cosmos itself has a definite beginning point in their separation. The prose cosmogonies tend to single this pair out as the starting point of the cosmos; the composer of the account under consideration here, who had been introduced to Christianity, in fact specifically draws an analogy between the cosmological position of this pair and that of the being that Christian metaphysics regarded as the "first cause" of the universe:

> Ki tā te Pākehā ki tāna tikanga na te Atua anake te tangata me Rangi me Papa me ngā mea katoa i hanga. Ki ngā tāngata Maori na Rangi rāua ko Papa ngā take o mua. (Grey xxxi; MS 43:893)

> According to Pakeha [European] tradition, God alone made man, Sky and Earth, and all things. To Maori people, Sky and Earth were the sources.

In the genealogical accounts, on the other hand, the basic patterns are already clearly and fully laid down in elements that precede sky and earth, that is, in such prior elements as night and nothing. The motive force that is characteristic of genealogical cosmogenesis (i.e., a set of regular and patterned progressions) thus appears at least relatively deeper in time than does the motive force that is characteristic of the prose cosmogonies (i.e., the actions of willful beings). The first things of the prose account are temporally secondary things in the genealogical account; this seems to hold as a general rule in Maori cosmogony, even though many other genealogical accounts do not proliferate terms as profusely as Te Rangikaheke's.

Te Rangikaheke's sense of the genealogical regress could almost be said to be infinitist. As noted before, the genealogical account makes recurrent use of mathematical epithets that culminate in the term "*tini*," which might be translated as "innumerable." Jenifer Curnow, who has extensively studied the writings of Te Rangikaheke, comments on these particular mathematical series: "Each sequence is numbered, and yet beyond number; its length can be counted to a thousand, but beyond that the period of time is so great it is myriad (*tuatini*)" (1985:124). Elsewhere she refers to these series as suggesting a "vastness of time" or even an "infinite sequence" (1985:123–24). Thus the genealogical account is punctuated by a term which suggests, if not an infinite regress, then one that is at least beyond enumeration.

The antinomy belonging to quality is, finally, the most complex and potentially interesting antinomy, though it also must be admitted that what is to be sought in the Maori formulations is most clearly by way of analogy only. At issue for Kant is the question of the qualitative decomposability of the "real" of the universe, and specifically the issue of whether this proceeds infinitely or ends in ultimate, indivisible substances. In the Maori formulations, all qualities are personified, and I do not see anything exactly equivalent to the venerable metaphysical concept of "substance." Yet one of the intellectual issues pervading Maori cosmogony, and many other traditional cosmogonies, is a concern with the number of kinds of things in the universe, coupled with an assumption that the qualities of some things arise as combinations of the qualities of others.

The intellectual operation that I will consider in the Maori case is that of epithetization, that is, the practice of adding qualifying epithets to main nominal terms in either the prose or the genealogical accounts. The analysis will thus consist not so much of introducing new material as of reexamining those we have already considered, but with an eye toward the ways in which "qualitative distinctions" are envisioned—and also toward a process that in these accounts is closely connected with such distinctions, that is, hierarchicalization. The underlying rules of genealogy and prose seem to differ fundamentally on this process of epithetization. In the genealogical account, the qualifying epithets are rather freely adduced, while in the prose cosmogony, there is a definite principle of limitation. The ostensible difference can be seen by recalling and comparing the appearance of some of the specific "people." In the prose account, Sky for example occurs as:

Sky, Big Sky

Sky in the genealogical account occurs as:

Big Sky, Long Sky, Short Sky, Dark Sky, Very Dark Sky, Lowering Sky, Dark Colored Sky, Glowing Sky, Gloomy Sky, Intensely Dark Sky, Gleaming Sky. (trans. of Grey 1; MS 44:915)

In the genealogical account of the ultimate origins of the universe, each primordial term in the genealogy is subjected to a series of qualifying epithets (numerical, spatial, or a third type connoting shades of lightness and darkness). In the prose account, extravagant epithetization occurs only once, specifically in relation to the ancestor of humanity, Tū, in consequence of his conquering in battle and eating of his brothers (in the event summarized above). The narrator follows the recounting of this event with the comment:

When his brothers were defeated by him, then his [Tū's] names were separated: Tū-ka-riri, Tū-ka-nguha, Tū-kai-taua, Tū-whakaheke-tangata, Tū-mata-whāiti, Tū-matauenga.
His names were made equal in number to his brothers. (trans. of Grey v; MS 81:55)

It might initially seem a bit presumptuous to infer any significance from this one prose occurrence of the process of epithetization. However, considering the use that is made of epithetization in the prose account, *there can be only one occurrence*—only one being with a highly "composite" character.

For here the epithetization—which also might be called, in Dumont's (1980) term, "encompassment"—is reserved for the expression of hierarchy, and very directly so in the sense that each epithet qualification must be specifically justified by the subordination of some specific cosmic entity (so that Tū's epithets are said to be equal to the number of beings he has subordinated).

Ultimately, both prose and genealogy in fact function to create a relation of superordination for one being to others in a set; but with respect to the compositeness of particular beings they work in opposite ways. The prose account creates hierarchy precisely through an economy of composition—the fact that one of the beings in the story, through the events that transpire, ends up more composite, or more encompassing, than the others. Genealogies, on the other hand, create hierarchy, not among the beings within the same genealogy, but for the one being at the end of the genealogy in relation to other beings with their own genealogies (cf. Valeri 1991). And in the latter strategy hierarchy is created more effectively precisely to the extent that the elements in the genealogy are subdivided (or should one say multiplied?) through epithetization, since the final being in any genealogy encompasses all that is contained in it. Thus, in sum, with respect to qualitative divisibility of main terms, the prose cosmogony seems once again to work by virtue of a principle of necessary limitation, and the genealogical by virtue of an attitude of (perhaps theoretically limitless) proliferation. And, once again, the different representations characteristic of the two cosmogonic formulations are representations of the same original "people."

The fact that the Maori cosmogony (in either form), and the cosmogonies of many other cultural traditions as well, is personified—that is, invokes "persons" as the idiom for dealing with the problem of the number and kinds of things in the universe—may stem from a human capacity for grasping individual persons as ensembles of qualities. Lévi-Strauss proposed at one point that proper names "form the fringe of a general system of classification: they are both its extension and its limit. When they come on to the stage the curtain rises for the last act of the logical performance" (Lévi-Strauss 1966:215). This statement is true only in certain contexts. Particularly in the case of exemplary and cosmically founding persons, there is another kind of process—not one that ends with an individual, but rather one that starts with an individual and decomposes the unity implied in this construct (infinitely?). The myriad characteristics and alternative appellations drawn in Christian litanies (for example, the litany of the Blessed Virgin) might be a process analogous in this respect to the epithetization of the various first elements of Maori cosmogony. Marcel Mauss once commented that

we have at our disposal, especially in mythology, cases of what I call
"mental reverberation," in which the image is endlessly multiplied, so to
speak. Thus Vishnu's arms, each the support of an attribute. Thus the
feather head-dresses of the Aztecs' priest-god, each feather of which is a
different fragment of the soul of the god. For here is one of the fundamental points both of social life and of the life of the individual consciousness: the symbol—an invoked genie—has a life of its own; it acts
and reproduces itself indefinitely. (Mauss 1979:21–22)

The only problem with Mauss's comment is that, in so tightly binding this
process to religious symbolism, it threatens overmystification, dismissing in
advance the possibility of analogies that might be drawn between this kind of
operation and those through which formal metaphysics has approached the
problem of the qualitative divisibility of the universe. For this is clearly a
problem common to, and in relation to which it is sometimes difficult to draw
a precise line of demarcation between, mythology and philosophy.

ANTINOMY AND COSMOLOGY

The above considerations sketch some possible points of contact between
the Maori dual representation of cosmogony and the Kantian characterization
of the antinomy of pure reason. It should be noted that there are complex issues
posed by the fact that Maori cosmogony is actually recited. Put simply, while
it may be possible to state, by way of ontological argument, that the universe
has no beginning, it is difficult to imagine how one would recite or "perform"
an account of such a universe. Seemingly intrinsic to performance is the act
of beginning. The basic logic of the Maori genealogical account seems to be
that of a regress of causes, even though, perhaps as necessitated by the constraints of recital, the regress lapses into a vague fade-out (or, in the directionality of the recital, a fade-in)—in some cases with an enigmatic first term
(the nothing), in some cases with an unpursued cyclicality (night). Some such
strategy might represent the best possible compromise between an attitude of
ontological infinitude and the pragmatic finitude of performance. There is an
even more significant sense in which Maori cosmology is "performed." For
in the Maori case one is confronting in cosmology an entire form of life: lived
reality is, at any moment, the present terminus of the ongoing world-genealogy
and world-historical tale. One finds in cosmology, for example, many of the
paradigms of ongoing political strategy and practice, which, in turn, grounded
in cosmology, embody the dual character thereof. Cosmology is, among other
things, the backdrop and idiom of Polynesian political theory, which seems
consistently to recognize two forms of political legitimation, that of ordered

genealogical succession and that of "usurpation." The former process involves a kind of necessity, succession being determined as a predictable consequence of genealogical rank (including seniority of birth). The other involves an interruption of this rule, in favor of legitimation by the willful and decisive actions of a given individual. Each of these processes abrogates the unity of process espoused in the other. The two forms of political legitimation are both thoroughly cosmologically grounded—the one in the regular, inevitable patterns of the original genealogy, the other in the tale of the decisive actions of the first beings, in which usurpers are typically genealogically junior members of lineages.

Starting from sociopolitical life, one could even envision in the antinomies a yet unexplored dimension of the classical Durkheimian project—that of sociologically grounding the Kantian topography of reason. Durkheim restricted his interest in Kant to the "Transcendental Analytic," the part of the *Critique of Pure Reason* that sets out the categories, and neglected the "Transcendental Dialectic," or the section that deals with the antinomies that develop when these categories are applied beyond the bounds of experience. Durkheim's main ambition with regard to the "Analytic" amounted to an attempt to ground the categories in society, for example, "the category of class was at first indistinct from the concept of the human group; it is the rhythm of social life which is at the basis of the category of time; the territory occupied by the society furnished the material for the category of space; it is the collective force which was the prototype of the concept of efficient force, an essential element in the category of causality" (Durkheim 1965:488).

Although I am satisfied at this point merely to make the observation that to describe cosmology in the Maori case is at the same time to characterize sociopolitical process, Durkheim, had he consulted the "Transcendental Dialectic," might have pursued the interrelationship much further, and in a specifically "sociological-reductionist" fashion. He might have claimed to have found, in the equal necessity of "regularity" and "spontaneity" to sociopolitical life, the ground of the ultimate equal compellingness of these forms of causality. And he might have found the social grounds for the other antinomies too—for example, in regard to space, in the fact that the social ethos of a given tribe demands, on the one hand, the conviction that its space, coterminus with all human value, is firmly circumscribed, and on the other hand, an opposed "other" (which demands its own other, etc.).

It is probably fair to say that many anthropologists of the present day have an ambivalent attitude toward the Durkheimian project: unable to go along completely, but glad that Durkheim made the arguments he did, for they present, if overzealously, the case for a sociological component of epistemology.

It seems likely that Kant would have rejected the social-functionalist teleology that underlies Durkheimian epistemology. But it is also worth noting that in abandoning metaphysics insofar as the interests of substantive knowledge were concerned, Kant nevertheless pronounced a belief that the metaphysical impulse, like everything in nature, must be "intended for some useful purpose," and bequeathed this impulse to a study that was more broadly conceived than formal epistemology; for "the question does not concern the objective validity of metaphysical judgements but our natural predisposition to them, and therefore does not belong to the system of metaphysics but to anthropology" (1983:102). But that would be another project; here it is enough to call attention to the several possible levels on which Maori cosmology appears to be under a constraint of performance that is more marked than—or perhaps merely of a character different from—that of Western metaphysics. And there are no doubt many other ways in which the two traditions differ.

But such differences do not mean that one tradition cannot shed light on the other, for the differences might be conceived as various deployments of certain possibilities and limitations inherent in cosmology as a project. The foregoing exercise suggests, among other things, certain possibilities of internal structure within cosmological/cosmogonic formulations. It does seem that the complete set of "theses," or alternatively the complete set of "antitheses," can be taken as forming a general strategy of internal cosmological structure, for on many levels the members of each set "go together." For example, a motive force of "spontaneity" would not presuppose an extended temporal duration, while a force of natural causation would seem *ipso facto* to induce a temporal regress of causes. There would seem to be a natural tendency toward proportionality between the degree of qualitative diversity attributed to the cosmos and the extent of the temporal/spatial continuum in which this is thought to develop. *On all these dimensions simultaneously*, the one Maori account, the prose account, seems committed to upholding finite domains, whereas the other account, the genealogical, allows cosmological speculation to proceed at least relatively further—and as though oblivious to any need to posit ultimate limits. There are further ways in which Kant's formulations might be of use in attempting to construct a cross-cultural perspective on cosmology. To the extent that antinomy is a recurrent characteristic of cosmology, one might extrapolate possible strategies of resolving antinomies. Three in particular suggest themselves:

1. To make noncontradiction the preeminent value, thus requiring individual cosmologists to choose dogmatically one side or the other. This seems to be, in Kant's view, the history of Western metaphysics: a permanent wavering, in the debates among different practitioners, between equally defensible positions.

2. To make completeness the preeminent value, or in other words, to make
the first imperative that of thinking out all the possibilities of cosmology, and
then, secondarily, to devise strategies to cope with the necessary consequences
of that mandate, one consequence of which is contradictory accounts. Maori
cosmology might lie somewhere in here. But it must immediately be cautioned
that such a suggestion should not be taken as lending support to the idea,
associated most closely with Lévy-Bruhl, of the existence of a form of non-
Western rationality that is indifferent to contradiction. In Kant's characterization of the antinomies, two imperatives of reason—consistency and completeness—end up opposed to one another. The choice of one imperative, in an
endeavor that precludes attainment of both, cannot count as implying an "indifference" toward the other. As alluded to at several points in this volume,
it is clear that, given the two Maori accounts, efforts are made to harmonize
them insofar as possible—to the extent that the general impression created by
the two accounts is often more of complementarity than of contradiction. If
the Maori allow, or indeed insist upon, opposed accounts both being given a
place, this would seem to be less a matter of indifference to contradiction than
of a positive valuation of rational exhaustiveness. Finally, it should be noted
that a part of Kant's resolution of the third and fourth antinomies consists in
his assertion that the contradiction in these antinomies is merely an apparent
contradiction. Both of the opposed pairs of propositions can be true, because
there is a shift in reference between them.[12] While it is not obvious from the
texts themselves that there is some such shift in reference, or in the "sense"
in which two accounts are respectively held to be true, such a possibility certainly cannot be ruled out.

3. To forswear thinking about such issues, or at least to forswear thinking
about them in the ways that give rise to the antinomies in the first place. This
would seem to form the main thrust of Kant's solution: "transcendental
idealism" is, among other things, an attempt to transcend some (in Kant's view,
very natural) assumptions that are brought to the cosmological endeavor in
its usual, precritical formulation, and which are, Kant argues, the source of
the "illusion" that is demonstrable in the antinomies. Kant's resolution thus
involves a rejecting of the problem itself in its usual definition. There is of
course much to be pursued, and which has been pursued by many scholars,
in the particulars of Kant's reconceptualization of the concerns of traditional
metaphysics. But it should be noted as well that this general kind of resolution—one that rejects or in some way attempts to transcend the usual statement of the endeavor—may not be unique to Kant. Both in the Western cosmological tradition and in some non-Western traditions can be found instances

of cosmological formulations whose essential move seems to be a positing of cosmological problems, and then a rejection (in the form of either total dismissal or radical reformulation) of the very problems that have been posed. Specifically, there is a general similarity between the general conclusion that Kant came to and the general conclusion that, according to Lévi-Strauss's analysis, the Ojibwa, Tikopians, and Bororo come to in their cosmological ventures (see the earlier discussion, pp. 19–23), namely, that at some point the salutary course in regard to those unknowable quanta of our speculations is to confine them to the unknowable, in order to fix our gaze on some finite set within the world that is available to our senses. The sentiment seems also to be in general spirit similar to the anticosmological countercurrent, depicted by Lovejoy, that was engendered by the very cosmological extravagance of the "Great Chain of Being," a countercurrent epitomized in the phrase of Pope (from *An Essay on Man*): "Know then thyself, presume not God to scan; / The proper study of mankind is man."

Maori cosmology is dualistic, and Kant presents a sophisticated characterization of the nature of cosmological thought that argues that this pursuit is in its nature dualistic; in this sense Kant's perspective may be of use in attempting to probe the inner logic of Maori and other similar cosmologies. But of even more direct importance is the suggestiveness of the Kantian perspective in relation to the issue of intercultural comparison—an issue that is at least implicitly present in any study of one culture by a member of another. There is perhaps a natural thrill in discovering exotic phenomena; and there is, in particular, a long-standing European tradition of viewing the South Pacific as a rich source of cultural exotica, a tradition which could be subtly or not so subtly invoked in portraying Maori dualistc cosmology. Here, however, Kant might give the enthnologist reason to pause, for he presents a perspective from which Maori cosmological dualism needs no special or esoteric explanation. In Kant's view, the dialectical character of cosmological thought is no less a fact in the Western cosmological tradition, though the history of metaphysics is the history of the attempt to deny it.

It is of course interesting to speculate about what Kant would have had to say regarding Maori cosmology. To be sure, "transcendental idealism" for Kant formed the only acceptable resolution of the antinomies; yet the recognition of the dogmatic irresolvability of the antinomies was the first step toward this resolution. Kant might have seen the Maori cosmological achievement as having something in common with that of Zeno, as embodied in the latter's famous series of cosmological paradoxes. For even if they did not invent transcendental idealism, the Maori seem to have at least recognized and thus escaped the futility inherent in attempting a dogmatic solution to such issues—an attempt which, suggests Kant (1983:66), "under the name of metaphysics has for centuries spoiled many a sound mind. . . ."

EPILOGUE: HAD DURKHEIM PURSUED THE "TRANSCENDENTAL DIALECTIC". . .

The following comments arise as a thought experiment revolving around the question of the kind of perspective that might have developed had Durkheim, in his dealings with Kantian philosophy, pursued, rather than ignored, Kant's theories about the nature of cosmology as set forth in the "Transcendental Dialectic." The neglect is evident in Boas too; it is as if anthropology, at its founding moment, chose to restrict the inspiration it drew from Kantian philosophy to the first division of the *Critique* only, the "Transcendental Analytic," or the section which sets out the scheme of "*a priori* categories of the understanding." The neglect is notable particularly in light of the fact that Kant himself saw the concerns of the "Dialectic" as necessary entailments of categorial knowledge as set out in the "Analytic." My explorations are motivated primarily by a belief that as the "Transcendental Analytic" served as one of the founding inspirations for what has become a major cross-cultural focus in anthropological theory—that is, the character of categorial knowledge—so the "Dialectic" might, analogously, prove a fruitful source of perspective in the attempt to analyze and understand ethnographic data related to its concern, that is, cosmology; I have also been motivated by the belief that anthropological theory, perhaps partly as a result of this particular founding neglect, is rather undernourished in terms of theoretical perspectives on this topic. Much of my presentation consists in the attempt to utilize aspects of the "Dialectic" in presenting and analyzing data that I have encountered in research on Maori cosmology and the cosmological formulations of other cultural traditions. While my interest in the character and history of the Kantian "Dialectic" flows in part from the "reflexive" concern that has come to be regarded as an intrinsic component of anthropology, there was an even more immediate spur in the efficacy I felt it to hold in the context of the actual practice of ethnographic analysis.

There can be no doubt that one of the moments particularly crucial to the character of contemporary anthropology lies at the end of the nineteenth century, in the projects of Emile Durkheim and Franz Boas, and that the theories of Immanuel Kant occupy a significant place in these projects. For if Durkheim is the source of the French and British anthropological traditions, and Boas of the American tradition, Immanuel Kant is the nearest thing to a common source for these two. Though Boas and Durkheim each developed his own notion of categories, they were united in the general idea that knowledge presupposes a priori categories. Boas carried this idea in the direction of linguistic categories as categories of knowledge. But the Kantian influence is more explicitly and formally evident in Durkheim than in Boas; for this reason my discussion will focus on Durkheim—though with the assumption that much of what is found might also apply to Boas.

Mauss once described the organization of the Durkheimian project in this way: "We have applied ourselves particularly to the social history of the categories of the human mind. We are trying to explain them one by one, starting quite simply and provisionally from the list of Aristotelian categories. . . . We describe certain of their forms in certain civilizations and through this comparison we try to discover their moving spirit, and the reasons they are as they are" (1979:59–60). Mauss goes on to describe the particular projects of the various members of the school; and in his discussion he mentions the following project, which approaches the concerns of the dialectic: ". . . that is how my late colleague, friend and pupil [Stefan Zygmunt] Czarnowski made a good beginning in—but alas did not complete—his theory of 'the fragmentation of the extended,' in other words, of one of the features, certain of the aspects, of the notion of space . . ." (1979:60). One is tempted to add that Zeno would have understood how one who chose the fragmentation of the extended as his topic might experience difficulty in completing the project.

The dominant concern of the "Transcendental Analytic" is with a priori categories of the understanding insofar as they constitute the possibility of natural science, that is, as they constitute the forms in terms of which the human subject synthesizes and judges empirical experience. The dominant concern of the "Transcendental Dialectic" is to expose the character of arguments that develop when the categories of the understanding are pursued beyond any possible experience (as, for example, the category of cause leads one to a regress of causes, prompting the idea of an uncaused cause or first cause). The basic claim was that, pursued in this way—which, for Kant was tantamount to the cosmological endeavor—the categories of the understanding end in antinomies or pairs of equally compelling arguments about the nature of the cosmos, a process and outcome which he referred to as the "antinomy of pure reason."

The particular notion of dialectic at issue here is thus rather specific, and should not be uncritically equated with the many other notions of dialectic present in contemporary sociological discourse, where the term has come to encompass nearly any sort of perspective that involves a movement between two positions or terms. At the heart of the Kantian dialectic is the notion of antinomies, or pairs of equally compelling chains of reasoning leading to and

supporting contradictory propositions. This notion is reminiscent of the dialectic of classical Greek pedagogy, that is, a strategy of argument in which a subtle
interlocutor leads a disciple through paired chains of seemingly unassailable
arguments eventuating in the disciple having to admit that he has assented to
contradictory propositions. Kant came to posit this dialectical form not as a
pedagogical strategy, but "transcendentally," that is, as part of the a priori structure of reason. Though he clearly regarded such a movement as a natural and
inevitable part of human reason, Kant held up as his prime example the tradition of dogmatic metaphysics—specifically its perennial concerns with such
issues as whether there is an infinite regress of causes or a first cause, or
whether matter is infinitely divisible or is composed of ultimate substances.
Metaphysics was a sort of *locus classicus* of the manifestation of this characteristic of reason.

There is a fascinating topic in the issue of why Durkheim allowed himself
to be inspired by only half of Kant's topography of reason, virtually ignoring
the other. This omission reveals some integral aspects of the character of
Durkheimian sociology, aspects which in a general way still seem to inform
the perspective of contemporary anthropology, sometimes with quite ironic
consequences.

But in one sense there is no mystery in the fact that Durkheim ignored the
"Transcendental Dialectic." For Kant himself was essentially dismissive of
the claims of this tradition. One of Kant's main projects was precisely to
demonstrate that the dialectic of traditional metaphysics could contribute
nothing to scientific knowledge. Though the metaphysical application of reason
is natural and inevitable—at points he seems to regard it as an application which
we are led to attempt by the nature of the categories themselves—its inescapable end point is antinomy, and thus the entire project must be discounted
as illusion. One part of the programmatic purpose of the *Critique of Pure
Reason* was to expose the limits of reason, and one of the conclusions was
that the categories should be restricted to judgement of experience. Unlike the
"Analytic," which attempts to characterize what science is, in the form of a
deduction of the conditions of its possibility, the relevance of the "Dialectic"
to science is essentially negative, that is, to expose the pseudo-scientific
character of certain apparent claims of reason, thus producing a rule of
exclusion.

Whether derived from Kant, or from some other aspect of the intellectual
milieu of his time, the attitude that Durkheim reveals toward traditional
metaphysical dialectic, though ostensibly less harsh in tone, in many ways
parallels that of Kant. One of these instances is found in Durkheim's *Evolution of Educational Thought*, a work written in the belief that "we are now

about to enter a new era" (1977:161), and in which Durkheim's own programmatic inclinations are particularly manifest.

> Just as we can see the origin of the enormous importance of dialectic and debate in medieval education, so we can now understand why this importance, which was justified at the time, is no longer relevant to today in its original form. This is because we have evolved an awareness of the nature and value of experimental reasoning. Today we know that there is an alternative method of proof, a different mode of argument; and it is now no less essential that we inculcate this mode of argument in our children than it was necessary to teach the scholars of the Middle Ages the art of dialectic. Moreover, the fact that experimental reasoning should have taken the place of dialectic was an entirely natural development inasmuch as the former is itself a sort of dialectic, albeit of an objective kind. Just as dialectic consists in a systematic confrontation of opinions, so experimental reasoning consists in a systematic confrontation of facts. (1977:154)

Though argued in somewhat different contexts—by Kant in a highly abstract epistemological treatise, by Durkheim in a consideration of practical issues of educational reform—the overall conclusions are related: the traditional dialectic is a kind of proto-science, which must be set in contrast to genuine science. For both Durkheim and Kant, moreover, it was an endeavor not of the hoary past but of a proximate force, the dispatching of which, or reformation of which, formed an immanent part of the inauguration of true science. It should not be forgotten that in asserting the desirability of raising sociology to a "positive science" Durkheim was clearly aligning his project with the evolutionary scheme of Comte. In Comte's view, positive science was the third stage, while metaphysics was the second stage—the stage that science defines itself in proximate opposition to in order to liberate itself from.

The other instance in which Durkheim reveals his attitude toward metaphysical dialectic is in his commentary, in *Pragmatism and Sociology* (1983:28ff.), on a more "embodied" formulation of cosmological paradox, that is, Zeno's famous paradox of the race between the tortoise and the hare. In his discussion of the "Dialectic," Kant accords a special prominence to Zeno, attributing to him the discovery of the fact that rational cosmological inquiry ensnares one intractably in unresolvable paradoxes—from which it is not a great leap to the Kantian antinomies. Durkheim's confrontation with this paradox arose in response to its invocation as a symbol of the spirit of the new philosophy of pragmatism—a philosophy which Durkheim found intriguing but threatening to the character of science and scientific sociology, not to mention French national culture. Both Henri Bergson and William James gave the paradox a new twist, though one which in certain respects was prepared by Kant. For they distinguished between the nature of ultimate reality and the nature of conceptual thought, and took Zeno's paradox as a statement about only the latter: it proved not that there was no motion, but that conceptual thought was incapable of grasping it. Reality was permeated with flux and change, and marked by an infinite number of unique forms and occurrences, whereas conceptual thought was led by the ideal of a finite number of reductive and static categories.

Durkheim was particularly wary of this claim of a "heterogeneity" between the nature of thought and its object, a claim which had as its consequence a fundamental skepticism of the idea that reality, and particularly "life," could be grasped through concepts. Durkheim saw the new cosmological and philosophical spirit as threatening to the foundations of rationalism, and, over against it, reasserted the ideal of the traditional Aristotelian category as the mainstay of all knowledge.

One is reminded of Kant's dependence upon Aristotle in the construction of the "Analytic." Kant (1965:17, 111) claims to have deduced all the "categories of the understanding" from functions of Aristotelian logic, and sees his table of categories as a modification and improvement of a list of the most fundamental categories that had been proffered originally by Aristotle. More will be said regarding Durkheim's confrontation with Zeno; for the present the main point is that there is a kind of parallel between the attitude expressed by Durkheim in this episode and that expressed by Kant in the *Critique of Pure Reason*. Durkheim regarded Zeno's paradoxes as presenting troubling, but not insurmountable, problems for categorial knowledge, whereas Kant enlisted Zeno as an ally in demonstrating specifically the limitations of categorial knowledge. But in their own ways, both Kant and Durkheim affirmed the notion of categories as the basic condition of knowledge, with Aristotle as exemplar; and for both, this possibility was affirmed over against the dialectics of illusion, with Zeno as exemplar. The incident is one that in an extraordinary way prompted Durkheim to probe his own intellectual roots; and we might add that the fact that Zeno had cast the logico-mathematical problem of divisibility in the form of the old and nearly universally known folktale of the race between the hare and the tortoise, turns out to be a not inappropriate vehicle for the confrontation as Durkheim saw it. For it was a confrontation between, on the one side, a set of deftly pitched enigmas, presented with the stylistic flare for which Henri Bergson and William James are both justly famous, and, on the other, the plodding and persistent, but, in Durkheim's mind, ultimately undefeatable, weight of the European rationalist tradition. The issues at the heart of this confrontation arise again in Lévi-Straussian theory, where there is almost certainly a Bergsonian influence (see chapter 1, pp. 34–35). James

(1977:102) was acutely aware of the significance of style in these debates: "The lucidity of Bergson's way of putting things is what all readers are first struck by. It seduces you and bribes you in advance to become his disciple. It is a miracle, and he a real magician." Through Bergson's philosophy James was led to renounce ". . . the current notion that logic is an adequate measure of what can or cannot be" (1977:101). In the same context, James says:

> M. Bergson, if I am rightly informed, came into philosophy through the gateway of mathematics. The old antinomies of the infinite were, I imagine, the irritant that first woke his faculties from their dogmatic slumber. You all remember Zeno's famous paradox, or sophism, as many of our logic-books still call it, of Achilles and the tortoise. Give that reptile ever so small an advance and the swift runner Achilles can never overtake him, much less get ahead of him. . . . (1977:102)

This passage is also overlain with Kant, not merely in the mention of "antinomies," but also more specifically in the comment about awakening from dogmatic slumber, a phrase which Kant uses to identify particularly significant ideas, including the discovery of the antinomies (see Kant 1983:5, 79).

There are, however, also some differences between Kant and Durkheim with respect to such paradoxes. For one thing, Kant saw the dialectical form of such paradoxes—even though a logic of "illusion" (which one would learn through the *Critique* not to attribute scientific claims to)—as a part of the character of reason that could not be avoided in an attempt to map its terrain fully. But there is more, for the dismissal of the scientific claims of metaphysics had certain positive consequences for Kant; and thus, if there are ways in which Durkheim's judgement is less harsh than Kant's, there are other ways in which Kant's judgement is less harsh than Durkheim's. For Kant, the dismissal of metaphysics was a dismissal that cut two ways. If the "Dialectic" showed that concerns of metaphysics could not be matters of science, science was then as powerless to disprove as to prove such concerns. For Kant, one of the consequences of setting the limits of science was a clearing of impediments to religious faith and the idea of moral freedom, issues which were of interest to Durkheim, but not directly implicated by him in the dismissal of metaphysics.

But, as noted earlier, there is another passage in Kant that opens the way for a less harsh, perhaps even positive, final judgement on the metaphysical impulse; and this one should be of special interest to anthropology. The full passage reads as follows:

> We have found that this merely natural use of such a predisposition of our reason, if no discipline arising only from a scientific critique bridles

and sets limits to it, involves us in transcendent dialectical inferences, that are in part merely illusory and in part self-contradictory, and that this fallacious metaphysics is not only unnecessary as regards the promotion of our knowledge of nature but even disadvantageous to it. There yet remains a problem worthy of inquiry, which is to find out the natural ends intended by this disposition to transcendent concepts in our reason, because everything that lies in nature must be originally intended for some useful purpose.

Such an inquiry is of a doubtful nature, and I acknowledge that what I can say about it is conjecture only, like every speculation about the first ends of nature. This conjecture may be allowed to me in this case alone, because the question does not concern the objective validity of metaphysical judgements but our natural predisposition to them, and therefore does not belong to the system of metaphysics but to anthropology. (1983:102)

Kant's notion of anthropology was certainly not in every respect identical with the present-day notion; for example, it had a certain kind of teleological connotation that many contemporary anthropologists might reject (though some forms of teleology, particularly of the functionalist type, are still very common in anthropological theory). But this passage is remarkable for several reasons. It manages to pose in elegantly simple terms what I think can still serve as the most fundamental question to be brought to an inquiry into cosmology: Why do people engage in this endeavor? One does not have to take on Kant's often caustic and illusionist attitude toward this enterprise to agree yet that there is a certain lack of immediately obvious point to it. Cosmologies often deal with spaces, places, and times that are not a part of sensory experience and which often also do not seem to possess any obvious utility. Yet it is often just these realms that are the most densely laden with human significance and value.

In the passage cited above Kant seems to envision the possibility that the metaphysical impulse answers to some telos other than scientific knowledge. It is here that we can particularly feel the irony of the fact that Durkheim ignored the "Dialectic." For Durkheim stepped forward to give what he considered a more adequate—that is, sociological—grounding to the categories of reason which Kant had set out. But then here we have an instance in which Kant admits to an impulse of reason which cannot be grounded in terms of the concern of the *Critique*, that is, in terms of the possibility of knowledge, and which he opens up to a more broadly conceived anthropology—and Durkheim fails to deliver. But at the same time there are a number of interesting quirks in Kant's extremely complex attitude toward cosmology, starting with the fact that metaphysical cosmological speculation is unavoidable yet to be avoided. In the passage above Kant admits to an inability to account for the metaphysical impulse; but in the course of his presentation offers many hints that are worthy of further development.

As noted above, the fact that the spirit of his age and project led Durkheim to ignore the "Dialectic" is a matter with intriguing consequences for the present. For the concerns of contemporary anthropology have come to include numerous interests that fit the spirit of the "Analytic" less comfortably than the spirit of the "Dialectic." These especially include paradoxes, internal contentions, and "multiple readings" within seemingly unitary texts or other symbolic schemata. The basic claim of the "Dialectic" is that reason of its nature cannot but generate contradictory answers when pursuing certain tasks. Yet these are precisely the kinds of issues that Durkheim was led to discount, a founding choice that has worked to deprive anthropology of what might be a fruitful addition to its current perspectives.

The sense of "something left out" that informs my project might also be seen as constituting another dimension of a specific set of dissatisfactions that has arisen in the study of categorial knowledge, a set of dissatisfactions for which the recent work of Lakoff (1987) forms an ambitious attempt at summarizing. Lakoff's work touches on a number of different problem areas, but the criticisms are unified in the general feeling that the idea of what categories are and how they work has hitherto been too tidy. These dissatisfactions have arisen largely by focusing inwardly, so to speak, for many of them have to do with complexities in the principles of inclusion of a given category (particularly those brought about by so-called prototype effects). Kant's "Dialectic," on the other hand, would lead to a concern with another kind of untidiness—one which arises in considering categories outwardly, that is, in terms of their consequences for the nature of consciousness in general. The fact that certain categories by nature seem to lead us beyond any specific empirical application of them forms at least a part of the condition that Kant points to in the opening line of the *Critique of Pure Reason*, with which I began my analysis: "Human reason has this peculiar fate that in one species of its knowledge it is burdened by questions which, as prescribed by the very nature of reason itself, it is not able to ignore, but which, as transcending all its powers, it is also not able to answer." Many of the dissatisfactions of the present are posed as a reaction, in one way or another, against analytical tendencies of structuralism, which tended to assume, not only tidy categorial schemes, but also systems of perfect mapping and/or transformations between schemata, both intra- and interculturally. In light of this situation, at least some of the dissatisfactions of the present have an antistructuralist flavor—ranging from a pointing out of weaknesses to the claim that structuralism is a fundamentally misdirected enterprise. In light of this situation, the Kantian "Dialectic" occupies an intriguing position; for while it is concerned with seemingly bizarre and irrational manifestations of reason, this focus emerges, not as rejection of the categorial view of knowledge on which structuralism depends, but rather in the attempt to demonstrate that such manifestations are an ineradicable accompaniment of knowledge constituted "structurally."

A final point should be made about the focus on Kant. Kant is chosen as a focus less because his perspective contains some previously unglimpsed truth than because it is a very rich and encompassing attempt at a statement on a set of issues that are as old as Western intellectual history, and which, as noted before, Kant himself traces back to the dawn of Western intellectual history, to the paradoxes of Zeno of Elea. But it is as if, historically, there has been a series of parallels in which the value of the outlook summarized in the "Dialectic" is recurrently submerged. We have already mentioned Kant's ultimate dismissal of its scientific pretensions in the *Critique of Pure Reason*, and Durkheim's neglect of this aspect of Kant. My own opening chapters deal with the perspectives on myth of Lévi-Strauss, in which I attempt to show that there are some very terse but highly significant insights that Lévi-Strauss develops out of a perspective directly reminiscent of Zeno's paradoxes or the Kantian antinomies. But here too we see a process of submergence. For while it is difficult to imagine a single anthropologist having had more impact than has Lévi-Strauss, yet the anthropological community's reaction to those particular parts of Lévi-Straussian theory that I treat is reminiscent of Durkheim's reaction to the Kantian "Dialectic," namely, total neglect, or nearly so. So for Lévi-Strauss as for Durkheim and Kant, I have the feeling of holding up for view the part that has been missed. But one must also quickly add that the points in question were treated by Lévi-Strauss himself in only the briefest of terms. So I have no doubt that my attitude toward Lévi-Strauss itself verges on paradox. For on one hand, I see his terse comments as containing some major innovations, which I attempt to carry forward. But on the other hand, given the way in which these concerns are so tersely dispatched, one is almost forced to see Lévi-Strauss as a part of the process of submergence, and in this sense as carrying on not only the positive program but also the exclusions that Durkheim laid down.

Chapter Six

The Quick and the Dead:
The Great Race in North America

Between the two corrals lay the world.
> —from a Jicarilla Apache cosmological narrative

ONE FINDS, then, in Maori cosmogony, formulations that achieve or assert a relation between unity and plurality. In the Arawa case, this is by means of a pervasive notion of separation (any distinct being achieves its distinctness through a process of separation from other entities), a theme that also has a place in the *Whare Wānanga* account though in a different and somewhat reduced way. In the Tūhoe case, there is the notion that a set of phenomenally distinct beings are approximations of (i.e., failed attempts at the creation of) a single ideal form. As different means of holding together a perspective of oneness and a perspective of plurality, either furnishes a fitting point to return to Zeno's paradoxes.

The various paradoxes attributed to Zeno for the most part seem to arise from the problematic of divisibility considered in various contexts or dimensions; and thus the even broader question can be posed: Might it not be possible to turn Zeno around, and use the various paradoxes as a sort of orienting framework or set of cues concerning the features in terms of which and dimensions along which cosmogonic thought is inclined to proceed? Of the four basic topics addressed in Zeno's paradoxes, three—*motion* (about which there are four paradoxes), *plurality*, and *sound* (i.e., the sound of the millet seed)—have already been mentioned; the fourth—*place* (*topos*)—will be added in the discussion that follows.

We begin with the paradox of motion (*kinesis*). Given his reputation as a skilled and subtle dialectician (see especially Kant's [1965:446ff.] discussion of Zeno) there can be no doubt but that Zeno would have leaped at the chance to try the "ped-antics" of his Achilles paradox on Jicarilla Apache cosmologists, one of whom gave an elaborate account of a ritual race. The following is my summary of the race as recounted in Opler 1938; material within quotation marks is quoted directly from the account in Opler:

"The reason for the first ceremonial race was that there was too much food of both kinds, meat and plants, at the same time. The food was all mixed up and people didn't know how to use it. The food did not come in season then as it does now." The sun and moon decided to hold a race; fruit and plants raced on the side of the moon, animals on the side of the sun. The night before the race both sides got together and sang songs "against the opposing side." Two corrals were prepared, one to the east and the other to the west. "Between the two corrals lay the world." The sun's side won, and there was much meat that year, but the crops failed. The sun and moon agreed that they would hold the race every year for four years, and alternated winning during these four years, ". . . because people can't eat meat all the time, and they can't eat vegetables all the time." After the fourth race, the race was given to the Apaches who were told, "If you stop holding this ceremony you will starve." However, the people forgot about the race.

Four large birds started the race again, with a prize of two pretty girls. The birds said, "Things should be different. Now we have everything at once. . . . All kinds of food should not be plentiful at one time. Let it be divided." As the runners assembled for the race, ". . . the others told Gopher, 'You'd better start now. You're so slow that the people will beat you if you don't.'"

> So Gopher, even before all the others had gathered, started off. After he started, Mouse, Frog, and many other animals and birds also started.
> Two of the best runners were Coyote and Water Beetle. They stood to one side and let the others run first. By the time they started, the others were far off and Gopher was nearly half way around. Before these two started, Goose and Sandhill Crane prayed over them and brushed them off with their long wings so that they would run fast.
> "Don't be discouraged. Don't stop," the birds told them.
> Then Coyote and Water Beetle started off towards the west. Both were running fast. Soon they began to catch up with the slower runners who had started ahead of them. . . .
> Now the four big birds came along. They were all in line. One couldn't get ahead of the others.
> They came to the place where Gopher was running. They all stopped. The white-headed bird picked up Gopher and put him on his back, for they felt very sorry for him.

He told Gopher, "Hold tightly. If you fall off it will be your own fault."

Then those four birds started on again. They passed Coyote and Beetle. About four miles from the finish line these four birds began to race in earnest. Each tried his best, but not one could get the advantage. They finished at the same time. But they were all far ahead of the other racers. They went directly past the two girls, paying no attention to them.

But the white-headed bird said to Gopher, "Get off my back now."

So Gopher got off and took one of the girls. Gopher took the girl who stood for the fruit, for the fruit comes from the ground.

Meanwhile Coyote and Water Beetle had been racing. Coyote was one step ahead and he crossed the finish line just a little ahead of Water Beetle. He took the other girl.

Beetle expected to get a girl too, but when he went to claim her, he saw that Gopher was already there.

"I thought we passed Gopher a long time ago," he complained. "So how did he get here first?"

But the four large birds said to him, "No, you must be mistaken. He was here ahead of us."

No one paid attention to Water Beetle.

The race was once again forgotten until some people again decided to have it. This time the sides that were chosen are the two bands of the Jicarilla, the Llanero and the Ollero. "In this way the Llanero and Ollero were formed, and they have raced against each other ever since." (from Opler 1938:80–86)

My summary has left out many of the details; moreover, the race forms only one phase of a long and intricate narrative of the origins of the cosmos. Although the events that transpire in the excerpted episodes resonate with many other episodes, here it will suffice to note that the theme of ambulation occurs in the very first part of the total narration, in the depiction of the creator Black Hactcin's decision to create the various beings of the cosmos, for example:

This is how animals and men first came to be made. Black Hactcin first tried to make an animal. He made it with four legs of clay and put a tail on it. He looked at it. He said, "It looks rather peculiar." Then he spoke to the mud image. "Let me see how you are going to walk with those four feet." That is why little children always like to play with clay images. Then it began to walk.

"That's pretty good," said Black Hactcin. "I think I can use you in a beneficial way." (Opler 1938:2)

In comparing Zeno's Achilles paradox with the Jicarilla account just presented, one finds that both formulations have attached grand cosmological arguments, arguments about the fundamental character of being, to what is basically the same folktale—one of the most widespread in the world—that is, a race between animals won by deceptions perpetrated by the inferior animal's helpers (see the earlier discussion in chapter 1 of the relation of Zeno's problem to the traditional folktale; in the Jicarilla case, it is the middle of the three races—in which Gopher wins and gets the girl—that is built up from this folktale). Many of the details are the same, including the head start for the inferior runner, whose inferiority—which really rests on a basic unfairness in the match and therefore makes the deception forgivable if not admirable— lies in the fact that a land animal is pitted, on land, against what is at best only ambiguously a land animal (the tortoise is a sea animal and the gopher is an underground animal, the differences—land/sea vs. above ground/underground—reflecting the more salient cosmological contrasts of the two cultural areas). They are two similar (that is, diametrically opposed) uses of the same folktale, namely, to argue cosmogony—one for it, the other against it.

As Zeno's Achilles utilizes the relation of difference (in speed) between the two runners to build up a more complex version of the paradox of motion than is present in the Dichotomy—so that the argument is developed from the simple demonstration that any one moving object can never reach a given point, to the demonstration *of the impossibility of a moving object overtaking another moving object*—so, analogously, in the Jicarilla account, the emphasis falls upon the relations that develop between the various entrants in the race, first by the sun and moon alternatingly overtaking one another. The race in fact becomes a means for the creation of more complex temporal periodicities (based on the combination of different individual periodicities), and more generally, an arena for the creation and display of similarities and differences based upon speeds, rhythms, modes, and spaces (e.g., sky vs. earth) of locomotion. A concern with the speed of the universe, or, more precisely, the relative speeds of its various constituents, can be seen in some episodes. For example, the human lifespan was originally correlated with the moon ". . . so that a life was only about thirty days long" (Opler 1938:44); numerous actions were motivated as attempts to improve the situation.

As alluded to earlier, there is some question about why there is an Achilles paradox at all. If one can prove that a given object cannot be in motion, there is a logical redundancy, if not a logical perversity, in then going on to apply essentially the same argument to prove that one moving thing cannot overtake another moving thing. It must be that, responding to the same love of intricate development that is characteristic of many cosmogonies, and which, moreover, is manifest at times (see the previous discussion of the cosmogonic genealogy) in subtle characterizations of negative or privative states, Zeno, in the Achilles, has given in to the cosmogonic impulse in mirror image, that is, in the developing of more complex nonperiodicities or denied periodicities. If, in the Jicarilla myth differences, in speed and form of locomotion serve as a means of display of "difference" more generally, it should be noted that the same tendency to see difference of speed as an axis of difference in general occurs in various developments of Zeno's paradox of motion. There are some tendencies of this sort in Plato's *Parmenides*. The idea that difference in speed betokens difference in kind of thing—or a corollary: that eliminating differences in speed would eliminate differences between things—seems implicit at one point in the treatment given to Zeno in that paragon of Enlightenment wit and wisdom, Bayle's *Dictionary*, that is: ". . . I say that if there was motion, it would be equal in all bodies; there would be no Achilles's and tortoises . . ." (1741:266).

There are numerous other fascinating themes posed in the Jicarilla account, including many manifestations of the broader American Indian disposition to interlink directional, spatial, and color schemes; and further motional schemes such as clockwise and counterclockwise running, and what seems to be an overarching contrast of the movable to the immovable (the North Star and the fire place). Part of the Jicarilla cosmologization of the tale of the race between the animals lies in the adducing of four protagonists rather than the more usual two. The number four almost everywhere in American Indian mythology, and certainly in this Jicarilla tale, carries the connotation of completeness. Moreover in the four main actors in the race, we have a kind of mapping of main regions of the cosmos: Gopher (underground), Coyote (surface of the earth), the bird helpers (sky), and Water Beetle (water). The sky and the underground, widely regarded in the Southwest as regions of great spiritual power, are linked in the cooperation of the bird helpers and Gopher. Anyone familiar with the mythology of the Southwest will know that the scarcity of water forms one of its most persistent obsessions; in this context it may not be accidental that the runner who, as a result of the deception, loses out on the prize (i.e., the possibility to reproduce) is the water animal. A race with *four* main protagonists allows numerous other innovations, one of which is a more complex and interesting deception. An important focus of the account is the race between Coyote and Water Beetle (a land and a water animal, as in the tale of the tortoise and the hare); but the centrality of the contest between these two figures in a sense turns out itself to be an illusion as the race between the land runner and the underground runner becomes more salient.

In relation to the cosmological "reduction" model, which I discussed in detail earlier, the means of the reduction is, in the Jicarilla case, novel; but the novelty of the solution lies in the combining of two themes that we have already seen. For in the Jicarilla case, the establishment of periodicity (which takes place through a race), on the one hand, and the reduction of being, on the other, are intimately fused, such that the former provides the means of the latter. The special genius of the Jicarilla solution lies in its avoiding of any permanent loss of being, through the consigning of two halves of the totality to alternating temporal periods, which amounts to the creation of seasonality. At the cost of allowing only half of all that is possible to be "on stage" at any one time, the necessity for any permanent loss to being is eliminated. While the temporal scheme in the Jicarilla case in one of cyclically alternating periods, and those considered by Lovejoy in *The Great Chain of Being* are evolutionary progressions, nevertheless the Jicarilla solution is in one significant respect reminiscent of Lovejoy's "temporalized" versions of the Chain of Being, namely: in the conclusion that everything that can be ought to be, but not necessarily all at once.

This Jicarilla account contains three phases, in the form of three main races, the race having been twice forgotten and revived. The first race is centered on the fixing of the order of nature through the delimitation of two main types of foodstuffs; the second deals with the original generation of the two great Jicarilla bands; and the third, with maintaining the present order of society on the same dual model, well prepared by the earlier two races—the principle of duality being, next to the race itself, perhaps the most recurrent theme in the account. The event of the race lies somewhere between two concepts frequently opposed in Western thought, that is, sport and ritual: on the one hand there is a competition; on the other hand, there is a precise periodic alternation of winners and losers. It should be noted that the running/race theme occurs within slightly different configurations in adjacent tribal areas as well; in Alfonso Ortiz's *The Tewa World* (1969), these and many other cosmogonic themes are considered specifically in relation to the issues that Lévi-Strauss has raised regarding "dual organization."

The Jicarilla account explicitly calls attention to another sort of reduction in the relation of these phases, that is, in the dimensions or the scale of the race. For the race used to be around the world, but "people now can't run around the world. So they just run between the two points which served as the starting place and the finish of the race around the world" (Opler 1938:86). The current race is a small-scale miniature of the original. The major relations—for example, earth and sky, sun and moon—are worked out first, and the more specific ones are seen as deriving from or being modeled upon these.

While the Jicarilla end up affirming motion and plurality and Zeno seemingly ends up denying them, the fate of the two considerations are, in both cases, seen as interlinked. And, moreover, the threat of conflation that is posed as the Jicarilla original situation ("too much food" which was "all mixed up") rests upon the same general assumption as affords Zeno's basic method of skeptical disproof, namely, the recognition that the necessary consequence of the unrestricted thinking of plurality is the conclusion that plurality cannot be.

The Jicarilla method of dealing with this consequence is to establish a counterposed principle that sets a limit to the probing. The genius of the Jicarilla solution is revealed in yet another way: by virtue of dealing with the problem through an abstract proportion (i.e., of whatever there can be, only *half* will be available at once) it avoids having to deal at all with specific enumerations of quantity (e.g., reduction from six to five, or indefinite to four, as are necessitated in the cases which we already noted). In contrast to finding a limiting principle or counterprinciple, the course followed by Zeno is precisely to carry on with the first principle *ad absurdum*. In that it involves both a first principle and a limiting principle for the first principle, the Jicarilla formulation is, in one sense at least, more complex than Zeno's. Both constructions, Zeno's paradoxes and Jicarilla cosmogony, have permanency as one of their goals. In the Jicarilla case, the original reduction through seasonality ushers in a world order that can be perpetually reaffirmed through the yearly race. And, within the Western intellectual tradition, in the realm of fundamental theory of time, space, and being, Zeno, in the formulation of his paradoxes, has achieved the status of nuisance for all time.

WHY A RACE?

There is a great deal to be explored in the cosmology of the race in North America, and we have a beginning in a journalistic account of the race by Peter Nabokov (1981), an account which moreover summarizes some of the ethnological and mythological background of the ritual race. Here I would like to set forth what amounts to some working hypotheses and perspectives that belong to a larger theoretical analysis I have in progress on this myth/ritual complex in North America and other parts of the world. My observations here are oriented around the question: Of all possible images around which to construct an account of the origin and nature of the cosmos, why choose a race?

One part of the answer would seem to lie in the significance of the skill of speed in various life pursuits, such as hunting and raiding, but also in the maintenance of communication through the vast and efficient messenger network that existed through much if not all of native North America (see Nabokov 1981:11ff., passim). Cosmogonies/cosmologies in general address the issue of "the one and the many," discreteness and interconnection; there could perhaps be no better natural idiom than the runner/messenger as the idiom not so much of the "one" or of the "many" as of the relationship between the two principles. The skill of the hunt involved not only a supreme control of one's own motion, but also the ability to discern distinct varieties specifically through the traces left by their particular forms of mobility.

Another level of analysis will have to do with body symbolism; and here two points seem particularly important. The first has to do with the theme that has been developed in the Durkheimian tradition, especially by Robert Hertz (1978), of the dualism of the body. But while there has been a tendency to carry the theme of the dualism of the body in the direction of opposition, contrast, and even conflict, the Jicarilla accounts can bring home the other side of this image: we have no more immediate and profound image of cooperation than that afforded by the symmetrical halves of the body in the act of locomotion— one of the great achievements of nature, the complexity of which is confirmed in the fact that modern robotics has not yet been able to achieve a robot that can walk.[1] Still, as Hertz and Lévi-Strauss bring to our attention, every bodily symmetry contains a potential asymmetry; the compellingness of the image of bodily symmetry in the Southwest may stem from the fact that this is a model of dualism that embodies the potential of both symmetry and asymmetry, as well as the uneasy relation between them.

The second main point regarding body symbolism begins with the fact that the experience of ambulation is intrinsically an experience of periodicity. The experience of the body is in fact an experience of numerous levels and kinds of periodicities, some of which are largely outside of a human capacity to modify, some of which are within this capacity. The periodicity intrinsically involved in ambulation—repeatedly putting one foot before the other—is a form of periodicity that is relatively controllable from within: we can speed it up or slow it down, and more so to the extent that we are able to engage in physical training of this ability, which, in the case of some of the societies of the Southwest, was frequently extreme. A number of rituals in North America proceed as if there is an attempt to extend that possibility of inner control to the cosmos at large; there are texts that suggest, for example, that a ritual running will hasten the rain, or the ripening of the crops (often involving the runners touching various food products of the earth), as though to align controllable bodily periodicity with the larger, outer periodicity of seasonal crops (e.g., see Parsons 1939:116, 207, 394–95, passim).

Ultimately we can ask whether it is a mere coincidence that Zeno and the Jicarilla Apache (as well as some of their other southwestern neighbors) have chosen to cosmologize the same tale, or whether there might be something that makes this little tale particularly suitable to cosmological speculation.

While a definitive answer to this question is not possible at this point, it is important to note that Zeno and the American Indians of the Southwest are not the only cosmologists to seize on this tale. As already alluded to, within Western intellectual history it is a tale that continues to reemerge in the context of cosmology. This tale, along with other "animal tales," has also been cosmologized in Africa, where it is combined with the theme of mixed messages which account for the present imperfection of the world (so that once again the theme of success and failure implicit in the tale resonates with the universe at large).[2] Walter Burkert (1985:234–46) provides some fascinating information and the beginnings of an analysis of "a curious foot race" run by "grape runners," the outcome of which portended the fate of their city in ancient Greece; Patai (1967) discusses ritualized races of the ancient Middle East that have intriguing parallels to those of the American Southwest.

Two other points might be added about the tale's cosmological potential. The first of these has to do with the relationship that, in the discussion of Maori material, we considered in terms of "freedom" and "necessity" as competing paradigms of "cause." The tale of a race between two animals is broadly spread in North America, occurring frequently as a "smaller" tale, which in some cases is quite reminiscent of the stories known to Western readers, though usually with other main protagonists, of whom Gopher and Coyote are especially common. Besides the choice of animals, certain other characteristics of the tale as it occurs in North America are distinctive to this part of the world. The theme of the wife-as-prize is not uncommon. Another common theme in North America is the race as a life/death wager: the winner will live and the loser will die. The ethos surrounding the race in many of the "smaller" tales seems clearly to be one of competition, with life and death consequences (whether in the immediate death of the loser, or in the winner's gaining the wife as source of the continuation of his life in progeny). Yet in some of the cosmologized races of the Southwest, the competitive element of the race is, minimally, much more ambiguous. The life/death character of the race is preserved, but in the sense of the running of the race as a life/death matter for the society as a whole: it is the society at large aligned for its own life.

> The ceremony was held so that the winners would marry the girls
> and raise children. Thus the people would increase. And the children,
> because the older people couldn't live forever, were taught this ceremony,
> so that people might continue to increase on the earth. And the children
> raced against one another so that the fruits and the animals too would in-
> crease and be plentiful. And each year this must be done or the fruits
> and animals will disappear and the people will starve. (Opler 1938:86)

The race, in short, ends up being at least as much of (what Western scholars would call) a ritual as it is a sport. In the Jicarilla text the race appears to involve competition and openness of outcome, on one hand, and on the other, a certain inevitability in the alternation of winning sides. The cosmological race somehow conflates or transcends the inevitability that Western scholars attach to the notion of ritual and the sense of indeterminacy of outcome that they attach to the notion of sport. The same can be said of many other American Indian "games," such as hoop and pole, which similarly are taken up in major ways within southwestern narratives about the origin of the world. The point I am suggesting might best be put comparatively: If, as I suggest in chapter 5, the Maori seem to handle the dilemma of "necessity" versus "will" in the universe by, in effect, creating two descriptions of the cosmos, one under each principle, certain American Indian groups might be seen as negotiating the same dilemma by focusing upon a single image that somehow embodies at different moments both kinds of "cause" in the universe. Hence the difficulty for Western scholars for whom the dualism—for which Kant's third antinomy is one academic objectification—is not only recognized, but also imposes the sense of an ultimate mutual exclusivity.

There is another possible comparison between Jicarilla and Maori cosmology, one which takes us back to my earlier comments on negation and affirmation (pp. 98–104). Many cosmogonies seem, in the end, to rest on a grand opposition in which *one of the terms is a privative term*; and it is characteristic of privative terms to have more than one opposite; or, to put it another way, a privative term will have a graded opposite—at least we seem to feel that this is so. In the Maori case, the original nothing calls forth as its opposite one thing (Sky and Earth originally as a single entity), two things (Sky and Earth separated), and/or a multitude of things (everything in the universe). But there seems to be a sense in which the *tini*, the multitude, is ultimately the fullest opposite to the nothing. And just as, in the idiom of matter, the multitude may, at least in certain contexts, furnish a stronger counter to the nothing than would one thing; so, in the idiom of motion, might running furnish a more adequate counter to motionlessness than would walking. Both the Maori and Jicarilla cases seem to imply a progression through various grades of opposition: in the Maori case we have one, two, many, perhaps infinitely many; in the Jicarilla case the first thing the creator Hactcins concern themselves with is their creatures' ability to walk; and only later are the creatures taught to race.

Several kinds of evidence in the Jicarilla case suggest that human running itself lies on a scale of motion that extends beyond humans. For example, the runners of the Southwest sometimes carry projectile points in their mouths, a practice which might suggest that running is juxtaposed to an image associated with a more rapid and continuous motion, that of an arrow.[3] The runners also frequently incorporate feathers into their costumes; and in the Jicarilla account the race that is run on the surface of the earth parallels a race of sorts that is run above the earth by birds. The race as it exists today is said to have been reinstigated by four large birds; and in the first reinstigated race these birds are, literally and metaphorically, above the race that they have set up. In their role as helpers, the birds in fact influence the outcome.

The race of the birds above serves as a sort of ideal model for the runners below in several ways, most obviously in the display of the birds' superior speed. An incident in the account suggests that the motion of birds may be internally graded into a slower, flapping (discrete?) form and a faster, flapless (continuous?) kind:

> The four birds were not going to try to win the girls. They had suggested the race for the others. They were going to run, but only to see how the race came out.
>
> . . .
>
> But the four big ones [birds] who had suggested the race soon drew away from the others [the other birds]. They were the swiftest and the ones with much power. They would look at a distant point and draw in their wings and they would already be there. (Opler 1938:84–85)

Besides serving as a model of speed, the flight of the four birds serves as a model of the basic nature of the race, specifically that it will be a race that no one wins, or rather that everyone wins—a race run for the sake of totality:

> About four miles from the finish line these four birds began to race in earnest. Each tried his best, but not one could get the advantage. They finished at the same time. But they were all far ahead of the other racers. (1938:85)

But I would add one more point about the cosmological potential of the "tortoise and the hare": It is as though it is intrinsic to this tale that it subverts its own obvious moral. Nominally about physical speed, it proceeds to disclose itself as a tale about thought, about cleverness (cf. Detienne and Vernant 1991:13)—so that while fast emerges as better than slow, smart emerges as better than either. It is ultimately a tale that exists to advocate clever thinking—a perhaps not inappropriate prescription given the cosmologist's daunting intellectual task.

THE OTHER PARADOXES

Since it figures centrally in the cosmogonic analytic of Lévi-Strauss with which this investigation began, the theme of motion has been considered in

some detail here. The foci of the other three paradoxes will be mentioned only
very briefly and in the most general terms, in effect leaving the main work of
exploring any implications to some future time—which is not, however, in any
way to suggest a lesser significance.

> Simplicius:
> Zeno's argument seemed to do away with place, putting the question as
> follows: if place exists, in what will it be? For every existent is in some-
> thing; but what is in something is in a place. Place therefore will be in a
> place, and so on *ad infinitum*: therefore place does not exist. (Lee 1967:37)

The concern with place in cosmogony is one that spans every level of formulation from the most concrete to the most abstract. In the *Whare Wānanga*
account (Smith 1913) separation of sky and earth is first broached in a way that
would seem to indicate the recognition of the necessity for a first "here" versus
"there":

> "Me wehe o tatou matua i konei, kia tau ke Rangi, kia tau ke Papa ki te
> whanga." (22)

> "Let us now separate our parents that Rangi and Papa may occupy dif-
> ferent places." (121)

Smith's translation is a bit loose; the line suggests that Sky is set in one place,
and that Earth is set beside Sky. A basic contrast of spatial placements and/or
configurations, in some versions expressed in the idea that Sky stands above
while Earth lies below, is frequently made explicit in the first great separation.

We have already noted that a main theme in the later phases of this account
is the attacks on the surface of the earth by Whakarū, which are responsible
for the origins of the bends in the rivers and other topographical idiosyn-
crasies—a theme matched by the Arawa account in the recounting of the battle of Tāwhiri against the beings of the earth. Among the various tales of the
culture-hero Māui is an account, having numerous parallels throughout the
Pacific, in which the land originates, alternatively, by being fished up from
the sea by Māui and his brothers; as in the previous examples the topography
of the earth is seen as originating in the degeneration of a previous form. In
the *Whare Wānanga* account (Smith 1913) we find the following incident:

> Ka mea nga tuakana kia kotikotia te ika; ka mea a Māui-tikitiki, "Ata
> waiho te ika na kia takoto ana, kia mataotao ka kotikoti ai." Kaore i
> whakarongo mai nga tuakana me o ratou hoa; ka rere ki te kotikoti haere
> i taua ika. Koia i kino ai te takoto o te ika nei—e tu nei nga pae-maunga.
> Mehemea i kore te takatakahia e nga tuakana, e kore e penei te takoto o
> taua ika nei. (66)

> The elder brothers now wished to cut up the fish; but Māui said, "Let the fish remain there quietly until it is cool, and then cut it up." But the elder brothers and their companions would not listen, and at once proceeded to cut up the 'fish.' Now hence is the broken nature [of the surface] of the 'fish' with its many mountains. If the elder brethren had not trampled all over it, the 'fish' would not present the [broken] appearance it does. (180)

These attempts account for the irregular features of the landscape today. Still later phases of cosmogony/history are replete with various voyages and treks, linking motion and place, in the course of which the great ancestors create and name the particular, distinctive features of landscape that figure in tribal identities (cf. Salmond 1982). Ancestral treks at various levels of time are stock-in-trade of cosmogony. There is the opportunity for exploring the different developments of this theme, one elementary contrast lying in the linear configurations found in some North American cases versus the circular configurations found in some Austronesian instances.

So central is the concern with place(s) in most cosmogonies/cosmologies, that to say that cosmology is interested in topology is a near tautology. Polynesia is not the only part of the world in which the plane on which humans live is envisioned as enshrouded by numerous layers of heavens; in such heavens within heavens one recalls Zeno's sense of the nature of place, such that any place must be within a place, and so on.

The paradox of "sound" (*psophos*) was alluded to earlier, but here it is quoted more fully:

> Simplicius:
> "Tell me, Protagoras," he said, "does a single grain of millet or the ten thousandth part of a grain make any sound when it falls?" And when Protagoras said it did not, "Then," asked Zeno, "does a bushel of millet make any sound when it falls or not?" Protagoras answered that it did, whereupon Zeno replied, "But surely there is some ratio between a bushel of millet and a single grain or even the ten thousandth part of a grain"; and when this was admitted, "But then surely," Zeno said, "the ratios of the corresponding sounds to each other will be the same: for as the bodies which make the sounds are to one another, so will the sounds be to one another. And if this is so, and if the bushel of millet makes a sound, then the single grain of millet and the ten thousandth part of a grain will make a sound." This was the way Zeno used to put his questions. (Lee 1967:109)

Surely sound is one of the main foci in origin accounts. It is almost infinitely modulatable simultaneously in various dimensions (pitch, volume, timbre, etc.), and this no doubt accounts for the commonness of themes of speaking, singing, chanting of the world into being, under the general paradigm that modulation of sound = modulation of being. Additionally, sound is the primary medium of human language, so all that belongs to language can figure in creation or origin accounts. And finally sound, particularly as music, is highly layerable, so that it has served as a model not only of modulation, separation, or differentiation, but also of the integration of the parts, the "harmony of the spheres."[4] Neither the Maori nor the Jicarilla origin account would appear to be a case in which sound is a central focus. And yet in Maori accounts there are sometimes "first rumblings" in the cosmogonic genealogy. And in the Jicarilla account there are sessions of—specifically dual or one might say "antiphonal"—singing between the two competing groups, so that the dualities of sound, place, and society become linked assertions.

Besides cueing one to the significance of the element of sound in traditional cosmogony, the Millet Seed, it should also be noted, has bequeathed an enormous legacy in the analytical study of perception, particularly as regards the concept of sensory thresholds. There is no evidence that Zeno had a concept of thresholds or that he recognized that the range of sensory apparati could constitute a separate problem—that is, a problem with a potentially different solution—from the problem of the divisibility of the object itself. The Millet Seed, however, does occur in Aristotle with the sense of two distinct issues: "A difficulty might arise as to whether, if every body is susceptible of infinite division, its sensible qualities, *e.g.*, colour, flavour, smell, weight, sound, cold and heat, lightness, hardness and softness, are also so susceptible, or is this impossible?" (1957:261). Aristotle's solution rests in part upon, as do many others of his treatments of Zeno, an implication of his distinction of potential and actual:

> . . . we must realize the difference between the potential and the actual;
> it is because of this that, when a grain of millet is looked at, the ten-
> thousandth part of it cannot be seen, although vision has covered it all,
> and the sound of quarter-tone escapes us, although one can hear the
> whole continuous scale; but the interval between the extremes escapes
> us. The same thing is true of all very small quantities in the other sensi-
> ble objects; potentially they are visible but not actually, unless they are
> isolated from the whole. (Potentially the one-foot length exists in the
> two-foot length, but actually only after its division.) Such small incre-
> ments, when isolated, might well be merged in their environment, like a
> flavoured droplet when poured into the sea. But it is important to realize
> that as the increment of sense is not perceptible by itself, nor isolable
> (for it exists only potentially in a more distinctly perceptible whole), so
> neither will it be possible actually to perceive its equally small object

when separated from the whole, yet it will be perceptible; for it is so already potentially, and will become so actually by aggregation. (1957:263–65)

The centrality to the human sciences of questions of sensory boundaries and thresholds is generally recognized, but at the same time the topic would profit from a study of all the particular transformations that it has undergone. It is more than just one particular empirical issue: it ends right at the center of many perspectives. For example, there is Boas' concern with perception of color and sound (e.g., see Stocking 1974). These issues were also at the center of the great confrontation between Charles Darwin and Max Müller, the latter of whom wrote: "The admission of this insensible graduation would eliminate, not only the difference between ape and man, but likewise between black and white, hot and cold, a high and a low note in music: in fact, it would do away with the possibility of all exact and definite knowledge, by removing those wonderful lines and laws of nature which change the Chaos into a Kosmos, the Infinite into the Finite, and which enable us to count, to tell, and to know" (1873:668).

The paradox traditionally labeled as "plurality" might also be called the paradox of "what is" (ta on), the latter being the specified subject—the issue being whether "what is" can be plural. It differs from the other paradoxes primarily in this designating of a maximally nonspecified subject. If, in the focus on motion, there is an analogy between Zeno's paradox of motion, on one hand, and the Jicarilla account considered above, on the other, then there is an analogy between Zeno's paradox of "what is," on the one hand, and what I called the metaphysical level of the Arawa account considered earlier, on the other. For the underlying, recurrent theme of separation in the latter would seem to indicate a concern with the divisibility of being considered immediately and generally, as opposed to the Jicarilla formulation, which considers the divisibility of being through a particular designated intermediary focus, that is, motion.

The foci of the four paradoxes all seem to be at the heart of at least some cosmogonic formulations; more commonly, several or all are intertwined in complex ways in the same formulation, perhaps one or the other being given particular prominence. It is as if Zeno were attempting to isolate the various foci that cosmogonic argument seeks to pile up or interweave, in order to confront them one by one, and thus systematically demonstrate the problematic character of this form of discourse.

THE ORIGINS OF THE ANALYTIC

It is possible that—in some way—that is what Zeno was trying to do: isolate the essential foci of cosmogonic argument. There is a long-standing issue in Zeno scholarship, quite analogous to one brought to the fore in the study of mythology by Lévi-Strauss, of whether there is a larger view or project—which Zeno himself never explicitly articulates—lying behind the various paradoxes, or, in other words, whether the paradoxes form some sort of "set." The most consistently drawn-upon theory of the unity of the paradoxes is the suggestion, found in Plato (*Parmenides*), that the paradoxes are various specific arguments designed to defend the teachings of Parmenides.

Our knowledge of Parmenides is even more tenuous than our knowledge of Zeno, partly because, in addition to the small and fragmentary nature of the texts, they are, additionally, poetically and otherwise obscure. The textual obscurities have given rise to a variety of extremely complex arguments regarding the substance of the Parmenidean doctrine. For present purposes, most of the finer issues can be put to the side. But there is one general point, on which there does not appear to be any great dispute, that is of great interest here: Parmenides' poem "On Nature"—which is all that really remains, and only in fragments—is by quantity at least half devoted to the rendering of a traditional cosmogony similar to and perhaps drawn from Hesiod's *Theogony* (see Kirk, Raven, and Schofield 1983:244, 254, 257).

Parmenides' poem is based on a contrast between two paths or roads, that of truth (*aletheia*) and that of opinion (*doxa*). The cosmogony is confined to, or, rather, constitutes the major theme of, the latter (*doxa*), while the first part of the poem (*aletheia*) appears to be defined over against the cosmogonic part.

The poem begins with the general declaration that it is necessary to learn two ways (from Fragment 1), following Taran's (1965) translation:

> It is necessary that you shall learn all things, as well the unshaken heart
> of well-rounded truth as the opinions of mortals in which there is no true
> belief. (1965:9)

The second main part of the poem, the cosmogonic part, begins with the basic point of the separation of light and night (Fragment 9):

> But once all things have been named Light and Night and these (i.e.,
> Light and Night) according to their meanings have been attributed to
> these things and to those, all is full at the same time of Light and
> obscure Night. . . . (1965:161)

Other themes that are touched upon in opinion are (Fragment 11):

> How the earth and the sun and the moon and the common ether and the
> heavenly milky way and the outermost Olympos and the fiery stars
> strove eagerly to come into being. (1965:166)

A number of comments on opposition and generation (Fragments 12, 17):

In the middle of these is the goddess who governs all things. For everywhere she is the beginner of union and of painful birth, sending the female to unite with the male and again to the contrary the male with the
female. (1965:166)

When woman and man mix the seeds of Love, the power which is
formed in the veins out of different blood, if it maintains proper proportion, produces well-formed bodies. (1965:172)

A comment that some scholars believe to be a reference to a theory of
embryology, that is, that different-sex embryos belong to different sides of the
womb (Fragment 17):

On the right, boys; on the left, girls. (1965:171)

And the summary line (Fragment 19):

So, according to belief, these things were born and now are, and from
now on they will grow and will afterwards perish. For each of them men
posited a distinctive name. (1965:172)

The first part of the poem invokes a contrasting view that appears to be defined over against the latter part (Fragment 8):

. . . that Being is ungenerated and imperishable, whole, unique, immovable,
and complete. It was not once nor will it be, since it is now altogether,
one, continuous. For, what origin could you search out for it? How and
whence did it grow? (1965:85)

Admittedly there are many problems with the precise meaning of such
statements, and also with the exact significance and intention of the contrast.

But, regarding Zeno, one interpretation, as noted earlier, suggests that the
paradoxes were attempts to defend the teachings of Parmenides against the
charge of absurdity by showing that the logical consequences of such notions
as plurality, motion, and change were no less absurd. There is also a more
"nihilistic" interpretation of Zeno, based in part upon certain fragments that
could suggest that Zeno turned his dialectical skills against the notion of the
one, as well as the notion of plurality. The nihilistic interpretation, while rejecting the idea of Zeno as mere apologist, does not necessarily reject the idea
that Zeno's doctrines were connected with Parmenides'. The nihilistic view
sees Zeno as doubly skeptical, and the point of the paradoxes to be something
more like an exercise in sophistry.

But, whichever, the overall significance for present purposes is simply this:
if two millennia later, the central elements of Zeno's paradoxes show up in

Lévi-Strauss's attempt to develop an analytic of *specifically* cosmogonic thought, this may be the case by virtue of something other than a mere quirk; for as suggested in the foregoing excursion, there is good reason to suppose that the paradoxes originated within an intellectual project defined—in some central even if not fully understood way—as just that: a critical analysis of cosmogonic thought (developed, incidentally, in relation to a cosmogony whose basic format is not wholly unlike that of the Maori). And, thus, the relation of (one part of) Lévi-Strauss to Zeno would rest on not only (as discussed in the first part of my argument, regarding "the Great Race"), a continuity of method, but also a continuity of object—or one might even say, a continuity of entire intellectual project.

In a curious way, the nihilistic interpretation of Zeno's teaching has some affinities with Te Rangikaheke's teaching, in which, similarly, it would appear that neither of the two ontologies emerges as wholly unproblematic. In the latter teaching, as seemingly the only alternatives, both conditions are retained by consigning one (that is, the "one" and "undivided") to a time in the past, so that there is a description of being that no longer fully obtains. But though confined in fullest expression to one end of time (but which end of time for the Maori is more real or important?), that first state is still always ritually and otherwise recallable. Moreover, by being the first state, that condition is permanently installed as the archetypal oneness that permits conditions of more particular (e.g., sociological) oneness. The significance of the underlying and embracive process of separation lies in the interrelating of the two conditions, so that things that are now discrete are still always also one by virtue of having once been so. The question can at least be posed, Can any society do fully without some version of both ontologies? There would seem to be the possibility of viewing cosmogony as comparative ontology, that is, a given society's comparisons, within cosmogonic formulations, of different possible ontologies.

Beyond the paradoxes there is also a kind of paradox in the fact that what is certainly the West's "longest running" cosmogonic analytic derives seemingly from an anticosmogonic outlook. It is a complex issue and may be ultimately related to the question of why the mythologies of some societies spend so much time talking about what is distinctly asserted to be not, or no longer, the case. In such instances, it may be that a specifically problem-savoring orientation provides the condition suitable for the isolating of key lines of argument, in order to confront them. Zeno does seem to have been successful in isolating, in the topics of the various paradoxes, several essential, recurrent foci of cosmogonic argument. The principle that defines the various paradoxes as a "set" may indeed be this: central foci of cosmogonic argument.

If this is so, does it mean that one should expect that these foci necessarily provide the dimension for describing all possible cosmogonies? No, there is no possible way to claim in advance that they should. And, moreover, four such foci could at most constitute only the very rudiments of a general perspective. But if it be acknowledged that the four foci that are isolated in the paradoxes are unlikely to provide anything more than the rudiments of a perspective, it should not necessarily be concluded that Zeno himself did not get very far in what might have been his project. For there is evidence that would suggest that most of Zeno's ruminations have been lost—that, for instance, Zeno had composed an entire book of paradoxes (see, e.g., Sorabji 1983:321; Barnes 1982:233ff.), of which what remains is only a small part. As regards Zeno, then, the Western intellectual tradition, quantitatively, may have sustained a loss of the same proportions as the disaster which befell the original Tikopian foodstuffs: only four have been salvaged. Once more reminiscent of Tikopia, Plato (*Parmenides*) has Zeno report that his original totality was *stolen*. And therefore, one who now finds some intellectual prospect for Zeno's perspective is faced immediately with the possibility of having to work with a drastically impoverished set of tools.

On the other hand, however, perhaps it is after all just as well that most of the paradoxes have been lost. The ones we do have are good ones, and not even solved. It is worth noting that, of the four paradoxes dealing with motion, one of these, that of the Flying Arrow, is often confused in the popular mind with that of the Dichotomy (as if the argument is that the arrow cannot hit the wall because of continually halving distances, whereas the real argument, whose details are irrelevant here, is somewhat different) (see, e.g., Lee 1967:53–55, 78ff.). Even in their sparsity they are sometimes mixed up. The truth of the matter is: we can't even handle the few miserable remnants we do have. It would appear that, as in the case of an individual memory, the process of collective historical memory is mercifully unreliable. As the intellectual history of the idea of "Zeno" shows, we can do more with him precisely because we have so little to work with.

Certain minds depend upon a sense of loss. If all had been saved, it is questionable whether, for instance, Nietzsche would have written, from the perspective of a culture which since that first creative moment had continually sought to abandon its endowment, his paean to Parmenides and the other pre-Socratic philosophers (*Philosophy in the Tragic Age of the Greeks*). Quite apart from the technical arguments that he presents regarding the deficiencies of later philosophy, one cannot help wondering whether Nietzsche's ratings did not tend to rise precisely in proportion to the fragmentariness and irrecoverability of the object. Even if there never were a complete book, someone would have had to invent the idea that there had been.

Worst of all, there is the possibility that what has been lost would reveal that our ancestors were bigger than we by less than some of us might care to imagine. Even from the few paradoxes that are left, a possibility distinctly suggests itself: far from the boundlessly fertile spirit that Nietzsche would have preferred, Zeno was pretty much a one-paradox author. But whether or not one really does possess the original totality, it might in general foster an attitude more favorable to scholarship and life to be convinced that whatever one has at hand is only the detritus of what was originally.

MAGICAL ARROWS, OR MAN THE HUNTER

Cosmological narratives are frequently also narratives about the very nature of knowledge and discovery. Idioms appropriate to the depiction of the cosmos dovetail with the figures through which the intellect represents its exploratory activity to itself. Such cosmological/epistemological dovetailing is suggested in the enigmatic fourth chapter of Detienne's *Creation of Mythology*, a treatise that in a broad way attempts to sketch a topography of human understandings of the past, and which seems to be aimed specifically at formulating an origin myth for the idea that *to talk about knowledge is to talk about distance.*

One of Detienne's most persistent concerns is the difference in forms and processes of knowledge that stem from the differences between written and oral/aural knowledge transmission. Writing in this view introduces the potential for certain kinds of fixidity precluded by oral/aural processes; for example, ". . . the very substantiality of the 'graphic' or printed manuscript allows a work to wait, for centuries if necessary, before producing its effect and finding readers, almost impossible to imagine. Whereas every oral production, if not immediately received by attentive ears and rescued from the silence that immediately threatens it, is destined for oblivion and instant annihilation as though it had never been spoken" (1986:39). While some forms of self-commentary are characteristic of all societies, the critical distance necessary for recovering and "interpreting" texts is a possibility that comes to be through writing. "That is precisely what changes with regard to the contemporaries of Xenophanes. There appears a distance that is either a wish to throw out material or a feeling of discontinuance but always that which makes possible criticism of tribal stories: that is, writing, like something alien, like another place whence is spoken and written the discourse on tradition" (1986:68–69).

The phrase "another place" of course exemplifies the bonding of the concept of distance to that of critical knowledge; Detienne's discussion is, tactically, replete with self-exemplifications of the tendency that he is investigating. And many of the specific exemplifications bring us back, both in the abstract and concrete, to the images displayed by Zeno. For example, the work of the student of myth is like a hunt: "However confused he may be in choosing between trickery and vagabond pleasure, the 'myth' hunter will not be surprised to find that in the land of beginnings, at this season in History, the 'pure' tracks as they are called in *L'art de la chasse* are mingled with others, mixed up and so faint that the scent, the technical term used by hunters, seems to have vanished. He will be even less surprised to find that his hare makes its form in the sites of illusion" (1986:63).

Whether or not one accepts the notion of a historical moment of origin for a certain kind of critical distance, this discussion is useful in calling attention to the existence of certain topographically inclined figures of speech which have had illustrious double careers, in cosmology and epistemology. Notable among these is the arrow in flight, invoked by Zeno as a multileveled image, perhaps suggesting the hunt, but in a removed sense: the hunt as the metaphor of the mind's activity.

While the arrow in flight is one of the best known of the Zenoian images, the particular way in which Zeno developed the mathematical argument has, in the case of the arrow, proved less than evident; and, at least in the popular mind, the image of the arrow in flight has simply been assimilated to the mathematical model associated with the Achilles and the Dichotomy. There are numerous commentaries on the purport of Zeno's technical argument; for present purposes, however, the concern is not with these, but with the image itself.

For Zeno is not the only cosmographer who perceived a certain mystery, as well as a cosmological import, in flying arrows. Arrows, darts, and other sorts of projectiles are an object of fascination and a vehicle of cosmological contemplation in many cultures. The arrow is a recurrent figure of speech in contemporary astrophysical cosmography, for example, in the grand phrase "the arrow of time."

One of the widest spread folkloric motifs in the world is the motif of an explorer who, in repeatedly tossing a magic arrow, or some other projectile, in front of himself and then continuously catching up to it, traverses hitherto unknown terrains (for a summary see, for example, Thompson motifs D1092, D1314.1, D1526.1, H125.4, H1226.2). There are several Polynesian variants (for a survey of these see Dixon 1916:75ff.). Among these are some rather obscure Maori texts in which the explorer follows a magical *teka*, or spear (Williams' Maori dictionary defines it as a "*dart* thrown for amusement"), in a search for notable women (the explorer's wives or sister) (Hongi 1896a, 1896b). The women are associated with greenstone, a preeminent cultural valuable, and the route of the journeys, among other things, accounts for the distribution of greenstone. Embedded in these same accounts are other central cultural themes, including the cooking and defilement of food.

Lucretius, in *On the Nature of the Universe*, at one point argues for the infinitude of the universe in a formulation that combines the ambulatory idiom (which he associates with the idea of finitude) with the flying dart (which he associates with the idea of infinitude). The scenario seems to project a sense of the locomotive limitation that humans feel vis-à-vis things in flight, for the argument is that, even if one can imagine a border to the universe beyond which one cannot walk, one can disprove such a possibility by invoking the image of a projectile in flight.

> Suppose for a moment that the whole of space were bounded and that someone made his way to its uttermost boundary and threw a flying dart. Do you choose to suppose that the missile, hurled with might and main, would speed along the course on which it was aimed? Or do you think something would block the way and stop it? You must assume one alternative or the other. But neither of them leaves you a loophole. Both force you to admit that the universe continues without end. Whether there is some obstacle lying on the boundary line that prevents the dart from going farther on its course or whether it flies on beyond, it cannot in fact have started from the boundary. With this argument I will pursue you. Wherever you may place the ultimate limit of things, I will ask you: "Well then, what does happen to the dart?" The upshot is that the boundary cannot stand firm anywhere, and final escape from this conclusion is precluded by the limitless possibility of running away from it. (1975:55–56)

In the course of the passage the dart becomes an intellectual dart, the pursuit an intellectual pursuit.

There is a !Kung Bushman myth about the origin of cooking fire that has been studied by Isaacson (1987) in the context of archaeological evidence and of Lévi-Strauss's concern with this theme. The first part tells of the chance discovery by the hero, ≠Gao!na, of food cooked by a character named /Kai/Kini, who, however, would always hide the fire sticks after cooking.

> After a while ≠Gao!na said, "Now we must make a game to play," and he made a *jani* toy, mounting it with a guinea-fowl feather, weighting it with a *tsi* nut. He tossed it into the air with his stick and, when it floated down, ran and caught it and tossed it up again and again without its ever falling to the ground. /Kai/Kini wanted to play. ≠Gao!na gave him the *jani*, but /Kai/Kini could not toss it high and did not get away from his house in following it. ≠Gao!na said the guinea-fowl feather was no good,

they must put a big paouw feather on it. This they did and the *jani* flew high. ≠Gao!na then opened the wind and the wind blew from the eastern side and blew the *jani* toward the west. /Kai/Kini followed and followed it, fascinated, tossing it higher each time he caught it. ≠Goa!na followed /Kai/Kini and, when they came to the place where the fire sticks were hidden, he seized them and ran with them into the veld. As he ran he broke them into little pieces and then threw them the whole world over. "All the world is going to get fire now," he said. "Fire, fire, go over the world." Since then there has been fire in every piece of wood and all men can get it out and cook their food. (Marshall 1962:233)

A recent interviewer (Streitfeld 1991) of novelist Mark Helprin reported, "All Helprin's fiction is written in the same manner. Standing in his expansive backyard, he demonstrates his method of composition by picking up an imaginary rock and flinging it. . . . "I take the last line," he explains, "and I throw it as far as I can. And then I walk to it. It's as simple as that." The common thread in these diverse scenarios is the theme of the projectile in flight leading the hurler across some major watershed in the development of the character of human intellect or culture. The popularity of the image is, no doubt, partly a reflection of a mere fascination with flight: the geometry (the pure line or curvature) of the projectile's course; the motion, color, shape, and speed of the projectile itself; or the possibility of escape from human confinement to the surface of the earth. But the projectile in flight appears also to be a kind of natural metaphor of discovery and transition—and of particularly transcending discovery, involving the crossing of some major horizon. This is the case, perhaps doubly so, in Zeno, where the impasse of the arrow is presented as the fulcrum for the transition to critical thought.

The image of the projectile-hurling explorer is an intriguing one, because it presents the process of discovery as something that is, in a way, within one's control (one tosses a part of one's life-equipment into some unknown region), and, in a way, outside of one's control (one tries to catch up with what one has instigated). Zeno's paradoxes are an important item of equipment from the Western intellectual tradition on the topic of cosmology. "Ether" is the possibility of rapprochement (which is not to say identity) between the different places of the universe. Zeno, in part because of his reluctance to be comfortable with the pedestrian certainties that surround him, provides one way for a comparative cosmologist to gain a toe-hold in the universe—or so I have attempted to show with this "trial balloon."

Notes

Works Cited

Index

Notes

CHAPTER 1. THE GREAT RACE

1. Perhaps the most recurrent general thesis about the nature of myth in Lévi-Strauss's theoretical writings consists in the notion, broached in "The Structural Study of Myth," that "mythical thought always progresses from the awareness of oppositions toward their resolution" (1967:221). The notion continued to inform centrally all Lévi-Strauss's later researches on myth, including "The Story of Asdiwal" and various parts of the *Mythologiques*. So central was this notion of the mediation of oppositions that in that same early essay it was implicated directly in an attempt to account for the proliferation of different myths in a given society—or in other words, to give an account of the age-old anthropological problem of "the growth of mythology": ". . . since the purpose of myth is to provide a logical model capable of overcoming a contradiction (an impossible achievement if, as it happens, the contradiction is real), a theoretically infinite number of slates will be generated, each one slightly different from the others. Thus, myth grows spiralwise until the intellectual impulse which has produced it is exhausted" (1967:226).

But despite the certain and universalistic tone in which these notions were proffered, it was but a short time until a countertheme began to show itself, that is, an interest in myths, or certain types of myths (generally cosmogonic in nature) that were perceived as though their purpose and nature were opposite to what was proclaimed in those first bold generalizations. In the counterperspective, the work of myth is seen as lying not in mediating oppositions or contradictions, but precisely in creating and insuring their possibility.

The notion of myth as generically mediatory was announced early and with fanfare. The countertheme crept in almost unnoticed. Or, perhaps it was precisely the certainty of the early pronouncements that necessitated that the later emendation—in the direction of an enlarged and diversified view—be put on record quietly and without drawing attention to itself. It would not be the first time that a great comparative mythologist found himself "boxed in" by his own architectonic inclinations (see my discussion of Max Müller [Schrempp 1983]). The former—mediatory—perspective became the charter of a certain type of mythological "normal science," spawning the desire both to apply the method and perspective to new data and to explore the development and nature of Lévi-Strauss's thought in itself. The counterperspective has not received such attention.

The presence of the counterperspective confirms in a way the perspective out of which it grew. For it turns out that Lévi-Strauss's analytic of mythology is thus itself constituted as an opposition—or even a contradiction—between two theories about the general nature of myth and the work that it does. It is almost as if the first (mediatory) theory of myth unwittingly projects, chiasmatically, a mirror image of itself in the form of an opposite theory.

But the opposition in Lévi-Strauss's theory of myth may also offer a valid insight into the nature of myth; the "world of myth" itself may be organized on different levels, at odds with one another. Behind all the myriad human disasters that form the subject matter of myth lies the possibility of an even greater human disaster, that is, the possibility—which can at least be imagined—that conditions under which the ensemble of scandals that constitute the human world could not exist.

2. There is an interesting discrepancy between the prose and diagrammatic representations of the Bororo situation, one that can perhaps be described in terms of the distinction made by Aristotle (in T1, above), namely, that "there are two senses in which length and time and, generally, any continuum are called infinite, namely either in respect of divisibility or of extension." For Lévi-Strauss's prose version of the original Bororo situation seems to be governed by the threat of infinity in respect to divisibility, inasmuch as the account posits two fixed outside borders to the continuum in the form of two clans (". . . we should run the risk of finding that between any two given clans or communities there was an unlimited number of other clans or other tribes . . ."). If one wants a diagram that corresponds to Lévi-Strauss's prose description, the one that is typically associated with Zeno's paradox of the "Dichotomy" will work perfectly. Other, less well-known paradoxes of Zeno (particularly the paradoxes that address plurality and place) indicate that not only was Zeno doubtful of the possibility of motion expressed in the form of a passage from one thing or place to another; he was also equally doubtful of the possibility of any two things or places. Zeno's doubts about the possibility of motion, plurality, and place are in many ways different expressions of the same master-doubt. In much the same way that Zeno was concerned with the problem that infinite divisibility presents to the possibility of any two things or places, so Lévi-Strauss is concerned with the logical problem that infinite divisibility presents to the possibility of any two clans.

But while Lévi-Strauss's *prose* version of the Bororo initial situation appears to be conceptualized in terms of the threat of infinity with respect to divisibility, the *diagrammatic* representation of the same original situation, as also that of the Tikopian original situation, appears to be conceptualized in terms of the threat of infinity with respect to expansion; "etc." in each case appears to signify that the line is to be taken as infinitely extendable to the right by the addition of further segments, the Tikopian line, always by equal-length ones, the Bororo line, always by increasingly shorter ones. As the prose description of the Bororo case corresponds to Zeno's Dichotomy, so the diagrammatic representation of the Bororo case corresponds to the Achilles; for the most fundamental difference between the ways in which the two paradoxes conceptualize the problem of motion consists in the fact that one does so in the form of infinite division and the other in the form of infinite extension.

There is in fact a basic ambiguity, or even impossibility, in Lévi-Strauss's diagram (Figure 2). The fact that the left and right terminal points of all six lines (the three representing the original totalities and the three representing the secondary totalities) are all aligned suggests that Lévi-Strauss thinks of these lines as representing a preset space whose outer borders are fixed in each case; that is, there is in each case the same fixed amount of space to be broken up and used in different ways. Without doubt the concept of phonological space constitutes one of the models standing behind Lévi-Strauss's interest in such continua, and the idea of phonological space clearly assumes a fixed space (determined by the physical limits of sound production) where the issue is then the variable ways and degrees of fineness with which this continuum is broken up.

But if in Figure 2 the outside limits are indeed to be taken as fixed, this directly contradicts the fact that, in the Tikopian and Bororo cases, the lines are also supposed to represent the threat of the limitlessness of the series (suggested in the prose description and the "etc." of the diagrams). The fixidity of the outer border could, in a way, be reconciled with the quantitative limitlessness of the series, through the sort of scheme suggested in Figure 1, in which increasingly finer segmentation takes place within the same fixed space by simultaneous proportional reduction of all individual segments. But even this solution introduces a diagrammatical inelegance, for the length of any individual segments ought to remain constant through the whole diagram; otherwise there is nothing to prevent the particular segments that are left in the secondary totalities from, so to speak, expanding back out to fill up the space that has been opened up between them. But ultimately more important than the problems with the diagram is a point that can be made regarding the relation between the notions of infinite extension and infinite divisibility. For while they are in some manner different, representation by extension and by division is—more so to the extent that one is dealing with space as representing something other than space, and where distances are therefore purely relative—so easily transposable that one can, as Lévi-Strauss has done, slip unwittingly from the one to the other.

CHAPTER 2. COSMOGONY TODAY, COSMOGONY YESTERDAY

1. One form of innovation in Lévi-Strauss's use of the Chain consists in its now having been sociologized and anthropologized. The object to which it is applied is society, and it has been made into a tool for cross-cultural comparison. The anthropologization of the Chain in the nineteenth and preceding centuries took the form of a Eurocentric hierarchy of races, whereas the twentieth-century anthropologization, in Lévi-Strauss, consists of a cultural relativization. While the application of the Chain as a cross-cultural analytic, to be sure, depends upon and implies some level of "phychic unity" within the various societies that are considered within this perspective, it is only the abstract logical form of the Chain that is imputed as a recurrent principle of thought.

The particular contents of the Chain (the species that are posited) as well as the size of the links—that is, how many it takes to, so to speak, reach across being—are treated as a cultural variable, as is evident even from the variety of chains comprised in the three totemic myths. The main point is that the Chain of Being has been replaced by chains of being. While it is not possible to attempt to trace out all the specific details of the historical process of the relativization of the Chain, nevertheless I would hazard the suggestion that a particularly critical figure in the transition will be Kant, whose particular form of universalism seems historically to have afforded the grounds, with respect to this and many other objects of analysis, for socially and/or culturally relativistic perspectives. In the *Critique of Pure Reason* the principles of the Chain as well as the concerns of Zeno (regarding, for instance, infinite division and extension with respect to motion and space) appear recurrently and are considered in great detail. The central interest in these principles, however, is no longer that which was characteristic of Zeno, and of Kant in his own earlier researches, namely, that of making propositions about the nature of the universe. The same principles appear now, not as theories about the cosmos as object, but rather themselves as objects of theories regarding the nature of human reason.

2. The question arises, What is the relationship of the Chain, as it appears in Lévi-Strauss, to his interest in classification? There is a kind of ambiguity in the way that the activity of classifying is thought of in anthropology: On one hand there is the notion that the purpose of classification is to "reduce to order" as if without a classificatory scheme the mind encounters an unmanageable number of unique impressions. But on the other hand the activity is pictured expansively: as discrimination and enumeration of what would otherwise form only an undifferentiated and run-together mass. A classificatory scheme is by nature relational; and the nature of the relation is necessarily such that there must be more things on one end and fewer on the other. On one end it expands and enumerates, on the other it gathers and reduces. It cannot lack either end, the "universalizing" or the "particularizing," because it is precisely in establishing the relation that its work subsists. Regarding the question of how Lévi-Strauss's implication of the Chain fits in with his interest in classification, perhaps it can be said that the Chain—or more specifically the principle of infinite division applied to being— functions to probe the nature and limits of the expansive, enumerative end of the classificatory relation. The point, however, may be less about actual systems of classification in a particular society than about the nature of order in general: for the sake of order, one must be prepared to settle for less than the maximum possible.

Totalization as an abstract notion is accorded central importance by Lévi-Strauss. But the notion has also been the object of criticism, one of the charges being that its meaning, in Lévi-Strauss's usage, is ultimately vague. The presence of the Chain in Lévi-Strauss is interesting in this respect, for, in contrast with the many suggestive but imprecise allusions, it potentially constitutes a formalized representation of a principle of totalization. Lévi-Strauss's analytic of the myths of the origin of totemism is not concerned, as are many of his analyses, with this or that fundamental opposition, but with opposition in general—that is, with the possibility of opposition. It is a metastatement about classification: in considering conditions that would render classification impossible, it is concerned precisely with the conditions *for* its possibility.

The form imparted by this totalizing principle is something more than or at least other than binary; it has to do with establishing or projecting a relation of proportionality (whether of equality or gradation) at once—that is, in a single mental act—across a comprehensive series of things or possible things (up to and including all possible things). As such it is not surprising that this form occurs in Lévi-Strauss's analyses specifically of totemism, where, in addition to the theme of axiomatic fullness or perhaps as a dimension of that theme, it would appear to be motivated by the fact that the original number of things is thought of as nonreducible (the founding members of a set, even if differentially ranked, yet possess the same irretractable right to some place in the system). Beyond this sense of the equal necessity of each of the members of a given set, sometimes the members do appear to be thought of as possessing equal rank.

Any implication of a binary logic in relation to such sets of original things would necessarily pose a threat to both the principle of the nonreducibility of the original number and (when it is present) the principle of the equality of the original things. Any binary formalization will necessarily contain within itself a logical means of reducing to two a set greater than two (or reducing it to one, if one thinks of a binarization as a bifurcation). But, the quasi-sacred character of the original set of things (even when, as a multiple of two, it could be easily binarized—e.g., the Tikopian four clans) may preclude any formalization that contains the possibility of the reduction of the original number. This of course may be a reason why such original sets are in some instances—as in those cited by Lévi-Strauss—established originally through subtraction from a larger original totality, rather than through a progressive division of an original monad (as is characteristic of many other cosmogonies, including Maori). Besides the threat of the reduction of an original number to a lesser number, any binary formulation inherently introduces numerous possibilities—indeed even propensities—toward hierarchicalization, a potential that in the case of some original sets is regarded as unwelcome.

The hierarchical potential or propensity would be particularly, and unavoidably, called up in any application of binary logic to sets that are mathematically odd (e.g., the five Ojibwa clans). In such a case a binary representation would necessarily be unbalanced—for example, on the first level, three deriving from one side, two from the other; at the second level, three simply carrying over from the first, and one branching again to form two.

Even if one viewed this binarization as an arrangement of "mere convenience" it is difficult to avoid thinking of the discreteness of the two entities that branch on the second level—and thus of the entities themselves—as being anything other than less deeply anchored in the system than the other three.

It would thus seem to be in the nature of some systems to demand a principle by which the entire set can be brought into a relation at once and on a single level, a principle that would thus have to be other than binary. An argument could be made that the proportion that is projected in the series, while not hierarchically binary, is yet binary in a kind of linear, additive way (i.e., in the proportional series ABCD the proportionality results from the equation A:B::B:C + B:C::C:D + C:D::D:E . . .). This can be accepted, and then what we mean by the Chain is specifically the mind's capacity to "chain" together such oppositions *all at once* in such a way that a totality is created as a proportional series, or a proportional series as a totality, and, more than this, that the totality then is the first formulation, since any particular opposition will derive its particular values from and owe its status as such to the larger comprehensive proportion (cf. Saussure 1966:113).

It will have been noticed that I have laid a strong claim upon Lévi-Strauss from two intellectual traditions, the one, that associated with the paradoxes of Zeno, and the other, that of the Great Chain of Being. Some clues point to one tradition, some to the other. The conclusion that is to be drawn in this case is not so much that Lévi-Strauss, in his intellectually cosmopolitan fashion, has eclectically combined elements from two traditions as that in some fundamental way the two traditions are the same. He can install himself in both traditions while diluting nothing. The underlying relationship between the traditions is suggested succinctly in Lovejoy, near the end of the work, in the comment that the principle of plenitude "ran on, in every province in which it was applied, into infinities—infinite space, infinite time, infinite worlds, an infinity of existent species, an infinity of individual existences, an infinity of kinds of beings between any two kinds of beings, however similar" (1960:331).

The reasons for the consideration of Lévi-Strauss's intellectual formulation in terms of the two different traditions lie partly in the historical interest itself, but, more important—in ways that will become clearer at later points—they lie in the fact that considering Lévi-Strauss's formulation in relation to two different traditions conjures up different sets of terms—and therefore a larger total inventory—of concepts and ideas for the study of cosmogony. Though the paradoxes of motion and the Chain are in many respects structurally the same, taking advantage of the different expressions allows us to see different possible angles of application, an argument not unlike Lévi-Strauss's for the necessity of consulting all the variants of a particular myth.

3. While "structurally" similar, Zeno's paradoxes and the Chain might not be in every respect identical. The main point here has already been raised in another context: much depends upon the way that one "thinks of" the implementation of the process of progressive infinite interposition. The infinite interposition can be thought of either as a progressive division, in which one can imagine that one is getting further away from the possibility of motion because of the alarming proliferation of midpoints that must first be traversed; or else it can be thought of as a progressive mediation, in which one can imagine that one is getting closer to the possibility of motion through a progressive lessening of the dimension of any particular gap. The latter is a kind of "divide and conquer" strategy; a gap of imposing magnitude is reduced to a series of gaps of small magnitude.

The paradoxes involve an application within the realms of pure mathematical space, whereas the Chain involves an application within the realm of "being" (by which here I mean to stress a positive content in the form of something like matter or "substance"). Within either a continuum of pure space or a continuum of being it seems to be possible to think of infinite interposition as either a progressive division or a progressive mediation. But there is apparently a kind of affinity between elements from the two pairs, so that it is easier to think of the interposition as division when it is applied to a space-continuum, and as a mediation when it is applied to a being-continuum. The affinity of mediation for the being-continuum stems perhaps from the fact that, within a being-continuum, any interposition represents (or posits) a "species"—some kind of "thing," "something" that occupies space and has mass, however minute; hence even a progressively finer or infinitely finer interposition nevertheless connotes or creates the impression of a "filling."

By contrast, any progressive interposition in a continuum of mathematical space merely means the positing of another mathematical point, which by definition is without dimension of either mass or extent; therefore it cannot as readily create a sense of a "filling" and tends to produce rather the sense of, witness Achilles, getting nowhere. Hence it is probably not accidental that it is within the space continuum that we get a proof for the impossibility of motion, and that in the being-continuum we get instances of something like a countertheme. For it is mainly in being-continua that we encounter the notion that progressive interposition leads not away from but precisely toward the possibility of motion—motion, that is, in the sense of a passage through all possible segments of the continuum. That countertheme is present incipiently (though its full possible implication was ultimately denied) in the traditional notion that nature itself does not move from one species to another *nisi per medium*, that is, except by creating intermediaries and, so to speak, leaving them in its wake. It is again present in the Darwinian version of "infinitesimal gradation," where the implication of passage is explicitly present. And it is present once more in the recognition of the threat of passage—and thus of the dissolution of the discrete in the continuous—in Lévi-Strauss's cosmogonic analytic.

CHAPTER 3. MAORI COSMOGONIC THOUGHT

1. My summary is drawn from an earlier and preliminary analysis that I did of this text (Schrempp 1985).

2. Variations on this theme are found, for example, in the Middle East (e.g., the Babylonian Enuma Elish, Hesiod's *Theogony*), India, South and Southeast Asia, and parts of the Pacific. A survey of some of them is presented by Numazawa (1984).

3. In instances in which cultures embody central dualisms, it is frequently the case that the dualism is not confined to a particular cultural level or type of manifestation. The contrasts that emerge between the Arawa and *Whare Wānanga* narrative accounts resemble in many ways the contrasts that emerge in the comparison of the Arawa prose narrative account with its corresponding genealogy (see chapter 5). The *Whare Wānanga* account is a prose narrative account, but it is largely a story of the creation of a genealogy.

4. Perhaps the epitomizing instance of an analytical application within the formulation of concrete social units is to be found in the case of Fiji. It is not that within the

total system there are not synthetic occurrences. It may be a background synthetic pattern that affords the possibility of analysis; and indeed it may well be the case that the reason for the social analysis is precisely to constitute the conditions under which society can represent itself in the form of an ongoing transactional synthesis. Whatever the ultimate reasons, we find in the Fijian case a pattern, essentially absent in Maori, of the self-description of social units through a potentially recursive analysis into formal land and sea components (see Sahlins 1978a:24ff.; 1978b).

The fact that the classifiers—land and sea—are potentially recursive itself is significant. According to Lévi-Strauss's totemic paradigm, classifications that implicate several levels of inclusiveness work by locating and exploiting different levels of markers that can be found within the classifiers—so that, for instance, when the turtle clan bifurcates, it will become the yellow turtles versus the gray turtles; or, for certain operations, the focus will be narrowed from the whole species thought of as classifier to certain *parts* of a given member of the species (e.g., the head) (see esp. 1966:67, and chapter 5). But as compared with the theoretically *near*-infinitude of such means of classification (which are, however, ultimately exhaustible and which require, with each demographic change, a special mental operation to locate an appropriate level and feature within the classifier), the Fijian case presents, not a near-infinite, but an infinite scheme of classifiers, and one which supplies new levels automatically. That is, because every opposition is the same opposition, the two terms forever reflect one another, always, so to speak, running infinitely ahead of whatever there is to be analyzed or synthesized. The possibility of such recursive classification constitutes one small manifestation of the dynamic nature of Polynesian systems.

5. The following comparative linguistic data would seem to be relevant: TON *ta?ili*, "fan"; EFU *taili*, "blow"; REN *taigi*, "blow gently"; HAW *kaahili*, "ceremonial standard"; TAH *taahiri*, "fan" (n., v.); RAR *ta?iri*, "id."; MAO *taawhiri*, "fan, etc." (cf. also *taairi*, "be suspended") (data furnished by Ross Clark, personal communication). The Hawaiian ceremonial standards (*kaahili*) take the form of, and have been interpreted as, enlarged and exaggerated fans.

6. I owe the example of the earth-diver, which may be the ultimate inspiration for my larger comments in this section, to William Hansen, who elaborated this example as one of my teachers a number of years ago.

7. Smith's comment is reminiscent of a comment by Lévi-Strauss in relation to the general "spirit" of a culture area that, in such matters as the emphasis on competitive status rivalry and display, has been frequently compared with Polynesia. Lévi-Strauss suggests that, in the view embodied in the myth of Asdiwal, ". . . the only positive form of existence is a *negation of non-existence*. . . . But let us note in passing that it would shed new light on the *need for self-assertion* which, in the potlatch, the feasts, the ceremonies, and the feudal rivalries, seems to be such a particular characteristic of the societies of the Northwest Pacific Coast" (1971:33).

CHAPTER 4: OTHER VARIANTS

1. Lévi-Strauss at one point in *The Naked Man* treats the relation of sky and earth, suggesting that the motif of the arrow ladder to the sky as it occurs in a certain North American myth can be viewed as the establishing of a continuum between two widely separated spheres (1981:467ff.; cf. Thompson F53, "Ascent to upper world on arrow chain"). Lévi-Strauss argues that ". . . through an accumulation of short intervals, the ladder of arrows uses discrete elements to create a continuum" (1981:469). The abstract issue here is the same Zenoian quandary that I treated in chapter 1, in the context of Lévi-Strauss's analysis, in *The Raw and the Cooked*, of a tale of a race. What is fascinating about the reappearance of the problem of the continuous and the discrete in *The Naked Man* is that this abstract Zenoian problem once again appears in the context of a tangible Zenoian image, in this case, arrows—leading me to speculate that if I had read the *Mythologiques* in a different order, my first chapter might have been about the arrow in flight, rather than the tortoise and the hare.

2. The document to which I had access was a photocopy held by the National Library in Wellington; the original manuscript is now in the manuscript collection of the National Library of Australia, catalogued as MS 4017.

CHAPTER 5: ANTINOMY AND COSMOLOGY

1. The present chapter is modified from an earlier article of the same name in *Myth and Philosophy* (1990), edited by Frank Reynolds and David Tracy, and appears here with the permission of the State University of New York Press. Earlier versions of this chapter were presented to the Departments of Anthropology at the University of Chicago and the University of California–Santa Cruz, and to the colloquium "Religion(s) in Culture and History" at the University of Chicago. I am particularly grateful for the critical commentaries provided by Frank Reynolds, Thomas Kasulis, and Jonathan Smith. While the project of relating Maori cosmology to Kantian philosophy is my own, I have taken on some of the other main foci of this paper from my teachers, whose influence I gratefully acknowledge. My concern with the two contrastive forms of cosmology is one that I inherited from Valerio Valeri, whereas my interest in the relationship between cosmology and political process has been influenced particularly by Marshall Sahlins.

2. The clarifications that follow are motivated in part by criticisms raised in Jonathan Smith's response to my presentation in the conference "Religion(s) in Culture and History."

3. There would be a worthy project in the investigation of the "antinomy of pure reason" specifically as a historical generalization. Such an approach would provide a refreshing alternative to the usual way in which the antinomies are subjected to critique—that is, in terms of the internal coherence and logical force of the specific arguments that Kant lines up against one another.

4. Examples of the sickly family theme can be found in White 1887. Lévi-Strauss discusses the mythological significance of ambulation at several points (e.g., 1967:212; 1974:464).

5. As embodied in such passages as:

> Then Tū sought for some plan by which to turn and subdue his brothers on ac-
> count of their weakness in the face of Tāwhiri's revenge over the parents, such that
> it had been he alone who had been brave enough to fight. (trans. of Grey xxxiii;
> MS 43:894)

6. For example, see Best 1925:991ff.

7. Numerous examples can be found in Best 1976:55ff.

8. The term here translated as "cloud" might alternatively be translated as "day."

9. See also Schrempp 1985:22–24, 35 n. 10.

10. "Indefinite," as a privative term, is potentially very ambiguous; here I utilize it to call attention to the absence of any indication that limits should exist. This usage of course is not equivalent to "infinite." Yet "indefinite" in this sense contrasts less strongly with "infinite" than it does when used in the other sense in which it is some-times invoked, that is, as implying an assumption of limits, but which have not yet been defined.

11. Even though Te Rangikaheke does not invoke the spreading plant image in his genealogy of primordial origins, it is interesting to note that he does invoke this image in his genealogy of his more recent ancestors, specifically those who migrated and settled New Zealand (see Schrempp 1985:27–28).

12. Kant's own attempt at resolution of the third antinomy should not be neglected in considering the Maori material. In an argument that figures centrally in his critique of "practical reason," Kant concludes that both poles of the dynamic antinomies can be true. Insofar as humans are phenomenal, their actions cannot be represented other than according to the causality of nature; but insofar as humans are noumenal, another principle—"freedom"—is possible. Since they have different referents, the (seemingly) opposed propositions are not contradictory.

Chapter 6: The Quick and the Dead

1. I presented some of the ideas in this chapter originally within a graduate course on American Indian mythology in the Folklore Institute of Indiana University in the spring of 1990. I am grateful for the comments of the many students in this course, and especially for some remarks by Cyndee Johnson which have led me to give greater em-phasis to the cooperation that is intrinsically embodied in ambulation. I also presented some of the notions in this chapter in "The Great Race in North America," a paper presented at the 1990 annual meeting of the American Folklore Society.

2. Though his ultimate orientation is one that the current age would reject, none-theless an interesting characterization of this African tale is to be found in Frazer (in Dundes 1984:80ff.).

3. On the arrow in flight, see p. 203, n. 1.

4. Two recent works that pose numerous potentials in regard to the issue of cosmology and sound are Feld 1982 and Basso 1985. The latter among other things finds a cosmos that hierarchicalizes various kinds of beings according to their degree of musicality, while the former suggests a metaphor common to Western and Kaluli discourse about sound, that is, that each discourse is built around the visual metaphor of "water" (or "wave") motion (Feld 1982:164–65).

Works Cited

Aarne, A. 1928. *The Types of the Folk-Tale.* Helsinki: Suomalainen Tiedeakatemia Academia Scientiarum Fennica. (FFC No. 74)

Aristotle. 1957. *On the Soul; Parva Naturalia; On Breath.* Cambridge: Harvard University Press.

Barnes, J. 1982. *The Presocratic Philosophers.* London: Routledge and Kegan Paul.

Basso, E. 1985. *A Musical View of the Universe.* Philadelphia: University of Pennsylvania Press.

Bayle, M. 1741. *A General Dictionary,* Vol. 10. London: James Bettenham.

Bergson, H. 1911. *Creative Evolution.* New York: Henry Holt and Co.

Best, E. 1924a. *Maori Religion and Mythology,* Vol. 1. Dominion Museum Bulletin No. 10. Wellington: Government Printer.

Best, E. 1924b. *The Maori,* Vol. 1. Wellington: Harry H. Tombs.

Best, E. 1925. *Tuhoe.* Wellington: Reed.

Best, E. 1976. *Maori Religion and Mythology,* Part 1. Rev. ed. Wellington: Government Printer.

Best, E. 1977. *Tuhoe.* Reprint. Wellington: Reed.

Best, E. 1982. *Maori Religion and Mythology,* Part 2. Wellington: Government Printer.

Biggs, B. 1976. The Position of Tangaroa in Maori Mythology. Unpublished paper.

Biggs, B., and D. Simmons. 1970. The Sources of "The Lore of the Whare-Wananga." *Journal of the Polynesian Society* 79, 22–42.

Biggs, B., C. Lane, and H. Cullen. 1980. *Readings from Maori Literature.* Auckland: University of Auckland, Maori Studies Department.

Boas, F. 1887. The Study of Geography. *Science* 9, 137–41.

Boas, F. 1905–6. The Mythologies of the Indians. *The International Quarterly* 11, 327–42; 12, 157–73.

Bourdieu, P. 1985. *Outline of a Theory of Praxis.* Cambridge: Cambridge University Press.

Burkert, W. 1985. *Greek Religion.* Cambridge: Harvard University Press.

Crump, T. 1990. *The Anthropology of Numbers.* Cambridge: Cambridge University Press.

Curnow, J. 1983. *Wiremu Maihi Te Rangikaheke: His Life and Work.* M.A. thesis, University of Auckland.

Curnow, J. 1985. Wiremu Maihi Te Rangikaheke: His Life and Work. *Journal of the Polynesian Society* 94, 97–147.

Detienne, M. 1986. *The Creation of Mythology.* Chicago: University of Chicago Press.

Detienne, M., and J. Vernant. 1991. *Cunning Intelligence in Greek Culture and Society.* Chicago: University of Chicago Press.

Dixon, R. 1916. *The Mythology of All Races,* Vol. 9: *Oceanic.* Boston: Marshall Jones Co.

Douglas, M. 1970. *Purity and Danger.* Harmondsworth: Penguin.

Dumont, L. 1980. *Homo Hierarchicus.* Rev. ed. Chicago: University of Chicago Press.

Dundes, A. 1984. *Sacred Narrative.* Berkeley: University of California Press.

Durkheim, E. 1965. *The Elementary Forms of the Religious Life.* New York: Free Press.

Durkheim, E. 1977. *The Evolution of Educational Thought.* London: Routledge and Kegan Paul.

Durkheim, E. 1982. *The Rules of Sociological Method.* New York: The Free Press.

Durkheim, E. 1983. *Pragmatism and Sociology.* Cambridge: Cambridge University Press.

Durkheim, E., and M. Mauss. 1972. *Primitive Classification.* Chicago: University of Chicago Press.

Eliade, M. 1965. *The Two and the One.* New York: Harper and Row.

Feld, S. 1982. *Sound and Sentiment.* Philadelphia: University of Pennsylvania Press.

Firth, R. 1961. *History and Traditions of Tikopia.* Memoir 33. Wellington: The Polynesian Society.

Firth, R. 1963. Bilateral Descend Groups: An Operational Viewpoint. In *Studies in Kinship and Marriage,* ed. I. Schapera. London: Occasional Papers of the Royal Anthropological Institute.

Formigari, L. 1973. Chain of Being. In *Dictionary of the History of Ideas,* ed. I. Berlin et al. New York: Charles Scribner's Sons.

Frazer, J. 1984. The Fall of Man. In *Sacred Narrative,* ed. A. Dundes. Berkeley: University of California Press.

Gadamer, H. 1975. *Truth and Method.* New York: The Seabury Press.

Gilson, E. 1940. *The Spirit of Medieval Philosophy.* New York: Charles Scribner's Sons.

Grey, G. 1853. *Ko Nga Moteatea.* Wellington: Robert Stokes.

Grey, G. 1855. *Polynesian Mythology.* London: John Murray.

Grey, G. 1974. *Polynesian Mythology.* Rev. ed. *Christchurch: Whitcoulls.*

Gyekye, K. 1987. *An Essay on African Philosophical Thought.* Cambridge: Cambridge University Press.

Hanson, F. 1983. Dynamic Forms in the Maori Concept of Reality. *Ultimate Reality and Meaning* 6, 180–204.

Henry, T. 1928. *Ancient Tahiti.* Bishop Museum Bulletin 48. Honolulu: Bernice P. Bishop Museum.

Hertz, R. 1978. The Pre-eminence of the Right Hand. In *Right & Left,* ed. R. Needham. Chicago: University of Chicago Press.

Hiroa, Te Rangi. 1958. *The Coming of the Maori.* Wellington: Whitcombe and Tombs.

Hongi, H. 1896a. The Lament of Te Rangi-mauri for Tonga-awhikau. *Journal of the Polynesian Society* 5, 112–20.

Hongi, H. 1896b. Tama-Ahua. *Journal of the Polynesian Society* 5, 233–36.

Hountondji, P. 1983. *African Philosophy: Myth and Reality.* Bloomington: Indiana University Press.

Isaacson, N. 1987. *The Significance of Fire in Human Evolution.* Unpublished senior thesis, Wesleyan University.

James, W. 1977. *A Pluralistic Universe.* Cambridge: Harvard University Press.

Johansen, J. 1954. *The Maori and His Religion.* Copenhagen: Ejnar Munksgaard.

Jung, C. 1977. *The Archetypes and the Collective Unconscious.* Princeton: Princeton University Press.

Kant, I. 1965. *Critique of Pure Reason.* Translated by N. K. Smith. New York: St. Martin's Press.

Kant, I. 1970. *Kant's Cosmogony.* New York: Johnson Reprint Corporation.

Kant, I. 1983. *Prolegomena to Any Future Metaphysics.* Indianapolis: Hackett.

Kelly, L. 1980. *Tainui.* Christchurch: Capper Press; originally published by the Polynesian Society.

Kirk, G., J. Raven, and M. Schofield. 1983. *The Presocratic Philosophers.* Cambridge: Cambridge University Press.

Lakoff, G. 1987. *Women, Fire, and Dangerous Things.* Chicago: University of Chicago Press.

Leach, E. 1970. Lévi-Strauss in the Garden of Eden. In *Claude Lévi-Strauss: The Anthropologist as Hero,* ed. N. Hayes and T. Hayes. Cambridge: M.I.T. Press.

Lee, H. D. P. 1967. *Zeno of Elea.* Amsterdam: Adolf M. Hakkert.

Lévi-Strauss, C. 1963. *Totemism.* Boston: Beacon Press.

Lévi-Strauss, C. 1966. *The Savage Mind.* Chicago: University of Chicago Press.

Lévi-Strauss, C. 1967. *Structural Anthropology.* Garden City: Anchor Books.

Lévi-Strauss, C. 1970. *The Raw and the Cooked.* Vol. 1 of *Mythologiques.* New York: Harper Torchbooks.

Lévi-Strauss, C. 1971. The Story of Asdiwal. In *The Structural Study of Myth and Totemism,* ed. E. Leach. London: Tavistock.

Lévi-Strauss, C. 1974. *From Honey to Ashes.* Vol. 2 of *Mythologiques.* New York: Harper and Row.

Lévi-Strauss, C. 1978. *Myth and Meaning.* New York: Schocken Books.

Lévi-Strauss, C. 1979. *The Origin of Table Manners.* Vol. 3 of *Mythologiques.* New York: Harper and Row.

Lévi-Strauss, C. 1981. *The Naked Man.* Vol. 4 of *Mythologiques.* New York: Harper and Row.

Lovejoy, A. 1960. *The Great Chain of Being.* New York: Harper and Row.

Lucretius. 1975. *On the Nature of the Universe.* Harmondsworth: Penguin.

Mahuta, R., G. Schrempp, and I. Nottingham. 1984. *A Whaikoorero Reader.* Occasional Paper No. 21. Hamilton: University of Waikato, Centre for Maori Studies and Research.

Marshall, L. 1962. !Kung Bushman Religious Beliefs. *Africa* 32, 221–52.

Matiaha Tiramorehu of Moeraki. Traditions of Natives. 9 June 1849. Item 4017. MS collection of the National Library of Australia, Canberra.

Mauss, M. 1967. *The Gift.* New York: W. W. Norton and Company.

Mauss, M. 1968–. *Œuvres*, Vol. 2. Paris: Les Editions de Minuit.

Mauss, M. 1979. *Sociology and Psychology*. London: Routledge and Kegan Paul.

Müller, M. 1873. Lectures on Mr. Darwin's Philosophy of Language. *Fraser's Magazine* 87, 659–78.

Nabokov, P. 1981. *Indian Running*. Santa Fe: Ancient City Press.

Numazawa, K. 1984. The Cultural-Historical Background of Myths on the Separation of Sky and Earth. In *Sacred Narrative*, ed. A. Dundes. Berkeley: University of California Press.

O'Flaherty, W. 1981. *The Rig Veda*. Harmondsworth: Penguin.

O'Flaherty, W. 1985. Ethical and Nonethical Implications of the Separation of Heaven and Earth in Indian Mythology. In *Cosmogony and Ethical Order*, ed. R. Lovin and F. Reynolds. Chicago: University of Chicago Press.

Opler, M. 1938. *Myths and Tales of the Jicarilla Apache Indians*. New York: American Folklore Society.

Ortiz, A. 1969. *The Tewa World*. Chicago: University of Chicago Press.

Parsons, E. 1939. *Pueblo Indian Religion*, Vol. 1. Chicago: University of Chicago Press.

Patai, Raphael. 1967. *Man and Temple*. New York: Ktav Publishing House.

Plato. 1981a. *Timaeus and Critias*. Translated by Desmond Lee. Harmondsworth: Penguin.

Plato, 1981b. *Timaeus*. Translated by R. G. Bury. Cambridge: Harvard University Press.

Reynolds, F., and D. Tracy, eds. 1990. *Myth and Philosophy*. Albany: State University of New York Press.

Sahlins, M. 1978a. *Culture and Practical Reason*. Chicago: University of Chicago Press.

Sahlins, M. 1978b. A Synthesis of Riches. Unpublished manuscript.

Sahlins, M. 1987. *Islands of History*. Chicago: University of Chicago Press.

Salmon, W. 1970. Introduction. In *Zeno's Paradoxes*, ed. W. Salmon. Indianapolis: Bobbs-Merrill.

Salmond, A. 1978. Te Ao Tawhito: A Semantic Approach to the Traditional Maori Cosmos. *Journal of the Polynesian Society* 87, 5–28.

Salmond, A. 1982. Theoretical Landscapes. In *Semantic Anthropology*, ed. D. Parkin. London: Academic Press.

Salmond, A. 1983. *Hui*. Wellington: Reed.

Saussure, F. 1966. *Course in General Linguistics*. New York: McGraw-Hill.

Schrempp, G. 1983. The Re-education of Friedrich Max Müller. *Man* 18, 90–110.

Schrempp, G. 1985. Tū Alone Was Brave: Notes on Maori Cosmogony. In *Transformations of Polynesian Culture*, ed. A. Hooper and J. Huntsman. Memoir No. 45. Auckland: Polynesian Society.

Schrempp, G. 1990. Antinomy and Cosmology: Kant among the Maori. In *Myth and Philosophy*, ed. F. Reynolds and D. Tracy. Albany: State University of New York Press.

Schwimmer, E. 1963. Guardian Animals of the Maori. *Journal of the Polynesian Society* 72, 397–410.

Schwimmer, E. 1978. Lévi-Strauss and Maori Social Structure. *Anthropologica* 20, 201–22.

Shirres, M. 1979. *Tapu: Being with Potentiality for Power.* M.A. thesis, University of Auckland.

Shortland, E. 1856. *Traditions and Superstitions of the New Zealanders.* London: Longman, Brown, Green, Longmans and Roberts.

Shortland, E. 1882. *Maori Religion and Mythology.* London: Longmans, Green, and Co.

Singer, D. 1950. *Giordano Bruno.* New York: Henry Schuman.

Smith, J. 1974. *Tapu Removal in Maori Religion.* Memoir 40. Wellington: The Polynesian Society.

Smith, S., ed. 1913. *The Lore of the Whare-wānanga.* Memoir 3. Wellington: The Polynesian Society.

Sorabji, R. 1983. *Time, Creation and the Continuum.* Ithaca: Cornell University Press.

Stocking, G. 1968. *Race, Culture, and Evolution.* New York: Free Press.

Stocking, G. 1974. The Basic Assumptions of Boasian Anthropology. In *The Shaping of American Anthropology*, ed. G. Stocking. New York: Basic Books.

Streitfeld, D. 1991. Soldier's Story. *Entertainment Weekly*, No. 76 (July 26), 30–34.

Taran, L. 1965. *Parmenides: A Text with Translation, Commentary, and Critical Essays.* Princeton: Princeton University Press.

Te Rangikaheke, W. 1849. Tama a Rangi, MS GNZMMSS 43, Auckland Public Library.

Te Rangikaheke, W. 1849. Tūpuna, MS GNZMMSS 44, Auckland Public Library.

Te Rangikaheke, W. 1849. Maori Religious Ideas and Observances, MS GNZMMSS 81, Auckland Public Library.

Thompson, S. 1946. *The Folktale.* New York: Dryden Press.

Thompson, S. 1955. *Motif Index of Folk Literature.* Bloomington: Indiana University Press.

Thornton, A. 1987. *Maori Oral Literature: As Seen by a Classicist.* Dunedin, N.Z.: University of Otago Press.

Tylor, E. 1958. *The Origins of Culture.* New York: Harper and Row.

Valeri, V. 1991. Constitutive History: Genealogy and Narrative in Hawaiian Kingship. In *Culture Through Time*, ed. E. Ohnuki-Tierney. Stanford: Stanford University Press.

van Ballekom, M., and R. Harlow. 1987. *Te Waiatatanga mai o te Atua.* Canterbury Maori Studies 4. Christchurch: Department of Maori, University of Canterbury.

Vernant, J. 1982. *The Origins of Greek Thought.* Ithaca: Cornell University Press.

White, J. 1887. *The Ancient History of the Maori*, Vol. 1. Wellington: Government Printer.

Whitehead, J. 1979. *Process and Reality.* New York: Free Press.

Wohlers, J. n.d. MS Ml., 234, Hocken Library, Dunedin, N.Z.

Wohlers, J. n.d. MS GNZMMSS 55, Auckland Public Library.

Wohlers, J. 1874. The Mythology and Traditions of the Maori in New Zealand. *Transactions of the New Zealand Institute* 7, 3–53.

Wohlers, J. 1895. *Memories of the Life of J. F. H. Wohlers.* Dunedin, N.Z.: Otago Daily Times and Witness Newspapers Co.

New Directions in Anthropological Writing
History, Poetics, Cultural Criticism

GEORGE E. MARCUS
Rice University

JAMES CLIFFORD
University of California, Santa Cruz

GENERAL EDITORS